Alexis Smith

Alexis Smith

Peter Shelley

BearManor Media

2024

Published in the United States of America by:

BearManor Media

1317 Edgewater Dr #110
Orlando FL 32804

bearmanormedia.com

Printed in the United States.

Typesetting and layout by PKJ Passion Global

ISBN—979-8-88771-449-3

Table of Contents

Foreword

Alexis Smith is a somewhat forgotten figure in movie history. She doesn't even rate a chapter in David Shipman's book series *The Great Movie Stars* even though the actress began in films in what he calls the golden years of Hollywood. Her being overlooked is perhaps because she was considered only a supporting player, though Smith played the leading role in *Undercover Girl* (1950). If technically she had smaller parts in terms of scene numbers, they were still sizeable in titles like "*The Doughgirls* "(1944), "*The Horn Blows At Midnight*" (1945), *Stallion Road* (1947), "*The Decision of Christopher Blake*" (1948), "*One Last Fling*" (1949), *Split Second* (1953) and especially *The Sleeping Tiger* (1952).

Smith was discovered by a Warner Bros talent while at college and signed to a seven-year contract in 1940. The studio tested her in small uncredited parts before she was cast in what was a break-out role in *Dive Bomber* (1941). From then the actress worked steadily, appearing with Hollywood's top leading men like Errol Flynn, Charles Boyer, Fredric March, Humphrey Bogart, Cary Grant, Joel McCrea, Clark Gable, and later Bing Crosby, and Paul Newman. She won no acting prizes and would have to wait for thirty years to do so. Her decade at Warners accounts for the bulk of her filmography. Smith described herself as a utility player, who was given the parts turned down by Bette Davis, Olivia de Havilland, Ida Lupino, Ann Sheridan, and Jane Wyman. She also had to compete with other actresses in contention for these roles, since Warners had a stable of women stars in their second tier. What probably gave her the advantage was beauty, and height, although Smith would say the latter could cause problems with shorter leading men.

She was initially typecast as a snow queen, a wealthy and arrogant woman presented in opposition to more earthy types. Smith uses a raised eyebrow to indicate amusement and disapproval. The actress demonstrated inexperience by using self-conscious self-touching and sometimes over-gesturing though some directors cleverly had her handle props and do business to hide these mannerisms. As she played more roles Smith was given the opportunity to warm up the persona and show her range. She could cry with tears, do accents and was particularly good at comedy but also able to express emotion in dramatic parts.

One frustration was that the actress wanted to play musical roles. Warners had her play a nightclub dancer in *Passage from Hong Kong* (1941), dance in *"Thank Your Lucky Stars"* (1943) and sing and dance with Ann Sheridan and Jane Wyman briefly in *"The Doughgirls"*. When she played singers in the Westerns *"San Antonio"* (1945), *"South Of St. Louis"* (1949), and *Wyoming Mail* (1950) and the sports drama *"Whiplash"* (1948) her vocals were dubbed. Finally, Smith's voice was used in *"Montana"* (1950). In *Frank Capra's Here Comes the Groom* (1951) for Paramount she sang for herself and danced briefly to "In The Cool, Cool, Cool of the Evening". The actress would never get a great musical film role. She would have to wait until the Broadway stage musical *Follies*.

Smith was usually a compliant player, accepting whatever was offered or assigned to her. As the years went on, she began to decline roles. For *The Return of the Frontiersman* the actress deliberately sabotaged her audition. When she declined the lead in "The Shoplifter", feeling it was an unsuitable role, Warners decided to terminate her contract. This happened at the time when the studio was laying off their stars. The U.S. Supreme Court had outlawed block booking which impacted film distribution and the popularity of television was taking a large percentage of the viewing audience.

The actress took a three-picture deal at Universal where she made *Wyoming Mail, Undercover Girl,* and *Cave Of Outlaws* (1951), and then operated as an independent before the offers stopped coming. Smith ventured into television doing guest appearances.

Then there was the stage, with the shows *Private Lives*; *Bell, Book and Candle*; her first musical *Plain and Fancy* and then *Wonderful Town*; *Critic's Choice* and *Mary, Mary* in summer stock; and a national tour of *Cactus Flower*.

Her career had a spectacular revival with *Follies* in 1972, which won her the Tony Award for Best Actress in a Musical and saw her on the cover of *Time* magazine. Being on the cover of *After Dark* magazine meant she had become a gay icon. Smith may not have had the greatest singing voice for musicals but she provided elegance and a sense of humor to her performances. Audiences embraced her, remembering the Hollywood star of yesteryear, and the actress countered F. Scott Fitzgerald's notion that there were no second acts in American life. Her subsequent Broadway stage roles in *The Women*, the musical *Platinum*, and *Summer Brave* were less successful. However, she played in the national tour of the musical *The Best Little Whorehouse in Texas* and a revival of *Pal Joey*.

Smith alternated between more television and the occasional film supporting role like *"Jacqueline Susann's Once is Not Enough"* (1975), *The Little Girl Who Lives Down The Lane* (1976), *Casey's Shadow* (1978) and *Tough Guys* (1986). One notable television appearance was in a recurring role in *Dallas* in 1984 and a return in 1990. She had tried being a regular on a series in 1973 called *Nightside* but it was not sold, and another called *Hothouse* in 1987 but it was cancelled after one season. Bob Hope said the actress invented the fountain of youth but by 1990 it was apparent that she had lost weight, perhaps an indication of the cancer that would kill her three years later. Her last film was Martin Scorsese's *The Age Of Innocence* (1993).

Smith's life was relatively free of scandal. In 1947 she was part of a delegation sent by the Screen Actors Guild to the American Federation of Labor convention in Chicago. The group presented a resolution calling for binding arbitration of the current Hollywood labor dispute which was passed. Fortunately, this action was not used against her as being Un-American during the Joseph McCarthy witch hunts. There was a rumor that the actress was a lesbian and that her marriage of forty-nine years was a bearded arrangement. However, while she had female friends, there was no confirmation that any were sexual relationships. The lesbian rumor perhaps came from a friendship with lesbian writer Rita Mae Brown and Smith playing a lesbian in *"Jacqueline Susann's Once is Not Enough"*.

This is the first book to span the actress' life and career to date although it cannot be considered a definite study. Not all of her work could be accessed. The films *The Great Mr. Nobody* (1941), *Here Comes Happiness* (1941), *Three Sons o' Guns* (1941), *Passage from Hong Kong*, and *"Always Together"* (1947) are all unavailable for viewing. Some of the television work is also unavailable such as guest appearances in *Stage 7*, *The 20th Century-Fox Hour*, *The Joseph Cotten Show: On Trial*, *Robert Montgomery Presents*, *Lux Video Theatre*, *The United States Steel Hour*, and the game show *To Tell the Truth*. Her appearance with husband Craig Stevens on *Person to Person* on May 20, 1960, is perhaps the one most regretted not being seen. For the unavailable material as much information as possible has been provided.

She did not write a memoir and neither did Stevens. Two sources that were very helpful were the chapter in Daniel Bubbeo's book *The Women of Warner Brothers* and a two part study by Jerry Vermilye in the 1994 editions of the magazine *Films in Review*. Other sources include the Internet Movie Database, as well as associated biographies and books on co-workers which allowed me to consider differing views of some of the events and situations. I also read articles and interviews that Smith gave to newspapers and magazines and watched interviews on YouTube. I accessed the archives of *The New York Times*, *Photoplay* magazine, and ebay.com and Getty Images for photographs of her at events. Additionally, ebay.com had stage show programs for me to gather information from.

The book is written as a biography, with the actress' career presented in the context of her life. Each film, television, stage and radio show appearance is mixed into the biography. Work is listed in the chronology they were made as opposed to when they opened or were released or broadcast, with that information also given. Titles are transcribed as they appear on screen. I have provided an analysis of the work when possible, positioning Smith's place in the project. I have commented on her look and performance and quoted any comments I have found by the star as well as those about her by director and co-stars. I have also given the critical reaction that the work received and information about any awards it earned. To complement the text, I have supplied stills, portraits, posters, and lobby cards from some of the films, theatre and television shows. In addition, the book comes with an appendix of the work and a bibliography of reference sources.

Chapter 1. Beginning

She was born Margaret Alexis Fitzsimmons-Smith aka Gladys Alexis Smith on June 8, 1921, in Penticton, British Columbia. Her parents were Gladys Mabel Fitzsimmons (aka Fitz-Simmons) and Alexander Smith. The girl was the couple's only child. Alexander was a Scot who owned a grocery store in British Columbia and Gladys was a Canadian secretary. Alexis was named after her father who wanted a boy, though she also said the name came when Alexander first saw the baby and thought it was a boy. She came from a family of adventurers. Her grandfather Fred was a gold miner in South Africa, and her mother's father, James mined for gold in Alaska.

The couple moved to Los Angeles when the child was one. Alexander had been offered a job as the manager of the West Stockley Company, a seller of canned foods. The move was favored by Gladys who felt the warmer climate and the educational opportunities would be better for their daughter.

The girl was said to be naturally bright and loved to study, since studying kept her mind occupied. Gladys believed that if girls kept their minds busy, they would not get into trouble. She attended Melrose Grammar School, Bancroft Junior High, and Hollywood High School.

Her mother had a love of literature and music, passions she shared with Alexis. Gladys read her daughter the literature classics as a daily ritual. She bought books that contained reproductions of famous paintings, and had the girl play a game called "Who Painted This One?" Alexis would read a book in bed every night while eating bread and butter and green onions. This was always the high point of her day. She swore that no matter what the ups and downs, good fortune or bad, Alexis would stick to her special kind of sandwiches.

As she got older the girl was given dance and piano lessons, and she became proficient in both. In 1931 at the age of ten she was hailed as an exceptionally talented pianist. Smith later said her pet aversion was prodigies yet there were some who said she nearly became one. The actress wouldn't agree to that label. In fact, Smith felt she wasn't a very good pianist at all, despite what the critics thought.

Alexis won a dance scholarship to the Edith Jane Studio aka the Edith Jane School of the Dance where she studied tap, ballet, and modern dance. The girl added singing to her repertoire, and it was said her lyric soprano voice was meant for opera. She quickly became one of the prize students in the class. Gladys accompanied her daughter to class but by the age of twelve, it was decided that the girl was responsible enough to go alone. The trip involved taking the Red Car, a public streetcar that ran through Los Angeles.

On one of the trips she noticed fellow classmate Frances Rafferty, who had joined the class the year after and got on the streetcar a few stops after her. When the girls started talking, they discovered they had much in common. Their spirited sense of humor and mutual love of dance and music would make them lifelong friends. Rafferty reported that Alexis had trouble with her height in class because she was a couple of inches taller than the other students. As a result, the girl had to play the boy's part. The two went to the ballet and the Hollywood Bowl together. It was such a sharing relationship that people took them for sisters. Alexis gave Rafferty a photograph inscribed with "May we be happy sisters for many years to come". The girls shared books, and clothes when they went on interviews.

She was equally close to her mother, who taught Alexis the importance of good health and nutrition. A steady diet that included ample portions of fruits and vegetables was important, coupled with regular exercise and daily vitamins. Although at times the girl resented Gladys' nutritional bent, Alexis would remain an avid nutritionist and exercise buff throughout her life. Gladys provided a daily packed lunch for the girl which included a raw carrot, which earned Alexis the nickname Rabbit, which she hated.

During the Depression the family's financial situation was not good. Gladys worked as a seamstress and designed all her daughter's clothes to reduce expenses. Unfortunately, this caused the girl to suffer more ridicule from her peers who wore expensive frilly dresses from the May Company or Sears. Alexis never told her mother of the humiliations she suffered at school. The girl was a well-behaved child who respected and loved both her parents.

Another trait that she inherited from her mother was neatness. Gladys was fervent about taking care of the home and Alexis was equally meticulous. Frances Rafferty said this made she and the girl like The Odd Couple as Rafferty was a slob.

By the age of thirteen Alexis had become an accomplished dancer and now she auditioned for the role of a dancer in the Hollywood Bowl's production of *Carmen* in 1934. The girl got the job and was paid $8.50. The following year both she and Rafferty danced in the Bowl's production of *Prince Igor* with a pay of $18.50. In her sophomore year at school Alexis choreographed and danced in *The Red Mill*.

At Hollywood High School at the same time were Lana Turner and Judy Garland but only briefly since they were both whisked away to Hollywood. The girl was so envious thinking it would be wonderful to be discovered for the movies.

When she was fifteen Alexis befriended another schoolmate, Gloria. Their friendship and its eventual abrupt termination helped her give a dramatic performance in the college play, which set the girl on the road to fame.

Alexis was growing fast and described herself as gangly. Her nose was freckled, and the blonde eyebrows and eyelashes were rather too light for beauty. The only make-up the girl wore was a little lipstick, used sketchily. She didn't even own a box of mascara. Alexis was so shy that she had never even had a date with a boy.

The girl got the idea to get a permanent wave, against her mother's advice.

Gloria was the same age but had the sophistication of someone far past her teens. She had had many dates but her only female friend was Alexis. But it soon dawned on the girl that Gloria had an agenda. She wanted Alexis as a friend to act as a foil for Gloria's own vivaciousness and allure. The girl was the perfect patsy. If there was a group of boys, Gloria would be the centre of attention, while Alexis hung around on the edges feeling awkward and self-conscious. If she spoke at all it was usually the wrong thing to say.

One day the two friends were at an ice-cream parlor after school and were enjoying banana splits. They were having a really nice time because Gloria was fun to be with when boys weren't around. A certain boy walked over to their table - a boy Gloria did not know. But this boy was drawn to Alexis, and she was thrilled. But after the girl asked him to sit with them, Gloria set out to vamp the boy away from her.

It was so sudden, so obvious and startling. Gloria ignored her friend completely and turned all her wiles on the boy. He was particularly attractive, but Alexis was sure Gloria wasn't really interested in him. It was just natural for her to act this way. And since she was pretty and vivacious and gay, he fell for it. The boy now forgot about Alexis. Quietly she left payment for her banana split on the table and stood up and left. Gloria and the boy noticed the girl leaving and looked shocked. Alexis walked all the way home which was a long walk. She felt hurt and resentment over her treatment and got some clear thinking done.

Alexis decided she would stop playing second fiddle to Gloria or to anybody. The girl would try in her own way to make herself an entity, just as Gloria had made herself one. But she wouldn't go about it like her friend. Alexis wasn't boy crazy and didn't really care that Gloria had tried to steal the boy away right under her nose. But she was tired of not being able to hold her own, ever, in any sort of situation. Alexis began a campaign.

The girl studied the people she liked and analysed that what attracted them to her was that they were positive sort of people. They didn't have arbitrary opinions and continually voiced them. There was something to them. When they spoke, they had something to say. When they did something, their actions had meaning. Alexis set about turning herself into a person of this sort. It wasn't easy. She had been very used to and dependent on Gloria for companionship, such as it was, and the girl missed it. But she stuck to her guns.

Later, when Alexis was a movie star, she would hear from that boy again. He called her and asked what his chances were for a date. Smith replied not so good. Not ever? he pressed. Not ever, she said. The boy sighed and commented that to think once he could have had her for the asking. What a fool the boy was. Alexis agreed sweetly and hung up the phone. Fate moved in strange, ironical yet often logical ways.

She studied harder in school and took more interest in her clothes. The girl began to experiment with make-up and with new ways of fixing her hair. She practiced the piano even harder and spent more time on her dancing. Alexis also enrolled in a dramatic class realizing that acting would give her much needed poise. The girl loved dramatics from the start.

One day, almost a year after that sad episode at the ice cream parlor, she was walking down steps at school with a group of girls and boys. Alexis suddenly realized she was the centre of attention, and it was a grand and glorious feeling to be popular.

The girl was interested in dramatics believing that acting incorporated all of the arts and all of life. She entered a city-wide oratory acting contest, which Alexis won. She moved onto the state competition, performing a scene from *Elizabeth the Queen*, playing both Queen Elizabeth and Lord Essex. The girl came in second place, losing to Jack Edwards, though the pair returned home on the same train. On arrival they found a brass band and a welcoming crowd at the station to honor the winner. The dejected Alexis didn't want to get off the train, but she was found by her father who gave a lecture on never quitting.

She auditioned for and lost the leading part in the school play *Who Killed Cock Robin?* to Nanette Fabray who was a senior but also a friend. Fabray said in those days both girls were very tall and very cool but no matter hard she tried, Fabray could never look quite as tall and cool as Alexis.

In her senior year she auditioned for the role of Lady Macbeth and won, her trembling hands interpreted by the drama teacher as emotion. After the performance a Hollywood agent came backstage and told the girl she was a great find. He promised to take Alexis around to the studios but then she never saw him again, which was a tremendous blow to her ego. The girl's mother tried to give solace, saying this is what Hollywood people did. The man was just being nice. However, the truth was that her parents had interceded. They did not like the proposal at all and didn't like to see their daughter's acting bug aggravated, which is what they felt he had done. She needed more school and not be afire with the hope of being launched at once on an acting career.

The agent had told her father that Alexis' amazing promise could mean thousands of dollars financially. But Alexander Smith said he had had no trouble supporting the girl for the last sixteen years and he had every intention of doing so until she finished school. Alexis' parents would not reveal all this to their daughter for another six years, after she had become a movie star.

Smith would say the method of her later eminence was astonishingly simple – be a good girl and mind your mother and father. She felt if her parents had given the girl free reign, she would have become just another low salaried Hollywood dancer, as many of her high school classmates had done. It was all glamorous and powerfully enticing to girls of that age and Alexis wanted to join them. But her parents insisted it was more school for her. She cried on her pillow but soon forgot all about it in the pursuit of good English and proper diction. If any girl didn't think it paid to mind their folks, Smith could tell them otherwise.

Alexis didn't think she would have a date for the prom because nobody had asked her. She finally got a date on graduation night at that last moment which really did a lot for her ego. The girl presumed that the boy had been through the whole class and she was the only one left. In the summer her beau then went to Oregon and sent her a souvenir shop drum on which he wrote "Listen to the beat of my heart."

She went back to Hollywood High School the first year after graduating on Alumni Day but though Smith received subsequent invitations, she was too busy working to go again.

By 1939 her parents had become naturalized U.S. citizens, through which she derived her United States citizenship. Alexis had developed into a beauty, standing at five feet nine inches, with a well -toned figure and shapely legs from her years of dance. She had honey-blonde hair and green eyes, and the girl's elegant allure was not lost on her male classmates. Alexis had not been allowed to date until she was sixteen and, even then, it had to be under the watchful eye of her father. He would always pick her up and bring her home until the girl was liberated at eighteen.

By the time she was at college anyone Alexis dated still had to be inspected by her parents. She often dated boys from the campus but never became serious about anyone. Her top priority was academics. Los Angeles City College was a strict school. Of the one hundred that entered only twelve would be left at the end of the second year. The only acceptable excuse for missing class was death. Alexis also continued with her dance classes wanting a well-rounded theatrical background of musical and dramatic training.

In 1940 the College theatre group's final semester production was *The Night of January Sixteenth* in which she played the lead. At the opening night, Warner Bros. talent scouts Milt Lewis and Vic

Orsatti were in attendance and took notice of her. A Paramount agent was also there but it was Orsatti who went backstage and invited the girl to make a screen test. But to his surprise she did not jump up and down with delight. Alexis said politely that she wasn't interested. The girl wanted to finish her year at college and then continue her study of music. Orsatti gave Alexis his card and said to call him once school was out. But she didn't because the girl was having too good a time that summer.

In August Orsatti telephoned her asking again about a movie career. He wanted to take her out to Warner Bros. She agreed if he thought this would mean a good contract. But if the best they could offer was $50 a week for six months, then the girl said to skip the whole thing. She really wasn't that interested in the movies anyway. Instead, Alexis planned to go to the University of California in Los Angeles to get a degree. When Orsatti told her he thought she had a good chance for an important career, Alexis agreed to go.

The next afternoon she dressed in a simple little shirtmaker frock, with no hat and no make-up. The girl had none of the accoutrements which might have impressed movie producers. Orsatti took her to Warner Bros where they met with Sally Baiano in the casting department. Again, Alexis didn't try to create any effect. She was just herself, friendly and unaffected. To her having a movie career wasn't a matter of life and death. Baiano agreed the girl had possibilities and decreed she should be camera tested.

It was arranged for her to work with drama coach Sophie Rosenstein to prepare for the test. When it was run Jack Warner expressed concern about Alexis' height since most of the Warners leading men were less than six feet tall. But she photographed well and had a kind of regal, sophisticated quality that was genuinely lacking in most of the studio's leading ladies. The girl was signed to a seven-year contract for $75 a week.

She was disappointed that it was Warners and not M-G-M where all the big stars were. But later would believe that the Warners product stood up so much better than the pure escapist fare of Metro. The top movie stars at Warners were Bette Davis, Humphrey Bogart, George Arliss and Paul Muni and they were essentially actors.

Alexis consulted with Jerry Blunt, her Los Angeles City College drama tutor, about the Warners deal. He said of course she was not ready but to take it as the opportunity may never come again. The girl was glad and declared to do her best. Blunt said when Alexis first came to his class, he did not think she would become a big star. But he could see the girl had talent in the class of young kids who were all tied up in knots with their arms and legs. For him a star came with years and work, and he was never in the least surprised when she made it and turned out to be the toast of Broadway. But if Alexis didn't get by, she wouldn't care too much. The girl would just figure out some other type of career. Orsatti responded that she was a funny sort. Alexis would explain her thinking. She believed it didn't pay to care too much about things. People who did seemed often to lose them.

There was a minor battle with the bosses over her name. They said nobody had ever heard of a star with the name of Smith. But the girl said that was her name and she was going was going to keep it. Alexis figured there were umpteen million Smiths in the country, and she was sure they would be on her side. This Smith was determined to remain herself.

She spent her first year doing tests with potential contract players and posing for cheesecake publicity shots. Her first still picture was posing in a leather print bathing suit. Then the girl started being cast in bit parts to pay her dues and learn the film business. She also was given training in the Warners drama school.

Chapter 2. Warner Bros.

One source has her uncredited film debut in the black and white Warner Bros. and The Vitaphone Corporation twenty-two minute musical short *Alice in Movieland* aka Broadway Brevities (1940-1941 season) (#2): Alice in Movieland (1940). However, the viewed film suggests that Smith's appearance as herself is in the version re-edited and re-released on December 21, 1946. This is because she is identified as a movie star which the actress was not in September, 1940, when the short was made. The film was shot at the Warner Bros. studios, with a screenplay by Owen Crump and Cyrus D. Wood based on a story by Ed Sullivan and directed by Jean Negulesco. It centres on eighteen-year-old Plainville girl Alice Purdee (Joan Leslie) who wins a free trip to Hollywood for a screen test.

Smith has a cameo, sitting a table at the nightclub Carlos' with Craig Stevens, her hair worn in a shoulder-length brunette style with a side part. She is spotted by maid Agatha Winters (Nana Bryant) as one of the movie stars in the audience for Alice's dancing act in the club's talent night. Another source claims that Smith's original appearance saw her in a black wig dancing the conga and then changing into a blonde wig to do a Viennese waltz.

The actress reportedly appeared uncredited in the black and white Warner Bros. biography *"Lady with Red Hair"* (1940) shot at the Warners studios from August 26 to October 10, 1940. The film had a screenplay by Charles Kenyon and Milton Krims from the story by N. Brewster Morse and Norbert Faulkner based upon the memoirs of Mrs. Leslie Carter. The director was Curtis Bernhardt credited as Kurt Bernhardt. The plot centres on Caroline Carter (Miriam Hopkins), a Chicago divorcee who is shunned by society in 1889 for being an adulteress and forbidden from having custody of her son. Smith is said to be in a wedding scene though there is not one in the print viewed. There is a post-wedding dinner, but the actress cannot be spotted in it.

The film was released on November 30 with the taglines "Girls, throw away those typewriters…Come out from behind those counters… Leave those dishes in the sink… Here's How To Be Rich And Famous!", and "She didn't have any experience, either, so…She Started At The Top…And Worked Her Way Up!" It received mixed reactions from Bosley Crowther in *The New York Times* and Clive Hirschhorn in "The Warner Bros. Story".

Smith can be seen in the black and white Warner Bros. B comedy *"She Couldn't Say No"* (1940) shot from October 2 at the Warner Bros. studios. The screenplay was by Earl Baldwin and Charles Grayson from the play by Benjamin M. Kaye which ran on Broadway at the Booth Theatre from August 31 to November, 1926. The film had been previously made by Warner Bros. in 1930. The new film's director was William Clemens. The story centred on Alice Hinsdale (Eve Arden), the secretary to New York lawyer Wallace Turnbull (Roger Pryor) who defends Kerricksville farmer Eli Potter (Clem Bevans) in a breach of promise suit that Wallace prosecutes.

The uncredited Smith plays one of the Kerricksville Phone Gossips in a montage. Seen in close-up with her hair in curlers, she gets the line "Why he's never lost a case" referring to Wallace. The film was released on December 7 with the tagline "She Was A Lawyer .. . And So Was He . . . So They Took Their Heart Troubles To Court!" It was lambasted by Clive Hirschhorn in "The Warner Bros. Story".

Next was the black and white Warner Bros. B film-noir *"Flight From Destiny"* (1941) shot with the working titles Invitation to a Murder and Trial and Error from late September to early November at the Warner studios. The screenplay was by Barry Trivers with uncredited contributions from Charles Kenyon and Robert Rossen based on a story by Anthony Berkeley. The director was Vincent Sherman with an uncredited assistance from Don Siegel. The story centred on sixty-one year-old Professor Henry Todhunter (Thomas

Mitchell) who only has a few months to live and decides to commit a socially useful murder. Smith is uncredited in a montage about Ketti Moret (Mona Maris), as a girlfriend saying, "I wish she were dead". The actress is seen in close-up wearing her hair with sculptured bangs.

The film was released on December 25 in New York and given a wide release on February 8, 1941, with the taglines "A Picture As Important As Its Title…As Human As Its Stars…As Bold As the Screen Itself" and "Here is a strange, powerful picture that's different from all other pictures …the way the Mona Lisa is different from all other paintings!" It was praised by T.M.P in *The New York Times* and Clive Hirschhorn in "The Warner Bros. Story".

To follow was the black and white Warner Bros. B romantic comedy *The Great Mr. Nobody* (1941) with the working titles The Stuff of Heroes and A Bashful Hero. It was shot from late November to mid-December at the Warner studios. The screenplay was by Ben Markson and Kenneth Gamet with uncredited contributions from Ivan Goff and Al Martin, based on the story "The Stuff of Heroes" by Harold Titus. The story had been previously adapted for the Warner Bros. 1925 silent comedy *How Baxter Butted In*. The new film's director was Ben Stoloff. The story centred on Robert 'Dreamy' Smith (Eddie Albert) who aspires to quit his job as newspaper publicity drudge and sail the world. Smith is uncredited as either a woman in an office or a waitress. Regrettably the film is not available for viewing.

It was released on February 15, 1941, with the taglines "There'll Never Be Another Hero Like 'Dreamy'…There Couldn't Be!" and "YOU KNOW HIM! Just another guy . . . until he met THE girl!" It was praised by Clive Hirschhorn in "The Warner Bros. Story".

She was next seen in the black and white Warner Bros. B romantic comedy *Here Comes Happiness* (1941) shot from November 28 to early December at the Warner studios. The screenplay was by Charles Tedford based on a story by Harry Sauber, which had been previously made as the Warner Bros. musical comedy *Happiness Ahead* (1934). The new director was Noel M. Smith. The story centred on Jessica Vance (Mildred Coles), the millionaire's daughter who ditches her fiancé Jelliffe Blaine (Richard Ainley) at her engagement party. Smith is uncredited as a blonde. This is another film that is unavailable for viewing.

The film was released on March 15, 1941, with the taglines "Here Comes Love! Here Comes Laughter! "Here Comes Happiness" and "Here Comes The Bride. There Goes The Gloom!" It was praised by Clive Hirschhorn in "The Warner Bros. Story". The film would be remade as the Warner Bros. musical comedy *Love and Learn* (1947).

The actress then appeared in the Warner Bros. black and white romantic comedy "*Affectionately Yours*" (1941) shot from January 14 to March 9, 1941, on location at Lisbon airport, LaGuardia airport in New York and at the Warner studios. The screenplay was by Edward Kaufman based on s story by Fanya Foss and Aleen Leslie, and the director was Lloyd Bacon. It centred on Richard 'Rickey' Mayberry (Dennis Morgan), a married New York reporter whose international assignments gives him ample opportunity to put the moves on the local females.

Smith is uncredited in the scenes where Ricky's ex-wife Sue Mayberry (Merle Oberon) tries to marry Owen Wright (Ralph Bellamy). She is in four scenes, in the background walking behind Oberon and going up a staircase, in Sue's bedroom with Sue and the bridesmaids, in the living room reacting when Sue leaves the house to go after Ricky, and on the apartment stoop when the crowd follows Sue outside. The actress plays one of the three bridesmaids holding bouquets. She wears her hair in an updo with a veil and flowers and has a light-colored dress by Orry-Kelly.

The film was released on May 10, 1941, with the tagline "Here They Come… And They're Affectionately Yours". It was lambasted by Clive Hirschhorn in "The Warner Bros. Story".

Next was the Warners black and white B romance "*Singapore Woman*" (1941) shot from January 20 at the Warner studios. The working titles were Singapore and Jinx Woman. It was a remake of the Warners romance *Dangerous* (1935). The new film's screenplay was by M. Coates Webster and Allen Rivkin with uncredited contribution by Robert Presnell Sr. The director was Jean Negulesco. The film centred on Victoria 'Vicki' Moore (Brenda Marshall), an alcoholic American heiress in Singapore who is romanced by rubber plantation owner David 'Dave' Ritchie (David Bruce).

Smith is uncredited as Miss Oswald, the secretary of the Pacific American Oil Company President Jim North (Jerome Cowan). She appears in four scenes: taking Jim's dictation, sending in solicitor Sidney P. Melrose (an uncredited Ian Wolfe), with Vicki at Miss Oswald's desk and trying to stop her from seeing Jim. The actress has an upswept hairdo, with glasses and different outfits by Damon Giffard. However Negulesco obscures our first view of her with foreground set dressing. Smith gets a few lines and is twice heard over the intercom.

The film was released on May 11, 1941, with the taglines "MARKED WOMAN OF THE ORIENT!" and "INTRIGUE! ROMANCE! MARKED WOMAN!". It was lambasted by Clive Hirschhorn in "The Warner Bros. Story".

In his book *Jean Negulesco: The Life and Films* Michelangelo Capua reports that the director was fired in the middle of production and the shoot completed by associate producer Harlan Thompson.

To follow was the Warners romantic comedy *Three Sons o' Guns* (1941) shot from February 9 at the Warners studios. The screenplay was by Fred Niblo Jr. and the director was Ben Stoloff. The story centred on Margaret Patterson (Irene Rich) and her 3 sons, Charley (Wayne Morris), Eddie (Tom Brown) and Kenneth (William T. Orr). Smith plays the uncredited role of an actress. This is another film unavailable for viewing.

It was released on August 2 with taglines that included "Public Declares it a HOWLIDAY!" and "You've Gotta Get Up . . . YOU'VE GOTTA GET UP . . . To See It!"

On April 16 United States soldiers were asked to choose the six most beautiful women from a field of 150, many of whom were Warner Bros. contract players. The six chosen were known as the Navy Blues Sextet, assigned to promote the Warners musical comedy *Navy Blues* (1941). The film was in production from mid-April to mid-June and set for a September 13 release. It was announced on May 1 that of the six chosen, five were in the film. They were Georgia Carroll, Loraine Gettman, Kay Aldridge, Marguerite Chapman, and Peggy Diggins. As the sixth, Smith was the only one not in the film. The Sextet toured theatres but after the actress was cast in "*Dive Bomber*" she was replaced by Claire James as James had also appeared in the film.

Smith on left and Errol Flynn on right in portrait for *Dive Bomber* (1941)

The Warners Technicolor war romance "*Dive Bomber*" (1941) was shot from March 20 to mid-May or June 3 on locations in Florida, Hawaii, and Los Angeles and at the Warner studios. The working title was Beyond the Blue Sky. The screenplay was by Frank Wead and Robert Buckner from on a story by Wead, and the director was Michael Curtiz. The story centres on Navy surgeon Lieutenant Doug Lee (Errol Flynn) who teams with Navy flyer Lieutenant Commander Joe Blake (Fred MacMurray) to develop a high-altitude deep diving suit.

Smith gets her first screen credit and is billed fourth under the title, playing the supporting role of Linda 'Sugar' Fisher, an old friend of Joe's. She has the biggest female part in the film, but the character has minor impact on the plot, which is mostly focused on the men and the aviation. Linda is interested in Doug, but the feeling is not mutual. Then Joe becomes interested in her at a party where she prefers to talk to Doug. When Doug invites her and her girlfriend Helen (an uncredited Ann Doran) on a double date, for Joe's moral, the men are more absorbed in talking about their diving suit.

Director Curtiz has Linda first shown primping her hair in a mirror before she sees Doug. When Linda sits and talks with him, Curtiz has shadows from people behind Doug distracting our view of her, as well as shadows from Doug when he stands. She kicks him in the leg from anger, and the role also sees her kissed by and dancing with Doug. One upswept hairdo has a left sided part.

Smith banters with Flynn and Linda gets some funny lines. On the double date Linda tells Helen, "You know I fly too but I'm not such a bore about it. I CAN talk about other things now and then." When Doug grabs her lipstick to look at it for the valve for their diving suit , she replies, "I don't think that shade will be becoming to you." Craig Stevens plays John Thomas Anthony but has no scenes with her.

The film was released on August 30 with taglines that included "Flying high, wide and handsome!" and "MEN WITHOUT FEAR

. . . CONQUER the STRATOSPHERE!". It was a box office success and was nominated for the Academy Award for Best Cinematography, Color. The film was praised by *Variety*, and Bosley Crowther in *The New York Times* who wrote that Smith looked good but he couldn't tell how she acted. It received a mixed reaction from Clive Hirschhorn in "The Warner Bros. Story".

Smith reported that Linda's scenes were shot near the end of production when it was decided that the story needed girls. They looked at any number of starlets before giving her a screen test. Once cast, she was given the full glamor treatment although the film has no credit for wardrobe. The actress found Flynn to the manliest, sexist person she had ever met. Smith was also fond of him, believing Flynn to be a better actor than he was given credit for. And the man was so much fun.

Michael Freedland in his book *The Two Lives Of Errol Flynn* writes that she was upset by the actor when it was time for her first close-up in the film. Flynn walked into the frame and stole the scene. Smith was said to have been distraught and ran crying to her dressing room, convinced the opportunity to make her a star had been lost forever. She went home that night in a fit of deep depression. When the actress returned to the set the next morning, she felt even worse. That is until Smith came to her dressing room to find a note in front of the make-up mirror. The envelope bore the name Errol Flynn and inside, written on his personal stationary, was an apology. It was so apparently sincere and charming that her anger dissipated.

Thomas McNulty in *Errol Flynn: A Life and Career* writes that Flynn cultivated the actress although she always denied a romantic relationship. Flynn supposedly insisted on her casting and claimed he wrote her scenes into the film. Flynn also spoke glowingly of Smith before the premiere, saying she was a lady you would be hearing a good deal from and soon. The actress might be described as vaguely Grecian in appearance, and there was lots of talent there.

She comments in Tony Thomas' book, *Errol Flynn: The Spy Who Never Was* that Flynn was a movie idol of her teens. Smith was intimidated playing opposite him but came to like him genuinely. He was full of tricks and flip and always had an entourage of girls. But Flynn could charm anyone - man or woman - and he was intelligent and had wit. She thought it was shame Flynn cared more for the bottle and for fun and games than he did for work.

Alan K. Rode in *Michael Curtiz: A Life in Film* writes that the director wanted to showcase the lissom Smith and she was given a prosaic part as Flynn's girlfriend.

After the film's success Warners now gave her the star build-up, labelling the actress The Dynamite Girl. This is a tag she detested. There was also a publicity stunt where Warners arranged for the President of Dynamite Guild of America to present her with the Guild's pseudo-Oscar. This was five sticks of phony dynamite. Smith was said to be full of tremendous energy and was likely to explode on the slightest impulse, like dynamite. However privately she felt the stupidity of the studio's publicity department was not to be believed.

Her next film was the Warners black and white B comic horror mystery "*The Smiling Ghost*" (1941) shot from mid-May to mid-June at the Warners studios. The screenplay was by Kenneth Gamet and Stuart Palmer with uncredited contributions from Ben Markson and Ralph Spence, from an original story by Palmer and an uncredited story by Philip Wylie. The director was Lewis Seiler. It centred on engineer Lucky Downing (Wayne Morris) who is hired to be the new fiancé of New Haven heiress Elinor Bentley Fairchild (Smith) to catch the titular ghost. Elinor is known as The Kiss of Death Girl because all her three previous fiancés have met horrible ends.

She is billed third after the title and plays a supporting role. Her hairdos have a side part that switches from right to left, and clothes by Leah Rhodes include a low-cut negligee and an ugly wedding dress. Elinor is presented as the wealthy and haughty tall blonde in opposition to the proletariat no-nonsense short brunette newspaper reporter Lil Barstow (Brenda Marshall). The disparity makes the conclusion as to who Lucky chooses inevitable, however Smith makes Elinor funny. After Lucky kisses her, she says in a wavering voice, "Whatever you're getting for this job, you're underpaid." To Lil, Elinor says, "You're in love with Lucky yourself. Every look you give him you could pour on a waffle."

The role sees Elinor kiss and be kissed by Lucky, and cry. This is the first time we see Smith employ self-conscious self-touching in her acting, though she only does it in one scene. Our first view of her has the actress in close-up but strangely director Seiler has the headscarf she wears partially obscure her face.

The film was released on September 6 with the taglines "A SWELL MYSTERY! (You'll never guess the ending!) A GRAND COMEDY! (It's mysterical! A chiller-diller!)" and "It's eerie! It's cheery!" It received a mixed reaction from Bosley Crowther in *The New York Times* who wrote that Smith made a decorative kiss-of-death girl. However, it was lambasted by Clive Hirschhorn in "The Warner Bros. Story".

Warners made this film in the hope of emulating the success of Paramount's comic horror films *The Cat and the Canary* (1939) and *The Ghost Breakers* (1940), with the latter also featuring Willie Best as a quaking manservant.

She was back to having an uncredited cameo role in the Warners B comic crime mystery *Passage from Hong Kong* (1941) shot from mid-March at the Warners studio. The screenplay was by Fred Niblo Jr. from a story "Agony Column" by Earl Derr Biggers, and the director was D. Ross Lederman. The story centred on Maria Calhoun (Lucille Fairbanks) who is pursued by pulp writer Jeff Hunter (Keith Douglas) by inventing a murder story in which he claims he was implicated. Smith plays a Nightclub Dancer who is said to perform in a black Cleopatra wig and harem girl costume. This is another film that is unavailable for viewing.

Smith in portrait for *Passage from Hong Kong* (1941)

It was released in September with taglines that included "A beautiful, figureful lady who will do anything for her purpose!" and "Not even murder could stop this mystery girl!" It was lambasted by Clive Hirschhorn in "The Warner Bros. Story".

Next was the Warners black and white B comic action adventure "*Steel Against The Sky*" (1941) shot from mid-August to mid-September at the Warners studios. The working titles were The High Tower and Bridges Built at Night. The screenplay was by Paul Gerard Smith from a story by Maurice Hanline and Jesse Lasky, Jr. The director was A. Edward Sutherland. It centred on bridge building supervisor Rocky Evans (Lloyd Nolan) and his brother Chuck (Craig Stevens) who both fall in love with Helen Powers (Smith).

Although she is top-billed below the title the actress plays a supporting role. It sees her kiss and be kissed by Chuck, have coffee spilled on Helen by him, and marry Chuck. Smith has some funny moments, when she is flirting with Rocky and how she suddenly gets up from a chair that Pete Evans (Edward Brophy) says their grandmother died in.

The actress also plays a scene where Helen lies that she does not love Chuck to save his estranged friendship with his brother. Smith's raised eyebrow acting may have the context of Helen being a flirt, and again she only uses self-conscious self-touching in one scene. Gowns are by Howard Shoup with costuming that includes a sheer raincoat that is worn in the climactic rainstorm. Director Sutherland gives the actress many close-ups and one extreme close-up at the end of the lying scene to show Helen's real feelings.

The film was released on December 13, 1941, with the taglines "Defying Sudden Death . . . Fighting for Life and Love . . . Matching Their Might Against Steel!" and "Love plays its song against steel; girders. Romance and action high up among bolts and beams."

Smith had wanted her friend Charles Drake to play Chuck, but the casting of Craig Stevens proved to be a personal milestone. She had known him slightly when they made *"Dive Bomber"*. He said they had met at the Warners talent school where the two took classes. But now their relationship reached a new plateau. The actress had made it a firm policy not to date men from the studio but during the shooting of the climactic scene of the film she changed her mind. The scene took a long time to film, and since it was shot at night, Smith accepted Stevens' invitation to eat together afterwards. He said that's when they got to know each other. The actor found her a lot of fun and she told him about wanting Drake in the film. Stevens knew Smith had no say in casting but found her admission amusing. She in turn found him to be a charming dinner companion.

Lloyd Nolan commented that the actress had a very original type of beauty, very fresh and sincere both on and off the screen.

On August 27 it was announced that she would star in "Blonde Bomber" for Warners, a story of naval aviation. The screenplay would be based on a story by Richard Macauley. It appears this film was never made.

Smith followed with the Warners A black and white musical mystery "*The Constant Nymph*" (1943) shot from late February to early April, 1942, at the Warners studios. The material had been previously filmed as a 1928 British silent romance, a British 1933 drama, and a British 1938 television drama. The new screenplay was by Kathryn Scola based on the novel and play by Margaret Kennedy and Basil Dean. The director was Edmund Goulding. The story is set in Switzerland and centres on fourteen-year-old Tessa Sanger (Joan Fontaine) who is in love with composer Lewis Dodd (Charles Boyer) the husband of her cousin Florence Creighton (Smith). She is billed third above the title and plays a supporting part. The actress' hair is longer here, and her gowns are by Orry-Kelly.

It appears Lewis has married Florence for her money, and she understands his music less than Tessa. Florence likes the dissonant modern music he plays at a concert, but Tessa knows his real talent is for romantic music. Florence is aware of Tessa's crush on Lewis and her jealousy turns to hatred. Smith expresses this in a scene that she performs archly, but the actress is better in later scenes when Florence begs Lewis for a second chance and finally accepts his love for Tessa. The role also sees her smoke, use an English accent, kiss and be kissed by Lewis, cry, and shake Tessa.

The film was not released until June 23, 1943, with taglines that included "HE LEARNED TOO LATE . . . that he preferred charming simplicity to sophisticated beauty!" and "He tried to divide his heart and broke theirs." Sources differ as to whether it was a box office success, but Fontaine was nominated for the Best Actress Academy Award. The film was praised by L.B.F. in *The New York Times* who wrote that Smith came through with an intelligent rendition and her dramatic scene with Tessa was especially ably done. However, it received a mixed reaction from *Variety*, and Clive Hirschhorn in "The Warner Bros. Story". *Lux Radio Theater* broadcast a sixty-minute radio adaptation of the movie on January 10, 1944, with Boyer and the actress reprising their film roles. "The Screen Guild Theater" broadcast a thirty-minute radio adaptation of the movie on March 20, 1944, also with Boyer and Smith.

She had to test for the film. In his book *Final Gig: The Man Behind The Murder*, George Eells reports that Gig Young had the workhorse assignment of being her test partner. When it was over it was said the actress was the talk of the studio because the test was so good. When Boyer saw it, he reportedly whistled, which was something extraordinary for the reserved actor to do. He described it as unbelievable.

In his book *Sisters: The Story Of Olivia De Havilland & Joan Fontaine* Charles Higham writes that director Goulding made things fun on the set by acting out the roles played by Fontaine and Smith.

Matthew Kennedy in *Edmund Goulding's Dark Victory: Hollywood's Genius Bad Boy* has the director describe Smith as so nervous. Craig Stevens reported that Goulding really gave the actress a big break by casting her in the film. He was very fond of Smith and wanted her for the role. She was aged twenty and had to play an older woman, but the director knew Alexis could do it. Stevens believed it was this role that finally got her noticed as an actress. She said there were two or three directors Smith had learned from and been challenged by and Goulding was the first.

She considered the film her big break with serious performers and not fun and games like Errol Flynn films. Goulding intimidated her despite his reputation as a 'women's director'. Smith felt the part was over her head because of the age difference but came to work as a piece of putty, and Goulding molded her. It was a marvellous experience, but she was terrified. The actress was also intimidated to be working with Boyer and was nervous about their first screen kiss. She was given a pep talk by Goulding and after four takes and fifteen minutes the director was satisfied with the kiss. Smith said they rehearsed only once because Boyer really knew how to kiss.

Boyer was reportedly unhappy with the film. He felt Florence was so humorless and unlikable that Lewis' love for her was unbelievable, consequently making Tessa's love for him also dubious. Smith's friend actress Audrey Totter reported that she was so excited to about the chance to work with Boyer but also concerned about the height difference. The actress was a good two inches taller than the leading man. For her screen test she went about on bended knee the whole time so Smith would appear shorter than him. Boyer was very nice and stood on a box during their scenes together, and she just adored him.

Goulding said that it wasn't a question of what the actress would be because she had already arrived.

Smith in portrait for "*The Constant Nymph*" (1943)

On March 21 it was reported that Smith would appear in Warners "Sweethearts of 1942", a screenplay by Hugh Wedlock and Howard Snyder. It appears this film was never made.

To aid the war effort she was among the Warners contract players who were sent to the Lockheed aircraft factory. They gave speeches and tried to get people to buy War Bonds.

Chapter 3. *"Gentleman Jim"*

Next was the Warners musical romance *"Gentleman Jim"* (1942) shot from May 20, 1942 to July 23 or August on locations in California and at the Warners studios. The screenplay was by Vincent Lawrence and Horace McCoy based upon the life of James J. Corbett. The director was Raoul Walsh. Beginning in San Francisco in 1887 it told how Corbett (Errol Flynn) uses dazzlingly innovative footwork to rise to the top of the boxing world. Smith is billed second above the title and plays the supporting role of Victoria 'Vicki' Ware, mining heiress. Her hairdos are all upswept and gowns by Milo Anderson include a seemingly historically inaccurate low-cut one and a hat that causes a shadow over the actress' face. The role sees her dance with and be kissed by Jim and try to slap him.

She makes Vicki funny in her initial reaction to Jim's advances, and the narrative has the heiress resent his conceit so as to be against Jim winning his fights. This leads to some strange reaction shots in two fights, where Vicki sits forward in her perverse enthusiasm for him to lose. Director Walsh shows the men's reactions to be equally cartoonish. Vicki gets a funny line when she yells, "You're all wet, Mr. Corbett" after he is knocked out of the barge ring and falls into the San Francisco Bay in the fight with Joe Choynski (an uncredited Sammy Stein). However, her enthusiasm changes from perversity to support in the climactic fight with John L. Sullivan (Ward Bond). Smith makes Vicki sweet when she finally admits to loving Jim.

The film was released on November 14 with taglines that included "The grandest story of the Naughty "Nineties" becomes the gayest picture of the Fighting "Forties!"" and "IT'S A KNOCK-OUT!" It was a box office success. The film was praised by Pauline Kael in "5001 Nights At The Movies" who wrote that Smith was quite entertaining. It received a mixed reaction from *Variety*, and T.M.P. in *The New York Times* who wrote that she carried the romantic interest very entertainingly, and Clive Hirschhorn in "The Warner Bros. Story". *The Screen Guild Theater* broadcast a thirty-minute radio adaptation of the movie on February 14, 1944, with Flynn, Smith, and Ward Bond reprising their roles.

There was no Victoria Ware in real life. From the start of his boxing career in 1886 until 3 years after his fight with John L Sullivan, Jim Corbett was married to Mary Higgins. After their divorce, he married Vera Taylor.

Ann Sheridan had been announced for the part of Vicki, but Raoul Walsh had also suggested Rita Hayworth.

In the film's pressbook Smith reported that her newest fur coat was one of the actress' best investments. Of richly shaved beaver, it was styled with melon sleeves and a tiny collar. It had deep armholes and plenty of fullness so was easy to wear over suits or heavy winter clothes. She was also bringing some of her clothes patriotically up-to-date, particularly sweaters. Smith was having a gold eagle embroidered on a red sweater, and navy blue star and chevrons of felt stitched onto a white one. It was not only a patriotic touch but also an extremely smart one.

In addition, she had a personal outfit redesigned by Warners' costumer Milo Anderson. Orry-Kelly was another fan of the actress. The designer said he could put draped sackcloth on her, and she would appear beautiful. Orry-Kelly said Smith was grace personified. When she walked, the line of her body was as straight as if the actress had an invisible cord strung from the centre top of her head straight to the floor. Yet the movements were relaxed and flowing without tenseness.

The pressbook also saw Smith's answer to the challenge of meat rationing – a recipe for beef with noodles where she made a little beef go a long way.

Flynn suffered a mild heart attack during shooting on July 15 although Charles Higham in his book *Errol Flynn: The Untold Story* reports that the actor had been continuously ill since March. Filming was suspended for a week and according to Michael Freedland in *The Two Lives Of Errol Flynn* the actress spoke to Flynn about it. She told him that it was so silly, working all day and then playing all night and dissipating himself. Smith asked Flynn if he wanted live a long life to which he replied "I'm only interested in this half. I don't care for the future.'"

Craig Stevens denied that she and Flynn were romantically involved, though Flynn was known to have affairs with his leading ladies. Stevens said Flynn had great respect for her, treating the actress with dignity and humor, and never made a pass.

By now she and Stevens were inseparable. When Smith wasn't seeing him she spent her spare time with friends, as well as reading and attending the ballet. Her friend Frances Rafferty reported one memorable night when they decided to splurge. The Ballet Russe de Monte Carlo were appearing in Los Angeles, and the pair obtained orchestra seats. The women got all dressed up and looked beautiful. They drove to the theatre, parked at the Biltmore Garage, and went on to have a great time at the ballet. Rafferty said it was one of the most wonderful evenings in their lives. Then they discovered that neither one of them had the money to retrieve the car from the garage. Luckily the men working there recognised the actresses, so they were able to get home, but it was still pretty embarrassing. The women returned to pay the men the next day.

Smith was tested for the role of Princess Maria in the Warners romantic comedy *Princess O'Rourke* (1943). Olivia de Havilland had refused the part but then played it.

She was next in the Warners black and white biographical adventure "*The Adventures of Mark Twain*" (1944) shot from July 7 to mid-September, 1942, on locations in Los Angeles and at the Warners studios. The screenplay was by Alan Le May. It was adapted by Le May and Harold M. Sherman based on works owned or controlled by the Mark Twain Company and Sherman's play

"Mark Twain", with additional dialogue by Harry Chandlee. The director was Irving Rapper. The film dramatized the life of immortal humorist Samuel Langhorne Clemens, better known as Mark Twain (Fredric March). The actress is billed second after the title and plays the supporting part of New England heiress Olivia 'Livy' Langdon who becomes Samuel's wife. We wait 58 out of the 130 minutes running time to see her and director Rapper introduces Livy with a close-up.

Poster for *The Adventures of Mark Twain* (1944)

Smith is styled differently here, with her hair parted in the middle and worn with period ringlets until age turns it white and worn off the forehead. Livy's clothes by Orry-Kelly include a notable plain-patterned dress. Perc Westmore's aging of Livy is done with more subtlety than that of Mark. March's hair is white relatively quickly, though Smith appears to wear less make-up from the beginning. Livy is shy but supportive of Mark and the role sees her kiss Jervis Langdon (Walter Hampden) and be kissed by Mark, cry, look dishevelled when faced with her child dying, and have a death scene. The actress gives a warm performance, with Rapper giving her many close-ups.

The film release was delayed until July 22, 1944, and the taglines included "All aboard, full steam ahead for the life story of America's greatest storyteller!" and "The Gol-Darndest American!" It was a box office success and nominated for three Academy Awards - Best Art Direction-Interior Decoration, Black-and-White; Best Effects, Special Effects; and Best Music, Scoring of a Dramatic or Comedy Picture. The film was praised by *Variety,* and Charles Higham and Joel Greenberg in "Hollywood In The Forties". It received a mixed reaction from Bosley Crowther in *The New York Times* who wrote that Smith was colorless and conventional, in the manner of film geniuses' wives, and Clive Hirschhorn in "The Warner Bros. Story".

The role of Lily was first announced for Olivia de Havilland, but she was replaced after being put on suspension by Warners for turning down another part.

For the later scenes Smith reported to the studio at 6:30 each morning to spend two hours in make-up having her face wrinkled, hair grayed and features etched with age. On other days she had to sit for long tedious hours in the studio-made rainstorm appearing beautiful and desirable when thoroughly wet and feeling miserable. The actress suggested very gently that anyone who thought it was easy might try it some rainy night on their own front porch. The early visits to make-up and nights spent studying lines interfered greatly with her romance with Craig Stevens which at this moment was very important indeed.

The film's pressbook said Smith's mother was the guiding genius of her present busy life - counsellor, comforter, best friend, and severest critic. Her father was the one she aimed to please the most. The actress was Dad's girl and she quoted him on any and all subjects during any friendly arguments on the set. It was her father whom Smith worried about when her dog chewed up the morning paper or dug into the family's victory garden. The highest compliment she paid herself was that he saw one of her films and liked the performance.

The actress was a home girl, sharing in the family's anonymity and its problems, economic, social, and educational. She liked puns and dolls, kept a scrapbook, and remembered favorite telephone numbers. Smith raided the refrigerator at night, talked pig Latin and liked to color Easter eggs.

On August 23 she announced her engagement to Craig Stevens, but no wedding date had been set. On September 22 it was reported the actress would appear in a serious part with Olivia de Havilland in "One More Tomorrow".

In October when Errol Flynn was accused of rape, she was one of his Hollywood friends who was said to have rushed to the actor's defence. Smith refused to believe he had raped any woman.

To follow was the Warners black and white musical comedy "*Thank Your Lucky Stars*" (1943) shot from October 14, 1942, to early January, 1943, at the Warners studios. The screenplay was by Norman Panama, Melvin Frank, and James V. Kern from an original story by Everett Freeman and Arthur Schwartz. It was directed by David Butler. The story centred on Eddie Cantor playing himself and movie star home tour guide Cantor lookalike Joe Simpson who are involved in a wartime charity show with an all-star cast.

Smith is listed twelfth after the title, with the stars listed alphabetically, and plays herself. She appears in part of one number, "Good Night, Good Neighbor" with music by Arthur Schwartz and lyrics by Frank Loesser. It opens with Dennis Morgan escorting Miss Latin America (Lynne Baggett] home to the Pan American Club For Women, singing to her and a chorus of residents. Then there is a segue to Club Chiquilla where Smith does an acrobatic ballroom dance with Igor Dega and Arnold Kent.

Her appearance is prefaced by being talked about by Tommy Randolph (Morgan) and Pat Dixon (Joan Leslie) with Pat referencing "*Gentleman Jim*". She is then seen behind the sheer curtain of the Club Chiquilla that is parted to reveal the dance in front of a band. Her costume by Milo Anderson is rather daring in that her midriff is bare in the floor-length, sleeveless, white-colored dress. Director Butler alternates between long and medium shot coverage of the dance, with the medium shots frustrating. Smith is brought out onto the stage by Morgan after the number for audience applause. She returns for the film's finale to dance with the boys, where all the numbers are reprised in a medley, including "Good Night, Good Neighbor" and the title song also by Schwartz and Loesser. The dances numbers were created and staged by Leroy Prinz.

The film was released on September 25 with the tagline "A Thousand Shows In One!" It was a box office success and nominated for Best Original Song Academy Award for "They're Either Too Young or Too Old". The film received a mixed reaction from *Variety*, and Bosley Crowther in *The New York Times*. The *Screen Guild Theater* did a thirty-minute radio version of the film which was broadcast on September 27, 1943. Although Dennis Morgan sang "Good Night, Good Neighbor" he made no mention of Smith's dance.

Each star was paid $50,000 for their appearance in this film, which was then donated to The Hollywood Canteen. The actress' dance was the only time she would ever do such an extended musical number on screen. Smith reported that when Leroy Prinz was asked why he had two boys dance with her, the choreographer replied he couldn't find just one strong enough to do the heavy lifting.

She commented on Warner's reluctance to cast her in a musical. The actress always played a character sitting in the audience applauding someone else who was little and cute. Hollywood liked cuddly little girls in its musicals, and she was not little or cute. Unlike Betty Grable and June Haver and Vera-Ellen, Smith was considered cold and statuesque. The only people she told about wanting to get up and there and perform like mad were the cop at the gate and the woman in wardrobe. However, another source claims the actress begged to do a musical, saying she could dance and sing, but no one paid any attention to her. Smith thought it all worked out very nicely and she had no complaints. A third source had her say that when the actress once heard a recording of her singing voice, she said "Forget it."

On January 11 it was announced that Smith had replaced Joan Leslie in Warners' "Broken Journey". It appears this film was not made.

On February 18 it was reported she would star in Warners remake of *The Animal Kingdom* which had been made by RKO in 1932. This was now titled "One More Tomorrow" which had been announced on September 21 the previous year with the actress to co-star with Olivia de Havilland. The new film was based on the Philip Barry play that had run on Broadway from January 12 till June, 1932. On March 29 it was announced that she would replace de Havilland in the wife role in the film.

The Warners romance "*One More Tomorrow*" (1946) was shot with the working title The Animal Kingdom from early April to early June with reshoots from mid-October to early November at the Warners studios. The screenplay was by Charles Hoffman and Catherine Turney with additional dialogue by Julius J. and Philip G. Epstein. The director was Peter Godfrey with uncredited work by Irving Rapper. The story was set in Connecticut from 1939 and centres on shiftless playboy Tom Collier (Dennis Morgan). He meets photographer Christie Sage (Ann Sheridan) who works for the liberal magazine The Bantam, which opposes everything Tom's family represents. Smith is billed fourth above the title and plays the supporting role of Cecelia 'C' Henry who marries Tom for his money.

C is the baddest girl she has played to date – scheming and manipulative who admits to having no principles – with the worst thing about her being a refusal to want children. She is in opposition to the good girl Christie. The role sees C smoke, kiss Owen Arthur (John Loder), dance with Tom, get a neck massage from him, and kiss and be kissed by Tom. The actress is gowned by Milo Anderson with outfits that include a veil-less wedding dress and a black negligee with bare midriff. She makes C's hauteur funny. Her best scene is perhaps the inevitable confrontation with Christie though Smith is equally strong in C's final scene with Tom where he rejects their marriage. Director Godfrey gives her many close-ups.

The film's release was delayed until June 1, 1946, with taglines that included "NEWS is Their Business! LOVE is Their Pleasure!" and "The Screen's Full Of Stars With Their Arms Full of Love". Sources differ as to whether or not it was a box office success. The film received a mixed reaction from T.M.P. in *The New York Times* who wrote that Smith was competent. But it was lambasted by Clive Hirschhorn in "The Warner Bros. Story". A *Lux Radio Theater* sixty-minute version was broadcast on June 9, 1947, with Morgan and Smith reprising their film roles and Jane Wyman playing Christie.

From left Dennis Morgan, Ann Sheridan, Jack Carson, and Smith on right in portrait for *"One More Tomorrow"* (1946)

The film's pressbook reported that Warners wanted the actress to be seen in a new way - as a siren – and dressed her accordingly. She never thought of herself as particularly seductive, and the negligee was too much or rather too little for her. Strictly peek-a-boo, it was a black lace net affair with practically no net and very little lace. When Smith stepped on stage in the outfit the well-mannered and interested crew gave off with "oohs" and "aahs" and she blushed. Then the actress made the revolutionary request to only wear the negligee for the scene when it was shot. For rehearsals she wanted to wear an old-fashioned mother-hubbard around it. Peter Godfrey, himself a blushing type, granted the request.

Smith also had trouble with the scene where she was hugged by Dennis Morgan. The actor was an old hand at movie hugging and rehearsed a very fine embrace, but Godfrey was not satisfied. The director hugged her to show what he wanted. But then cameraman Bert Glennon said that hug was bad for focus, and *he* hugged the actress the way he felt it should be done. Producer Benjamin Glazer joined the group, feeling he knew a better way and hugged her. She felt a little crushed by all this hugging and suggested that perhaps it would be better if Morgan and Smith just shook hands and let it go at that.

She was announced to appear in the Warners romantic adventure *Northern Pursuit* (1943) playing Laura McBain opposite Errol Flynn. However, Julie Bishop was cast instead.

On May 6 it was reported that New York show girl Mary Dowell would write a chorus girl yarn for Warners for the actress. It appears this film was "Here Come the Girls" which Warners announced on May 30 for her, Ann Sheridan, Ida Lupino, and Jane Wyman. On June 9 it was announced that she had been assigned to "Conflict" as the lead opposite Humphrey Bogart. Smith had replaced Nancy Coleman. Production was to begin on June 14.

The Warners mystery "*Conflict*" (1945) was shot from June 15 to August 25 on location in the Los Angeles National Forest and at the Warners studios. The screenplay was by Arthur T. Horman and Dwight Taylor from an original story by Robert Siodmak and Alfred Neumann. The director was Curtis Bernhardt. The story centred on engineer Richard 'Dick' Mason (Bogart), trapped in an unhappy marriage, who murders his wife Kathryn (Rose Hobart). The actress is billed second above the title and plays the role of Kathryn's younger sister Evelyn Turner. Her hair is shorter now and the costumes by Orry-Kelly include a mink coat. Evelyn presumably appeals to Dick more than his wife not only because she is younger but also because she is more of an innocent in her thinking about love.

The role sees Evelyn kiss Dick, fish, dance with Prof. Norman Holsworth (Charles Drake), and cry. Smith's best scene has Evelyn interrogated by Dick about her love for him. She uses emotion in her answers and some hysteria at Dick's questions which presumably comes from her grief over the missing sister. However, there is also the possibility that Evelyn does love Dick the way he loves her, though she denies it. The scene gets a nice button when he gives her one of Kathryn's handkerchiefs for Evelyn's tears, and she says, "That's what I meant when I said she'll always be between us." Director Bernhardt has an extreme close-up of the actress as part of Dick's dream.

The film's release was delayed until a premiere on May 13, 1945, with a general release on May 29. The taglines included "SUSPENSE . . . SUSPICION . . . MAN-WOMAN DESIRES!" and "Now Warner's big Humphrey Bogart thrill . . . will he kiss or will he kill?" It was a box office success. The film was praised by Brog in *Variety* who wrote Smith lent interest, and Bosely Crowther in *The New York Times*. However, it received a mixed reaction from Clive Hirschhorn in "The Warner Bros. Story".

It was reported that Eleanor Parker had originally been considered for the role of Evelyn. Smith said she disliked playing what the actress described as frigid females like Evelyn.

Bogart and his wife Mayo Methot celebrated their fifth wedding anniversary on August 21 during production. Stefan Kanfer in *Tough Without a Gun: The Life and Extraordinary Afterlife of*

Humphrey Bogart writes that the actor showed Smith and the other cast members the anniversary presents they had given each other.

Her next film was the Warners black and white musical biography "*Rhapsody In Blue*" (*The Story of George Gershwin*) (1945) shot from July 19 to October 12 at the Warner Bros. studios. The screenplay was by Howard Koch and Elliot Paul from an original story by Sonya Levien with uncredited additional work by Harry Chandlee, Clifford Odets, and Robert Rossen. The director was Irving Rapper. It was set in New York where the ambition of composer Gershwin (Robert Alda) destroys his relationship with singer Julie Adams (Joan Leslie) and socialite Christine Gilbert (Smith). She is billed third after the title and plays a supporting role. We wait for 70 out of the 140 minutes running time to see Christine. She is a divorced American painter living in Paris where Gershwin visits and who he brings back to New York.

Christine is another female character presented in contrast, here with Julie. She is more elegant and more beautiful than Julie, though we never get to see Christine's painting. The idea that George becomes a painter, one she thinks is better than her, seems to be more of an insult to Christine. He proposes to Christine but not to Julie, whom he only sees as a friend and work colleague. But Christine's rejection of him shows her both as an independent woman and someone who realized his career will aways come first. She has a wonderful moment at a party being pushed aside by the guests who clamor to hear George play the piano.

The role sees her dance with and be kissed by George, interact with a dog, smoke, and cry. Christine gets two memorable lines – one a howler and one camp. The howler is "Love is harder to learn than orchestration, and far more important". The camp line comes after George kisses her, "That's just what I didn't want to happen." Christine has a memorably sad exit underlined by the use of the song "The Man I Love". Gowns are by Milo Anderson. Director Rapper gives the actress many close-ups.

The film release was delayed. It premiered on June 27, 1945, and was given a wide release from September 22, 1945, with taglines that included "Warners' Crowning Glory!" and "The Great Story of George Gershwin and His Great Music!" It was a box office success and was nominated for the Academy Awards for Best Sound, Recording and Best Music, Scoring of a Musical Picture. The film was praised by *Variety* but received mixed reactions from Bosley Crowther in *The New York Times* and Clive Hirschhorn in "The Warner Bros. Story" who wrote that Smith's performance was indifferent.

Robert Alda on left and Smith on right in a portrait for *"Rhapsody In Blue" (The Story of George Gershwin)* (1945)

One source said she liked her part because, while a heavy of sorts, she got to do the unexpected. Another source claims the actress was unhappy. It was another of those superficial so-called sophisticates that had been fun to do at first because she got dressed up. Now all Smith had to do was raise her eyebrows and act when the director yelled 'Action'. A third source quotes her as saying the film was fun at first but then, ugh!

Her friend Frances Rafferty commented on the actress playing a variety of ice queens. She had the aristocratic face and was beautifully sculptured, and had that quality of being dignified, formal and aloof, which helped her play those parts well. But this was not the woman Rafferty knew.

In *Photoplay* of September she was one of the stars who told of "The Lesson I'll Never Forget – ". As an actress she met dozens of people during an average day. But Smith never had time to get to know them. So, when someone she had admired turned out not to be worthy of it, the actress was hurt and disappointed. One evening she went to a dinner party, smarting under her special personal disappointment. Smith found herself sitting next to a friendly and interesting man and told him all about her bruising experience. He smiled with understanding then said something very important. You must learn to give your hand to many – your heart to only a few.

At the time this didn't mean anything much to her, but she kept thinking about it afterward. Smith had to translate it for herself. Be friendly to everyone. Save your real heart for your nearest and dearest. Don't squander your real emotions. It would be months before the actress learned that her dinner partner had been Dr. Bert Frohman, one of Hollywood's foremost psychoanalysts. He taught her much that night.

She was tested for the role of Fanny Trellis Skeffington in the Warners romance *Mr. Skeffington* (1944). Bette Davis was unsure if she wanted to play the part which led to Smith being tested. When Davis heard of the test, she confronted the actress saying the idea that *she* could play the part was perfectly ridiculous. If Davis was not right for it, then Smith certainly was not. Davis would eventually play the part. Smith would never appear in a film with the queen of Warners. She described Davis as feisty, dynamic, very opinionated and strong in her ideas, a good actress and so unique at that time for not being a pretty girl. Despite the confrontation, Smith said Davis was always pleasant and very, very nice to her.

In the October *Photoplay* she was profiled by Maria Raymond as "American Original". On October 29 the actress was named for a principal part in the Warners forthcoming Jack Benny film "The Horn Blows at Midnight".

The black and white B comic musical fantasy "*The Horn Blows At Midnight*" (1945) was shot from late November, 1943 to late January, 1944, at the Warner studios. The screenplay was by Sam Hellman and James V. Kern based on an idea by Aubrey Wisberg. The director was Raoul Walsh. The story centred on a trumpet player in a New York radio orchestra (Benny) who dreams he's an angel deputized to blow the Last Trumpet at exactly midnight on Earth. Smith is billed second above the title and plays the supporting part of Elizabeth, a harpist in the orchestra and an angel secretary in Heaven. Her hair is worn in a new curly style with bangs.

The role sees Elizabeth play the harp, cry, get kissed by Archibald Dexter (Reginald Gardiner), and hold one of the legs of The Chief (Guy Kibbee) as he hangs from the top of a building. Costumer Milo Anderson differentiates between the two Elizabeths by giving the harpist a black dress and the secretary white outfits. The actress' comic crying is unfunny, but she is funny reacting to the frantic conducting of Archibald. Smith can be contrasted here with the other major female player, Dolores Moran as Fran Blackstone, since Moran is better at playing comedy.

The film's release was delayed until April 20, 1945, with taglines that included "Benny's from Heaven and the laughs are out of this world!!!" and "It's toot-toot terrific." It was not a box office success. The film received a mixed reaction from *Variety*, and Bosley Crowther in *The New York Times*, and was lambasted by Clive Hirschhorn in "The Warner Bros. Story". It was remade as a sixty-minute episode of the television series *Omnibus* which was broadcast on November 29, 1953, with Dorothy Malone as Elizabeth. A sixty-minute radio version was done for *The Ford Theater* broadcast March 4, 1949, however Smith was not in it.

Ida Lupino had been originally announced to play the female lead in the film.

Raoul Walsh originally thought she was too tall to play an angel. The only angels he knew were cherubs and they were short. Producer Mark Hellinger also thought Elizabeth should be dark and soulful and not blonde and beautiful. But with the objections overcome the actress was cast. Smith admitted that angeling was new to her and hoped Walsh had some ideas. But the director just instructed the actress to be herself. If Jack Benny, with his face could play an angel, so could she.

To create Heaven vapor was pumped into the set but it temporarily overcame her, and Smith required the attention of the first-aid man. She helped out the wardrobe department for her angel costume, loaning them material which the actress had intended to use to make curtains for her home.

In the film's pressbook she was said to be able to really play the harp and ice-skate. Smith was also an accomplished cook who could provide for fifteen of the family clan at Christmas.

Robert Blake who plays Junior Poplinski reported that Benny was not happy with her as his leading lady and had lobbied Warner Bros. for a different actress. Whether or not this was partially based on the difference in their ages is unclear. Although in the film they are undoubtedly Platonic lovers, Benny was twice her age in real life. However, Milt Josefsberg in his book *The Jack Benny Show: The Life and Times of America's Best-Loved Entertainer* writes that Benny gallantly absolved Smith of any blame for the film's financial failure. Benny said even if they had Olivia de Havilland, Ann Sheridan, Jane Wyman, and Bette Davis collectively as his love interest, it would still have been a flop.

She reportedly adored working with Benny and they became great friends.

The actress was featured in an article in *Life* magazine of December 13 entitled "Ballerina Smith: Alexis Turns Dancer". Photographer Gjon Mili was said to have noticed her walking gracefully by on the Warners lot and decided he wanted to photograph Smith as a dancer. The tall, placid girl performed as an agile dance mimic, doing all kinds of dances in a pretty and lively manner. But then she had been dancing since childhood. The actress describes herself half-seriously as a disappointed ballerina and Mili thinks she should star in a life of Isadora Duncan.

For the photographs he has her in three phases of a Hungarian Czardas in a bright Hungarian dress and braids. In a short golden tunic Smith does acrobatic handsprings in leaps and skips and poses that Isadora Duncan made famous. In a short demure ballerina's dress, she does a classic entrechat. In flowing gown, the actress moves dramatically in the way of modern dance. And in a scanty flashy Latin costume, she wiggles her way through a hot spot rumba.

Chapter 4. Her stock at Warners

By 1943 the actress' stock at Warners had risen and she was now considered competition to Ann Sheridan, Jane Wyman, and Eleanor Parker. The leading film roles were being offered to Bette Davis, Olivia de Havilland, and Ida Lupino. But Smith also had to compete for parts with the second tier of Warners ladies that included Joan Leslie, Priscilla Lane, Geraldine Fitzgerald, Betty Field, Brenda Marshall, Nancy Coleman, Faye Emerson, Dorothy Malone, and Dolores Moran.

Smith described herself as fresh out of school and delighted to be a movie star. As the studio liked her, she had no worries. There was no fighting for jobs. But in a sense the security was damning. You could become complacent and never get off your ass to become serious about the craft of acting. It was a big factory, and the actors were commodities, like cans of soup.

The actress never felt any animosity towards Warners so there was no real frustration. To her it was lovely. Maybe she was too naïve or a little too immature, but Smith was having a very good time and being paid a very substantial amount of money. Later she had a great deal of integrity about the work and would have liked to have done better roles. But the actress wasn't pushy.

Films were pretty much escapist entertainment, and she was pretty much a utility girl at Warners. Anything Ann Sheridan or Ida Lupino or Jane Wyman didn't want to do Smith fell into. Warners would start with Davis, then Lupino, then Sheridan, and if they didn't want it, she got it. The actress got what she called the dreck. Smith would have liked something that was hers from the start. People thought she was typecast but the actress believed she typecast herself. Smith wasn't creative and the creative ones at Warners – John Garfield and Davis and de Havilland - didn't allow the studio to do that to them. She didn't blame Warners at all.

The actress was a guest on the 30 minute *The Jack Benny Program For Grape-Nuts and Grape-Nuts Flakes* radio show broadcast from the Marine Corps Camp at El Toro California on January 16, 1944. Benny says in the next week he will start shooting a new film for Warners with Smith as his leading lady so this was presumably recorded in November, 1943. She reports Benny misled her to believing the actress was just going to meet the camp marines and not be on his show. She didn't even know he had a program. Smith listened to the radio including Fred Allen who was always talking about Benny. She said if Allen was lying about him, he should see a lawyer. But if he was telling the truth, Benny ought to see a doctor. The actress is heard to kiss Dennis Day then Phil Harris pretends to be a boy so he can get kissed too. She and Benny play a scene from *The Constant Nymph* where he impersonates Charles Boyer. Smith laughs when stumbling over one line, and then speaks in double-time as their skit time runs out.

She was back on the Jack Benny radio show that was broadcast on January 23 from the Army Air Station at Muroc, California. He picks up the actress from her home to go to Muroc. For the show Benny wants them to do a love scene from their film and kiss her. She tells him what Ann Sheridan told her about his acting ability after they made the Warners 1942 comedy *George Washington Slept Here* together. All the time he was making love to Sheridan, Benny was looking right into the camera, as if his option was hanging on the lens.

When he wants to rehearse their scene for the radio show, Benny wants to kiss her goodbye twice. Smith points out that in the film he only kissed her goodbye once and suggests that, instead of the kissing, why don't they stay in and play a game of gin rummy. When Benny answers he wants a little excitement, she agrees, with the joke being his kissing is not exciting. When they rehearse the scene, the actress keeps changing his name to things like clap saddle and albatross. He finally kisses her.

She was sent to Washington in a group of Warners movie people invited to attend President Roosevelt's Birthday Ball to raise money for the March of Dimes. His birthday was on January 30 and the March of Dimes his favorite charity as it was devoted to the fight against infantile paralysis. The group travelled on the Super Chief from Los Angeles and Smith said she felt liked a little kid. The actress sat in a drawing room which felt very luxurious. The train stopped for fifteen minutes in Albuquerque and when she looked out the window there were Navajo Indians. They stopped in New York which was the most glamorous place Smith had ever seen. Los Angeles was a country town by comparison.

Smith on left, with Craig Stevens, Jane Wyman, and
Jack Carson on right in still for "*The Doughgirls*" (1944)

Her next film was the Warners black and white comedy "*The Doughgirls*" (1944) shot from early March to mid-May at the Warners studios. The screenplay was by James V. Kern and Sam Hellman with additional dialogue by Wilkie Mahoney from the stage play by Joseph Fields. The play had run on Broadway at the Lyceum Theatre from December 30, 1942, to July 29, 1944. The film's director was also James V. Kern. The story centred on Vivian Marsden

Halstead (Jane Wyman), Edna Stokes Cadman (Ann Sheridan), and Nan Curtiss Dillon (Smith). The three friends share a hotel suite during the World War II housing shortage in Washington, D.C. and Vivian and Edna discover their marriages are not legally valid. Nan is not married to her fiancé Flying Lieutenant Tom (Craig Stevens) because his getting the measles has delayed the ceremony.

Smith is billed second above the title and plays a supporting role. Nan interacts with a dog, sings and dances "Jeepers Creepers" by Harry Warren and sings "The Wedding March" by Felix Mendelssohn both with Vivian and Edna, speaks with a Brooklyn accent, imitates Vivian and Sergeant Natalia Moskoroff (Eve Arden), smoke, has a nude sunbath though it is suggested rather than shown, plays the piano, and is kissed by and marries Tom. The actress has her turn at screaming lines, the way director Kern has all the actors do. However, she makes Nan funny, in the way she pronounces "Mr Umbriago" and has a slapstick moment. Nan is pushed onto the floor by Edna opening the door Nan is eavesdropping to. She gets a funny line after being given a Japanese officer's uniform epaulette from Breckenridge Drake (Alan Mowbray) – "Now who do I know with one shoulder?" However, Smith can't make Nan's monologue about Tom getting measles work as she delivers it in a Brooklyn accent. Gowns are by Milo Anderson

The film was released on November 25, 1944, with taglines that included "IT'S A SCREAM ON THE SCREEN!" and "IT'S A HONEY OF A FUNNY . . . .about love and money!" It was not a box office success. The film was praised by P.P.K. in *The New York Times* but received a mixed reaction from Clive Hirschhorn in "The Warner Bros. Story".

The three actresses were friendly while making the film. with Wyman saying they were swell gals, Sheridan stating not one was a cat, and Smith adding, "S'wonderful". They also remained friends after the shoot with the actress a steady visitor to Sheridan's Encino ranch and Wyman's house to coo at her baby. In addition both Sheridan and Wyman gave little parties now and then in honor of Smith and her soon to be husband.

On March 20, she was named among the best-dressed women of the country by the Fashion Academy of the Waves, Wacs, Spars and Marine Corp. The actress was chosen to represent the field of motion pictures with the awards presented at a tea at the Café du Bois in New York. The news came when she was in production on *"The Doughgirls"* and Smith said she was very proud to have been included in the selection this year. The secret of being well dressed was to keep clothes chic and uncluttered, with an eye to line and simplicity rather than to trim with bows, ruffles, and jewelry. The actress tried to wear clothes that were becoming and flattering to *her* rather than slavishly following a trend.

She also spoke about her height which had not upset her in the least. Tall schoolgirls wrote to her weekly bemoaning their height, their gawkiness, long coltish legs, and their beau problems. Smith now claimed to having no such problems when she was at school. If you were tall, you were also usually slim, and clothes just naturally looked better on you than short girls. Long legs had never been a liability and as far as the boys were concerned, Alexis just went with the tall ones. Studying ballet helped her achieve grace and it was important to have good posture and a beautiful carriage. A tall girl that slouches was not a pretty sight.

Fans wrote to the actress about clothes, and she had a couple of tricks. Smith watched her hats and tried to stick to flat types, like berets or tams that didn't give the feeling of soaring into space. She avoided spiked heels not wanting to look like a stilt-walker. French heels were high enough for anyone.

It was reported that her seventy-one-year-old Canadian grand-mother, Mrs. Catherine Fitz-Simmons, visited the set of *"The Doughgirls"* on the actress' birthday. Since the birthday was June 8 this suggests the shooting dates extended beyond mid-May. Other-wise, grandmother came to celebrate Smith's birthday early. She had hoped for a quiet little appearance, but no sooner had the actress arrived then the cast burst into "Happy Birthday To You". Next were speeches from Sheridan, the director, and producer Mark Hellinger, before a cake. Pictures were also taken for her, the kind that developed at once, and were signed by the stars.

At the end of shooting she, Wyman and Sheridan presented director Kern with a megaphone with the inscription, "For service far beyond the line of duty".

Smith said she had been working hard and admitted to being happiest when busy. That was why the actress kept right on working as long as Warners had film parts for her. It wasn't always easy to be up early in the morning and to go to bed early at night so she could be sure of getting up early the next morning. Smith felt fatigue after doing intense dramatic scenes but that was the sort of thing an actress encountered. She wanted to get along in Hollywood and would work hard to do it.

The actress appeared in the *Lux Radio Theater* production of *Old Acquaintance* which was broadcast on May 29 on CBS. This was a 36 minute version of the Warners 110 minute 1943 musical romance. She played the part of Kit, originated by Bette Davis in the film. The show was produced by Cecil B. DeMille. Smith is too young to play the character when she ages to be forty though her voice makes her sound older than the real age of twenty-two. The radio version has Kit slap Millie (Miriam Hopkins) rather than shake her as in the film. After the show was a curtain call chat with the stars. The actress reports she made nothing in her first job in the theatre because it was a college show.

The next film was the Warners black and white musical comedy *hollywood canteen* (1944) shot from June 5 to August 31 on locations in California and at the Warners studios. It was written and directed by Delmer Daves. The story centred on two soldiers Corporal Slim Green (Robert Hutton) and Sergeant Nowland (Dane Clark) on leave who spend three nights at the club. The stars are billed after the title alphabetically and Smith is thirty-fifth. In a cameo she is funny reacting to the Sergeant's primeval advance in the canteen corridor before his efforts are undermined by other servicemen who appear around them. Wardrobe again was by Milo Anderson.

The film was released on December 15 with taglines that included "62 Stars in Warners' Biggest Ever!" and "Songs Galore!". It was a box office success and was nominated for the Academy Awards for Best Sound, Recording; Best Music, Original Song for "Sweet Dreams Sweetheart"; and Best Music, Scoring of a Musical Picture. The film was praised by *Variety* but was lambasted by Bosley Crowther in *The New York Times*.

The actress and Craig Stevens finally married on June 18, 1944. It had been delayed multiple times due to the groom having a back injury. Stevens had served a year in the United States Army Air Corps' First Motion Picture Unit known as the Culver City Commandos, acting in propaganda and training films. The injury sent him to hospital and resulted in an honorable medical discharge six months prior to his wedding.

The ceremony was held at the Church of the Recessional at Forest Lawn with 300 persons attending, including Errol Flynn, Frances Rafferty, and Rosalind Russell. A reception was held at the Smith residence in Hollywood. Stevens reported that at the reception, Flynn spoke to him as he were the brides' father. He said if Stevens didn't do right by the girl he would have to answer to Flynn. The couple then left on a brief honeymoon.

Stevens reported that they bought a home in the Valley and had no furniture. There were two chairs the actress' mother had given her and they ate off apple boxes. Stevens visited George Montgomery who was married to Dinah Shore and saw how Montgomery made his own furniture in his garage. Smith asked her husband to do the same, knowing he loved to do things with his hands. Stevens took several courses and wound up making about fourteen pieces of furniture for their home.

A fan magazine interview with the actress had her report she believed in good luck. As a little girl Smith decided just how life should be - and it all came true. She became a motion picture star and found her Prince Charming. Even her wedding was exactly as the actress had dreamed it. The Smith and Stevens union would go on to rank as one of the longest in Hollywood history. However, she did not want to start a family. At least not for the moment. The actress had made one sacrifice for her new husband – no more onion sandwiches because he hated them.

On July 1 she was named as the lead in the proposed Technicolor production "San Antonio" opposite Errol Flynn. On August 11 it was reported that Smith was now back from her honeymoon and had been assigned the role of Nora in "Of Human Bondage" which was then in production. The black and white drama *W. Somerset Maugham's Of Human Bondage* (1946) was shot from mid-July to late October at the Warners studios. This was a remake of the RKO 1934 romantic mystery. The remake had a screenplay by Catherine Turney. The director was Edmund Goulding. The story centred on Philip Carey (Paul Henried), a London medical student with a club foot who falls for the beautiful but ambitious waitress Mildred Rogers (Eleanor Parker).

Smith is billed third after the title and plays the supporting role of Nora Nesbit, essayed by Kay Johnson in the original. She is heard before being seen in Paris in 1897 and we learn Nora is a widowed novelist. Nora is contrasted with Mildred, the latter being rude and common. She is affectionate and supportive, telling Philip she loves him, but he rejects her for Mildred. The role sees her cry and be kissed by Philip. Nora gets a striking, black-colored outfit with a large hat among her Milo Anderson designed wardrobe. However, she gets lumbered with lines like "I never thought ours would come to an end without any fault of mine at all" and "If you don't mind, I think I'll walk on alone. I'm afraid I'm going to weep." The actress at first uses masculine physicality for Nora but this is not repeated.

The film's release was delayed until July 5, 1946, with taglines that included "The World-Famous Story Of An Infamous Love!" and "Do you think you understand Love?" It was not a box office success. It received a mixed reaction from *Variety* and was lambasted by Bosley Crowther in *The New York Times* who wrote that Smith was stiff, and Clive Hirschhorn in "The Warner Bros. Story". The film was remade again in 1964 with Siobhan McKenna as Nora.

It was reported that the actress' part was greatly reduced in editing. Nora had more scenes as a married woman when Philip re-unites with her in the United States.

Matthew Kennedy in his book *Edmund Goulding's Dark Victory: Hollywood's Genius Bad Boy* writes that the director instructed Smith on his kind of acting. One day she reported to work and was laughing with the crew. Goulding ordered her to stop laughing because they were to shoot a serious scene. He instructed her to concentrate, and the actress did.

Her next film was the Warners Technicolor western "*San Antonio*" (1945) shot from September 21 to early December on location in California and at the Warners studios. The screenplay was by Alan LeMay and W.R. Burnett and the director was David Butler with uncredited work by Robert Florey and Raoul Walsh. The story was set in Texas in 1877 and centred on Clay Hardin (Errol Flynn), a cowboy who falls for Jeanne Starr (Smith) a tough dance hall girl working for the local villain.

She is billed second above the title and plays a supporting role. Jeanne sings and dances two numbers at the Bella Union hotel. The singing is dubbed by Bobbie Canvin although the actress recites one verse. The songs are "Some Sunday Morning" with music by M.K. Jerome and Ray Heindorf and lyrics by Ted Koehler, and "Somewhere in Monterey" with music by Charles Kisco and lyrics by Jack Scholl. Although the hotel has a stage, director Butler has Jeanne perform "Some Sunday Morning" on a staircase and walk among the audience before ending up on the stage. Our view of Smith is obstructed by having some of the audience in the foreground and there are cutaways to Clay. "Somewhere in Monterey" is performed on the stage, with the audience in the foreground in two shots and another where the orchestra is in the foreground. There is also an extended cutaway to Clay talking to Roy Stuart (Paul Kelly) and one to Sacha Bozic (S.Z. 'Cuddles' Sakall) as Jeanne dances, and Butler uses a medium shot of the dancing.

From left Florence Bates seated, S.Z. 'Cuddles' Sakall standing, Smith seated, and Errol Flynn on right with his leg on a chair in still for *San Antonio* (1945)

Her clothes by Milo Anderson are appropriately theatrical and hairstyles include period ringlets. The role sees Jeanne slap and dance with Clay, throw crockery at Clay, be kissed by Legare (Victor Francen), be kissed by Clay, and have her hair primped by Henrietta (Florence Bates). The actress makes Jeanne funny, and Butler gives her props like a handbag, hairbrush, and bunch of flowers to fiddle with which obscures her self-conscious self-touching mannerisms.

The film was released on December 28, 1945, with taglines that included "Strong Men . . . Brave Men . . . Real Americans - and their Women!" and "Warner's Adventure of the Century!" It was a box office success and was nominated for Academy Awards for Best

Art Direction-Interior Decoration, Color and Best Music, Original Song for "Some Sunday Morning"". The film received a mixed reaction from Cars in *Variety,* and Bosley Crowther in *The New York Times* who wrote that Smith was handsome and elegant. It was lambasted by Clive Hirschhorn in "The Warner Bros. Story".

W.R. Burnett pitched Marlene Dietrich to play Jeanne, but Jack Warner did not want to pay her fee, especially when he had so many actors under contract. The film's long production was due to the illness of both Flynn and Smith. It was reported that she was absent due to a mysterious viral ailment that dragged on for weeks.

Michael Freedland in *The Two Lives of Errol Flynn* writes that the actor cared for her welfare on the shoot. If he felt the director was demanding too much, Flynn made it very plain he was on her side. The actor would say "Steady, old sport" and remind Butler she was only human. In repayment Smith did her best to cover up the excesses of Flynn's drinking, which was anything but easy. She saw that when the actor came to set, he was not a pretty sight. Flynn would stay up all night drinking and arrive red-eyed and his face blotched. He was nearly always on time, though had a hangover and the remains of a drunken stupor. The actress arranged for the service boys who hovered around set to provide Flynn with a constant flow of hot black coffee. But she couldn't understand how having the coffee made him worse. That is until Smith learned he had arranged for the boys to lace the coffee with brandy, for an agreed fee.

The actress was named by a group of San Antonio cowhands as The Girl With The Loveliest Calves and was photographed feeding a four-day-old calf sent to her by the Texan's City Mayor. However, the little fellow seemed more interested in milk than lovely calves or movie stars.

Craig Stevens reported that she liked doing westerns because the ones Smith did were on the light side and had humor.

The film's pressbook states that when she was not working the actress still studied at the Falcon School of Dance. This was the same school where she had danced fifteen years prior. Proud of their alumni, the school frequently called her up to present cups or trophies at the fencing and dancing festivals. The pressbook also notes that Smith was a tea drinker, never acquiring the taste for liquor that some of her screen characters had.

On January 10, 1945, it was reported that Warners had cast her with Craig Stevens as the leads in "Shadow of a Woman", a mystery drama by Virginia Perdue previously titled "Dangerous Marriage". Joseph Santley was to direct and William Jacobs the producer with shooting to begin in March. However, on January 26 it was announced that the actress had refused the role and was put on suspension. Andrea King was cast instead.

She appeared on the *Command Performance* radio show broadcast on March 1. When Jack Carson goes on a tour of the Hollywood homes in Beverly Hills, he finds the actress at a party at the home of Basil Rathbone. She asks Carson to sit next to her. When he admires her dress, Smith says it's just a tea gown, and he replies, "Love that cream and sugar." Carson says her name brings out the poet in him and recites, "When I first saw dear Alexis, you hit me liked a shot in the solar plexus." She also reads in the play that Arthur Treacher has written for Rathbone's theatre group about fox hunting. The actress plays the part of Lady Guinevere, but Carson prefers they play the balcony scene from *Romeo and Juliet*.

On March 4 it was reported that her suspension had been lifted and she was now cast in the second lead in the forthcoming "The Two Mrs. Carrolls". Smith would play the role of Cecily Harden which had been essayed on Broadway by Irene Worth. The play had run from August 3, 1943, to July 2, 1944, and August 13 to February 3, 1945.

The Warners black and white crime drama "*The Two Mrs. Carrolls*" (1947) was shot from late April to late June, 1945, at the Warners studios. The screenplay was by Thomas Job from the stage play by Martin Vale. The director was Peter Godfrey. The story centred on American married artist Geoffrey Carroll (Humphrey Bogart) living in London who meets Sally Morton (Barbara Stanwyck) on holiday who will become his new wife. Smith is billed third above the title and plays the supporting role now named Cecily Latham.

We wait 19 of the 100 minutes running time to see her as the daughter of Isabel Latham (Isabel Elsom), a client of Charles Pennington (Pat O'Moore). Cecily asks Geoffrey to paint her portrait though as a ruse to romance him. Again, the character is a study in contrast with Sally, who is shorter but warmer. Sally had refused to see Geoffrey after learning he was married but Cecily has no qualm about seeing him when he is married to Sally. The screenplay has some funny potshots at Cecily but she gets some good lines too. To Geofffey, "Are you one of those frightening people who always tells the truth?" and to Isabell about Geoffrey, "I've never been insulted quite so delightfully."

The role has Cecily speak with an English accent, kiss and be manhandled by Geoffrey, and smoke. The actress makes Cecily's hauteur funny. The Milo Anderson wardrobe includes a coat with leopard print collar and trim, and a mink. Her best scene is perhaps where Geoffrey tells Cecily she can't leave him. Smith transitions from humorous disbelief to fear at his mad intensity.

The film's release was delayed until March, 1947, with taglines that included "Never try to deceive two women!" and "Don't Dare Miss This CLASH!" It was not a box office success. The film received a mixed reaction from *Variety*, and Clive Hirschhorn in "The Warner Bros. Story". However, it was lambasted by Bosley Crowther in *The New York Times* who wrote that Smith's performance was gaudy.

The Warners publicity campaign had theatre owners hold contests in which female patrons were to decide whether they looked more like Stanwyck or Smith. The actress said that she learned a lot of screen technique from Stanwyck.

Her next film was the Warners Technicolor musical biography *Night And Day* (1946) shot from June 14 to October 30, though production ceased during October 6 to 12 due to a strike. Filming took place on locations in California and at the Warners studios. The screenplay was by Charles Hoffman, Leo Townsend and William Bowers adapted by Jack Moffit based on the career of Cole Porter. The director was Michael Curtiz. This was a fictionalized biopic of composer Porter (Cary Grant) from his days at Yale in the 1910s through the height of his success to the 1940s. Smith is billed second above the title and plays the supporting part of Linda Lee, a friend of Porter's cousin Nancy (Dorothy Malone), who marries him. Linda wears her long hair down.

The character is reminiscent of Christine Gilbert in "*Rhapsody In Blue*" (The Story of George Gershwin), in her failed relationship with another composer. Here Porter won't accept Linda's financial help because he wants to achieve success independently. Even after they marry, Linda is ignored while Porter gets attention from the public and friends or works. Linda's home is also invaded by chorus girls rehearsing who go into the bedroom and use her lipstick. When Porter again chooses work over her, she leaves him. However the narrative has a happy ending, where Linda returns. She runs to the crippled Porter as he walks to her with the aid of sticks, while the title song is sung off-screen. Grant's hard expression perhaps undermines the romance of the moment, though has context given Linda's abandonment of her husband.

She gets a howler to Porter, "You've put me in a small corner of your life and every once in a while you smile at me." Linda also gives him a cigarette holder with the camp inscription, "As Ever, Anything Goes". The role sees her kissed by Porter, be a nurse in World War 1, cry, interact with children, knit, dance with Monty (Monty Woolley), and run. The knitting and fiddling with a handkerchief are possibly directorial devices to conceal the actress' fidgety hands and self-conscious self-touching elsewhere. Her gowns by Milo Anderson include pastel shades, and a nurses outfit and army uniform. Director Curtiz gives Smith some close-ups.

The film was released on July 2, 1946, with taglines that included "Cary Grant as Cole Porter" and "The Story Of Cole Porter, With Those Cole Porter Song Sensations!". It was a box office success and nominated for the Academy Award for Best Music, Scoring of a Musical Picture. The film was praised by Abel in *Variety*, and T.M.P. in *The New York Times* who wrote that Smith performed with a great deal of charm. However, it was lambasted by Clive Hirschhorn in "The Warner Bros. Story" and Pauline Kael in "5001 Nights At The Movies". The Porter story would again be told in *De-Lovely* (2004) where Ashley Judd played Linda.

Cary Grant on left and Smith on right in still for *Night And Day* (1946)

Porter was known to be homosexual in a marriage of convenience, but the Studio Production Code of the time could not allow this to be portrayed. However, the actress noted that film biographies were rarely accurate. They would pick a flamboyant person and then run into a stone wall. The certain aspect of their life that really made them interesting was impossible to present because of censorship.

Warren G. Harris writes in his book *Cary Grant: A Touch Of Elegance* that the real life Linda chose Smith to be her screen counterpart. In their book *Cary Grant: The Lonely Heart* Charles Higham and Roy Moseley report that the actor approved of her casting.

She recounted her first scene with Grant where they had to kiss. It seemed just a short time ago that the actress was a schoolgirl, seeing him at Saturday matinees on Hollywood Boulevard. In the balcony she and her girlfriends would swoon. Now Smith was in a state of shock. She completely forgot all her lines and the actress didn't know what she was doing for several minutes. Who could have blamed her? Smith had never been so flustered in her life. When she looked at Grant, the actress couldn't even remember her name.

In Nancy Nelson's book *Evenings With Cary Grant: Recollections In His Own Words And By Those Who Knew Him Best* Smith said there was such an intense quality and focus about his work. It was all encapsulated in that moment. He was mesmerizing and very exciting. It was so strong that you felt you were his whole universe.

She observed Grant was a perfectionist who agonized over many things the actress might have considered incidental. He would keep changing the dialogue, so she had to memorize different-colored pages of script every day. Then there would be meetings in dressing rooms where Curtiz would pull out cardboard boxes filled with the different-colored pages, sifting through them to find a version that would work.

Grant was particularly fretful over the scene in Kensington Gardens where Porter re-meets Linda who is now taking care of a bunch of children. The actor believed the idea that Porter felt the children were hers was a gag excessively overdone. He repeatedly rewrote the scene while Smith and the other actors sat in their dressing rooms to await the call for another stab at the action.

In another scene in a theatre where one of Porter's shows was in progress, Curtiz told her to link arms with Grant so Linda could express her pleasure at the performance. The actress obeyed but as her arms were bare, Grant suddenly drew back as if having been stung. He asked if she had body make-up on. Smith did. The actor was wearing a Savile Row suit that could not be replaced because of the war. If it got covered in body make-up it would be ruined. Curtiz scrapped the arm-linking.

She recalled how Grant also reprimanded Curtiz concerning the cuffs of a shirt he was asked to wear. There was a quarter of an inch showing and it should have been an eighth of an inch. Grant removed the shirt and returned to his dressing room, refusing to continue until the cuffs had been adjusted. The actress thought this was silly but then reflected that this kind of attitude was indicative of the actor's work. She would rather have him be fussy about a quarter of an inch on a cuff and gave the performance he did. It was that care and attention that carried him through everything Grant did. His acting wasn't an eighth of an inch off.

Smith found Grant a marvellous screen actor but was intimidated by him in many ways. She felt paranoid about the constant reshooting, wondering if it was her fault and feeling not on a par with the man as a performer. One of the reasons Grant was unhappy with the film was that he had worked with Clifford Odets the previous year on the RKO romance *None But the Lonely Heart* (1944). Suddenly the actor had to deal with lines that were virtually meaningless.

The scene where Porter composes the title song struck her as absurd. As he sat at the piano in hospital Porter was supposedly inspired by the rain dripping down to create a line in the verse. Linda was to stand and look at him lovingly, but the actress found her costume as Porter's romantic inspiration ridiculous. She wore a terrible nurse's unform and heavy white regulation shoes. Smith couldn't stop laughing but Grant couldn't see the joke.

However, she was quoted in Marc Eliot's book *Cary Grant: A Biography* that he was the best movie actor that ever was. There was a term 'romance with the camera' and the actress doubted anyone ever had as great a romance with the camera as Grant.

In Richard Torregrossa's book *Cary Grant: A Celebration Of Style* Smith said he was this monumental star and a very serious actor.

In Scott Eyman's book *Cary Grant: A Brilliant Disguise* she said he never gave too much to a scene. Grant was a minimalist. He was making love to the camera. His co-stars somehow got in the way, but Grant was only interested in how it all looked up on the screen.

In Nancy Nelson's book the actress said he also gave her some advice about marriage that she never forgot. Grant said never get divorced. You may as well stick with one person because you just keep marrying the same type over and over again. Craig Stevens reported that when he visited the set his wife introduced him to Grant. Grant told him that he had a great girl and recommended Stevens stay married. Stevens took his advice.

Smith reported that Cole Porter came to the set one day when they were shooting on the estate location. The band was rehearsing on the grounds and the drummer was Mel Torme. Porter wore white flannel pants and a blazer and a scarf, looking exactly as Cole Porter should have looked.

On September 4 it was reported that Warners had bought the screen rights to "Man Without Friends", a novel by Margaret Echard. The story involving a girl reporter who solves a murder mystery had been earmarked for the actress. It appears this film was not made.

On January 21, 1946, it was announced that she would star in Warners "Stallion Road" based on the novel by Stephen Longstreet. Production was scheduled for early spring. Errol Flynn and Humphrey Bogart had been planned to play the male lead that was now to be essayed by Ronald Reagan. The director was James Kern aka James V. Kern. On February 12 it was reported that Smith and Reagan were out, and Bogart was back in to play opposite Lauren Bacall. The film was to be produced by Alex Gottlieb.

On February 17 Joelyn Littauer in an article in *The New York Times* entitled "Three Of A Kind" wrote about the actress and her marriage. She commented about being anxious to rejoin her husband after being in New York. When a single toothbrush on the rack began to make you look lonely and sentimental, it was time to be on your way home. Looking back on her career, Smith confessed to liking her last film, *Night And Day*, the best because of its leading man. She was hoping to get a change of roles, tired of being a neurotic complex woman of thirty-five. For once it would be nice to be just a plain healthy American girl. Asked if the actress had to make a choice between a mighty career or her husband, she didn't hesitate to choose him. Smith was good for ten or fifteen more years and then what would she have? She couldn't see getting much happiness from a few faded memories and a scrapbook of yellowed clippings. While in town the actress saw the Broadway show *Anna Lucasta*.

Chapter 5. *Stallion Road*

Lauren Bacall refused the Warners black and white drama *Stallion Road* (1947) and Smith was back in it. The film was shot from April 2 to July on locations in California and at the Warner Bros. studios. The screenplay was by Stephen Longstreet and the director James V. Kern with uncredited work by Raoul Walsh. The story centred on novelist Stephen Purcell (Zachary Scott) who competes with Californian veterinarian and rancher Larry Hanrahan (Reagan) for the affections of horse breeder Rory Teller (Smith).

The actress is billed second above the title and plays a supporting role. Her hair is shorter and worn with a side part, and clothes by Milo Anderson and Leah Rhodes include jeans and long pants. The role sees Rory interact with a child, interact and ride horses though it seems a stunt double is used for some high jumps and a fall, ride a motorbike, and be kissed by Stephen and Larry. Smith makes Rory funny, especially when having bitchy banter with Daisy Otis (Peggy Knudsen) who is interested in Larry. Director Kern gives her a few close-ups.

The film's release was delayed until April 4, 1947, and the taglines included "UNTAMED! Powerful Drama of Reckless Love!". Sources differ as to whether it was a box office success. The film received a mixed reaction from Bosley Crowther in *The New York Times* who wrote that Smith played with sleek and monotonous haughtiness, and Clive Hirschhorn in "The Warner Bros. Story." *Lux Radio Theater* broadcast a sixty-minute adaptation of the movie on October 4, 1948, with Scott, Reagan, and the actress reprising their film roles.

The role of Rory was also declined by Eleanor Parker. Smith said she had fun making the film and got to wear blue jeans. Ronald L. Davis in his book *Zachary Scott: Hollywood's Sophisticated Cad* writes that both Scott and Reagan adored her which made doing scenes with the actress easy.

From left Ronald Reagan, Smith, and Zachary Scott on the right in portrait for *Stallion Road* (1947)

In their book *Jane Wyman: A Biography* Joe Morella and Edward Z. Epstein report that a scene with her and Reagan caused an issue with the film moral codes of the day. They got off horses and had to kiss as they lay in the grass under a tree. Kern instructed Reagan to get up on one elbow as it was not allowed for them both to be in the prone position. He had to play the whole love scene on one elbow.

On May 20 it was reported that Warners had purchased the screen story "And All For One" by Thomas Ware as a vehicle for Smith. It dealt with a New York model who is subjected to the public sponsorship of six society bachelors. The film was scheduled for production in the fall, but it appears the film was never made.

On July 19 it was announced that Warners had assigned her to play the lead opposite Dennis Morgan in the musical "My Wild Irish Rose". However, she was replaced by Andrea King. This might have been the musical Smith has longed to make, since King sings in the film.

On August 22 it was reported she had been assigned by Warners to appear in the Henry Blanke production of the Wilkie Collins melodrama "The Woman in White" published in 1873. Peter Godfrey would direct the film starting in September. In September the actress was among the delegation sent by the Screen Actors Guild to the American Federation of Labor convention in Chicago. The group was shunted from meeting to meeting before being allowed to present a resolution calling for binding arbitration of the current Hollywood labor dispute. It passed unanimously but was never enforced.

The black and white mystery romance "*The Woman In White*" (1948) was shot from late September to early February, 1947, at the Warners studios. The screenplay was by Stephen Moorehouse Avery, whose novel had been filmed previously as two silent shorts, four silent features, and the British B *Crimes at the Dark House* (1940). The story was set in England in 1851 and centred on Walter Hartright (Gig Young), a young painter who stumbles upon an assortment of odd characters at an English estate where he has been hired to give art lessons.

Smith is top-billed after the title but plays the supporting part of Marian Halcombe, the poor cousin of Laura Fairlee (Eleanor Parker). Her hair is now longer, perhaps aided by a wig, and reads as brunette. She speaks with an English accent, and the role sees her use a telescope, be kissed by Sir Percival Glyde (John Emery) and Walter, interact with a monkey, scramble over the walls of the estate with the possible assistance of a stunt double, cry, handle a pistol, and interact with children.

Marian gets a howler to Walter, "What you're not telling me speaks louder than your words!" However, she also gets a funny line to him at breakfast, "Oh I advise you as a friend to have nothing to do with the cold ham and wait till the omelette comes in." Director Godfrey hides the actress' self-conscious self-touching sometimes by having Marian fiddle with handkerchiefs. Her best scene is perhaps when confronted by Count Alessandro Fosco (Sydney Greenstreet) who attempts to hypnotise her. Smith conveys fear and some madness before underplaying her line, "You incredible fiend. You murderer." Godfrey expresses the hypnotism with extreme close-ups of Greenstreet and her, and otherwise gives the actress some close-ups. Milo Anderson gets a special credit for her gowns which include a hooded cape.

The film's release was delayed until May 7, 1948, with taglines that included "Born in Shame! Living in Mystery!" and "She hid her black secret under a cloak of white!" It was not a box office success. The film received a mixed reaction from Bosley Crowther in *The New York Times* and Clive Hirschhorn in "The Warner Bros. Story" who wrote that Smith gave a boring performance. There would be a 1949 Swedish remake, adaptations for television, and a 1981 Russian feature.

Craig Stevens reported that Smith was mesmerized by Greenstreet, who memorised the entire script and knew everyone's role. He was just fascinating to be around.

In 1946 she was voted the Worst Actress of the Year by Harvard Lampoon. Smith agreed that the films she did were becoming poor vehicles and her performances didn't hold up. Later the actress would maintain this opinion and add that they didn't improve with age. She didn't identify with the woman Smith saw on screen. She never believed that was her and would have much rather read a good book.

On March 14, 1947, Warners named the actress to play opposite Dane Clark in "Whiplash" a prize-fighting film which Lew Seiler would direct. Harry Frank Jr. had written the scenario from a story by Kenneth Earl.

The black and white sports drama "*Whiplash*" (1948) was shot from mid-March to May 23 on locations in New York and at the Warners studios. The screenplay was by Maurice Geraghty and Harry Frank Jr. adapted by Gordon Kahn from the Earl story. It was centred on Michael Gordon aka Mike Angelo (Clark), a struggling artist who becomes a New York City prize fighter.

Smith is billed second above the title and plays the part of nightclub singer Laurie Durant, the wife of the ring promoter Rex Durant (Zachary Scott). She sings one song, "Just for Now" by Dick Redmond but is said to be dubbed by Bobbie Canvin. Canvin also presumably dubs Smith when Laurie hums the song. Director Seiler stages the club performance with foreground audience blocking our view of Laurie and cutaways to Mike. She has short hair and her wardrobe by Milo Anderson includes bathing suits. The role sees Laurie kissed by Mike and Rex, smoke, drive a car, slap Mike, and dance with Mike. She is funny rejecting Mike's request for a date, "I'm rotten company" and Seiler appears to try to conceal her self-conscious self-touching with having the actress fiddle with a cigarette lighter in one scene. The actress' performance has more emotion in her voice here, and Seiler gives her close-ups and one extreme close-up.

The film's release was delayed until December 24, 1948, and the taglines included "Caught in the grip of love that marks like a whip!" and "Sure I know you're a two-timer! . . . but I'm going to kiss the two-timing out of you!" It is not known whether the film was a box office success. The film received a mixed reaction from T.M.P. in *The New York Times* who wrote that Smith provided suitable decoration.

She was photographed on the set taking lessons in the art of self-defence from fellow actor Fred Steele who plays Duke Carney and was a former middleweight champion. It was reported that the actress found little rapport with Clark, perhaps because of the discrepancy in their heights, though sources claims that he was the same height as she. Smith appears in a Warner Bros. Breakdown scene where Clark blows a line and she laughs.

The Random Notes About Pictures And People in *The New York Times* of March 30 by A.H. Weiler referenced the actress under the heading "Versatile". It recalled her previously stated desire to play a plain healthy American girl with she now apparently gotten her wish. This was evident in *Stallion Road* where Smith played a distaff horse breeder whose wardrobe ran chiefly to dungarees. She was also currently on screen as a villainous home wrecker with an appropriately varied clothes collection in *"The Two Mrs. Carrolls".*

On April 3 it was reported that the actress and Errol Flynn were to appear in "The Adventures of Don Juan" for Warners. The film had been on and off the Warners schedule since 1939 and was a romance laid in Spain in the late fifteenth century. The project had been shelved two years ago because of the 1945 writer's strike. However, when the film eventually went into production in October Viveca Lindfors was the female star.

Her next film was the Warners black and white B comedy *"Always Together"* (1947) shot from late May to early July at the Warners studios. The working titles were Head Over Heels, Love at First Sight and Need for Each Other. The screenplay was by Phoebe and Henry Ephron and I.A.L. Diamond, and the director was Frederick De Cordova. The story centred on Donn Masters (Robert Hutton) and his new bride Jane Barker (Joyce Reynolds) who are given a million dollars. Smith played the uncredited part of The Bride in one of two fictional films either "Million Dollar Darling" or "Yesterday Is Gone". Sources differ as to whether these films are watched by Donn and Jane or are imagined by Jane. Regrettably the film is unavailable for viewing.

It was released on December 10 with taglines that included "An eyeful of glamour - A fortune of fun" and "It's that "JANIE" team with more zany joy!" The film received a mixed reaction from Bosley Crowther in *The New York Times* and Clive Hirschhorn in "The Warner Bros. Story".

She appeared uncredited as herself in the Warners eleven-minute comedy short *So You Want to Be in Pictures* (1947). This was written and directed by Richard Bare and centred on aspiring actor Joe McDoakes (George O'Hanlon) who blows his first part at Warners and must settle for being a stand-in. The short was released on June 7 and received an Academy Award nomination for Best Short Subject, One-reel.

The actress appeared in *The Screen Guild Theater* radio production of "My Reputation" which was broadcast on July 7 on CBS. The twenty-four-minute show was an adaptation of the 1946 Warners romance which starred Barbara Stanwyck as Jessica. Smith played a thirty-three-year-old recent widow who meets an army major (Wayne Morris) while skiing and, despite pressures from friends and family, becomes romantically involved with him. The show was produced and directed by Bill Lawrence.

On August 1 it was reported that director Irving Rapper had been removed from the Warners "Christopher Blake", the screen version of Moss Hart's Broadway play. He had objected to the casting of the actress and Robert Douglas in the leading roles of the film, which was still to be produced by Ranald MacDougall. On August 18 it was announced that filming would begin on September 1 with the same two actors in the leads and the director Peter Godfrey. The title role was to be played by Ted Donaldson, and the film dealt with the effects of parental separation on a youngster.

The Warners black and white romance "*The Decision of Christopher Blake*" (1948) was shot from late August to October 24 at the Warners studios. Producer MacDougall also wrote the screenplay based on Moss Hart's play, which he had also staged, that ran on Broadway from November 30, 1946, to March 8, 1947. Christopher Blake is twelve years-old and his parents Evelyn 'Evie' (Smith) Blake and Ken Blake (Robert Douglas) are about to break up their marriage and get a divorce.

She is top-billed after the title but plays a supporting role, doubling as Christopher's dream idea of Ruth, his father's sculptress mistress. As Ruth the actress wears a raven long black wig and has a beauty spot. Her wardrobe by Milo Anderson includes a wobbly hat and a full-length black sequin gown with split skirt and floor train.

From left Smith, Ted Donaldson, and Robert Douglas on right
in portrait for "*The Decision of Christopher Blake*" (1948)

The role sees Evelyn interact with a child, cry, and get kissed by Ken. Ruth flies through the air though with the possible use of a stunt double. She is funny, imitating Mr. Caldwell (John Hoyt), and Evelyn gets a funny line to Ken, "To keep from being unhappy you'd be willing to sacrifice yourself to a marriage that obviously means nothing to you. It's a very flattering offer." Smith makes the relationship with the boy warm, and director Godfrey gives her some close-ups.

The film's release was delayed until December 23, 1948, and the taglines included "The Kind of Woman A Man Couldn't Trust . . . But a Boy Could!" and "How Daring A Decision Could One Boy Make . . . to kindle or kill a love like this!" It was not a box office success. The film was lambasted by Bosley Crowther in *The New York Times* who wrote that Smith was bland and slightly bored, and Clive Hirschhorn in "The Warner Bros. Story".

The role of Evelyn Blake was offered to Norma Shearer, then Barbara Stanwyck. Mary Wickes plays Clara and in his book *Mary*

Wickes: I Know I've Seen That Face Before Steve Taravella writes about Irving Rapper being attached as director. He says Rapper wanted Gary Cooper and Shearer. When Warners said no, he suggested Joel McCrea and Stanwyck. When they again said no the director quit. He felt that this was a very serious piece, an important piece, and Rapper felt he wouldn't get that with Smith and Robert Douglas.

In the film's pressbook it was reported that she had to do Ruth's flying through the air on wires twenty-one times. The actress' ambition was to get away from roles in which she had to cry and turn to musicals where Smith could sing and dance. In her offscreen moments she haunted antique shops looking for furniture for the San Fernando Valley home the actress had bought with Craig Stevens. She had also resumed daily ballet lessons after a broken foot had healed.

Smith appeared in the Warners ten-minute documentary short *Camera Angles* (1948) which was shot in October. Directed by Gene Lester it centred on magazine photography and the promotion of Hollywood stars.

On October 23 it was reported that she and Craig Stevens had been invited to be present for the second annual royal command film performance on November 25 in London. It was expected that they would arrive on November 17 on the Queen Mary. The ship sailed from New York on November 12 and returned on December 10. While in New York the actress saw the musical comedy *High Button Shoes* and considered the Jerome Robbins Mack Sennet ballet the high spot of her trip. On December 29 she attended the Los Angeles premiere of the crime romance *The Paradine Case* (1947).

In 1947 Warners had bought "Sunburst" a screen story about the adventures of a taxi driver, by Dietrich V. Hanneken and Aleck Block. It had been assigned to Ranald MacDougall for production and to star Smith and Dane Clark. However, the project was shelved. Later it would be made as the romantic thriller *Embraceable You* (1948) and star Clark and Geraldine Brooks.

The actress reported that every time she saw John Garfield on the lot he would ask if Smith had been on suspension yet. She said no, perhaps forgetting the "Shadow of a Woman" experience in 1945. He yelled at her that the actress had no guts. If she had refused a role or what Smith considered a bad script, she would be put on unpaid suspension until the film was made with someone else.

On January 8, 1948, it was reported that Warners planned to remake "Daddies" a 1919 stage comedy and Warners 1924 silent by John. L. Hobble. It would be retitled "Four Wise Bachelors" with her starring and Alex Gottlieb to produce. However, it appears this film was not made.

The next film was the Warners black and white B romantic comedy *"One Last Fling"* (1949) shot from early February at the Warners studios. The screenplay was by Richard Flourney and William Sackheim based on a story by Herbert Clyde Lewis. The director was Peter Godfrey. It was set in New York and centred on Larry Pearce (Zachary Scott) who manages a music store and whose wife Olivia (Smith) returns to her former job there.

Although she is top-billed before the title the actress plays a supporting role. Her hair is shorter here and wardrobe is by Milo Anderson. The role sees Olivia interact with a dog, scream, kiss and be kissed by Larry, dance with Howard Pritchard (Jim Backus), laugh, appear with hair dishevelled after sleeping on a sofa in a hotel hallway, and cry. She makes Olivia funny, even if Smith is not as good in comedy as Zachary Scott. Milo Anderson gets a special credit for her wardrobe.

The film's release was delayed until June 30, 1949, and the taglines included "It's One Long Laugh!" and "Love's in full swing!" It recovered its production costs. The film received a mixed reaction from H.H.T. in *The New York Times* who wrote that Smith was decorative, no more. It was lambasted by Clive Hirschhorn in "The Warner Bros. Story."

The film's pressbook reported that she was now devoting her afternoons to dancing under the instruction of Buddy Eason, assistant to LeRoy aka Leroy Prinz, the Warners dance director. The actress teamed with James Mitchell, a fellow dance student at the Los Angeles City College where they had danced in school plays together. Both were said to be experts at ballet, tap, adagio and modern, and were preparing routines with an idea towards convincing the studio that they would be a good team in musical films.

Her next film was the Technicolor western *"South Of St. Louis"* (1949) made by United States Pictures and distributed by Warners. It was shot from May 27 on locations in California and at the Warners studios. The screenplay was by Zachary Gold and James R. Webb. The working title was Distant Drums. The director was Ray Enright. It was set in Missouri during the Civil War and centred on Kip Davis (Joel McCrea), one of three Texas ranchers who seek revenge on raiders.

Smith is billed second above the title and plays the supporting part of Rouge de Lisle, a saloon girl who sings three songs dubbed by Bonnie Lou Williams. They are the traditional "Yankee Doodle" where director Enright uses foreground audience and a cutaway from her performance, "Too Much Love" with music by Ray Heindorf and lyrics by Ralph Blane sung to Kip at a table with cutaways to him, and "It Must Be Fun to Have a Soldier". The latter number has Rouge walking among the audience with some foreground blocking and she holds up her dress to show legs in the performance. "Too Much Love" is also reprised with Enright again using Kip in the foreground to Rouge's singing.

Her hair is colored red and worn long so is presumably a wig, with an appropriately tacky wardrobe by Milo Anderson, and she has a beauty spot. Rouge speaks with a Southern accent and partners with Kip to run guns to the union soldiers. She is contrasted with Deborah 'Deb' Miller (Dorothy Malone), who Kip is more interested in romantically. Deb is a brunette who does not wear make-up, dresses dowdily, and works as a nurse in a Union military hospital. Rouge gives the impression when she performs of being a loose woman, flirting with men in the audience. Kip proposes to Deb, but she declines, preferring to be a nurse to his wife on a ranch. She also moves away from Kip after the death of Bronco (Art Smith) and falls in love with Kip's friend Lee Price (Douglas Kennedy). Rouge and Deb have a confrontation when Deb comes to see Kip to help Lee against Charlie. Rouge beseeches Kip to help Lee and he implies loving her. The narrative ends with Rouge named Mrs. Davis, wearing conventional clothes and no make-up, and taken to Kip's ranch.

She has a funny line, explaining her name is Rouge because she comes from Baton Rouge. To Kip, "You wouldn't call a lady Bat." When Rouge goes after Kip, Charlie Burns (Zachary Scott) tells her, "He ain't got nothing but the clothes on his back", to which Rouge replies, "It's all in how you wear 'em." The role sees the actress play drunk with slurred speech, touch Kip's face with champagne, break a champagne glass, cry, and be kissed by Kip. She gives a funny arch performance, and director Enright photographs her in soft-focus, perhaps to add to Rouge's artificial allure.

The film premiered in Texas on March 1, 1949, and was given a wide release on March 6 with taglines that included "Warner Bros.' Thundering New Triumph!" and "Men Fought Like The Devil To Win Her … They'd go to the devil to keep her!" It was a box office success. The film was praised by Clive Hirschhorn in "The Warners Bros. Story" but received a mixed reaction from Bosley Crowther in *The New York Times* who wrote that Smith went through the motions of a heart-of-gold barroom queen.

She said working with McCrea was wonderful because he was taller than her. It was the first time the actress could wear heels and she could look up at the actor, with an elongated neck to kiss him.

Smith on left and Joe McCrea on right in
portrait for "*South Of St. Louis*" (1949)

Although as a contract player Smith said she had no selection of roles, one the actress had her eye on was Dominique, the heroine of The Warners romance *The Fountainhead* (1949). This was a much sought after part, and others considered were Lauren Bacall, Barbara Stanwyck, Bette Davis, and Ida Lupino. Patricia Neal was cast instead. Later Smith said she didn't regret missing on the film because it was not a success. The actress said reading Ayn Rand and filming her were two different things.

She next did another Technicolor western "*Montana*" (1950) shot from late August to mid-November on locations in Arizona and at the Warners Ranch. The screenplay was by James R. Webb, Borden Chase, and Charles O'Neal based on a story by Ernest Haycox. The director was again Ray Enright with uncredited work by Raoul Walsh. The story was set in 1879 and centred on Morgan Lane

(Errol Flynn), an Australian sheepman looking for grazing space, who is opposed by local ranchers and the wealthy cattle-woman Maria Singleton (Smith).

She is second billed above the title and again she is a redhead with long hair with a Milo Anderson wardrobe featuring rancher's skirts and a fancy gown for a dance. Maria speaks with a slight Southern accent as she is from Texas. The film features the actress finally singing a song with her own voice, "Reckon I'm in Love" by Mack David, Al Hoffman and Jerry Livingston, with Flynn. Maria gets a funny line to Rodney Ackroyd (Douglas Kennedy) "Well? If you can think of anything more contemptible to say then I've already said to myself, say it and get out!"

The role sees her ride a horse, interact with a dog, slap Morgan, break crockery with a pillow in a fury, be kissed by Morgan, handle a gun, face off against a herd of sheep, and shoot Morgan. Maria is assertive in opposition to Morgan's sheep and the climax presents her heroically before the final romantic submission. Director Enright seems to use Maria fiddling with a whip and a scarf to help disguise Smith's self-conscious self-touching and gives her close-ups.

The film's release was delayed until 1950. It had its premiere in Montana on January 10 and was given a wide release on January 28 with taglines that included "Their bullets riveted a new star to the flag!" and "Hard riding! Hard shooting! Thrill to this super western movie soon to appear at your local theatre!" It was a box office success. The film was praised by Brog in *Variety* but lambasted by Bosley Crowther in *The New York Times*.

In *Errol Flynn: The Untold Story* Charles Higham quotes Smith that one morning the actor arrived literally reeling from the effects of alcohol. The camera operator reported that Flynn's eyes were too bloodshot to be photographed. Late one afternoon Ray Enright wanted a shot of him walking down a dusty street. The actor started in a kind of zigzag but, because he was such a big star, nobody commented on it. The director said to do it again as the light was not good in the first take. Flynn did it again twice but still zigzagging. Enright finally threw up his hands in despair.

Another night at six p.m. the actor was loaded and clowning around. This made Smith angry, and she thought his behavior terrible. It was difficult for her to concentrate on the scene, so they rescheduled it for the next morning. When the actress arrived at work, she was given a letter of apology on Flynn's personal stationery. What he wrote was sweet and beautiful, very long and personal, and utterly typical of him. Smith forgave him at once.

In *Errol Flynn: The Life And Career* Thomas McNulty has Jack Warner claim that in the film's final scene the actor was so drunk that he insisted on playing it flat on his back and refused to kiss his co-star. The scene was re-shot, but Flynn remains on the ground after Morgan is shot by Maria, and he kisses her.

On December 8 she was photographed with a Christmas Seal Corsage designed by the Society of American Florists. The combination of fresh flowers and colorful stamps supported the battle against tuberculosis.

It was announced on December 24 that Warners had loaned her to M-G-M to play the leading feminine role in "Any Number Can Play". The star was Clark Gable and the director Mervyn LeRoy. The film would go into production in January and the story by Edward Harris Heth dealt with the relationship between a professional gambler and his son.

Chapter 6. *Any Number Can Play*

The black and white romance *Any Number Can Play* (1949) produced by Arthur Freed was shot from January 4 to late February, 1949, at the M-G-M Culver City studios in Hollywood. The screenplay was by Richard Brooks. Smith is second billed above the title and plays the supporting role of Lon Kyng, the wife of Charley Enley Kyng (Gable), who wants him to give up his gambling-house. Her hair is back to being short but there is no credited costume designer. Lon is the mother of the teenager Paul (Darryl Hickman), which the actress is really too young for, but the lack of make-up seems designed to make her look older.

The role sees Lon kissed by Charley, laugh, and push Alice Elcott (Audrey Totter) out of her way. She disappears during the climactic card game but returns for the finale. Lon gets a howler line about her one hundred complaints, "A hundred nights you weren't here when I wanted you." Smith has emotion in her voice.

The film was released on June 30 with taglines that included "Red-Head Trouble! Blonde Trouble! Brunette Trouble! -but GABLE is ABLE!" and "GABLE'S GREAT! . . . FIGHTING . . . LOVING . . . GAMBLING". It was a box office success. The film received a mixed reaction from *Variety* and A.W. in *The New York Times* who wrote that Smith was genuinely appealing. It was lambasted by John Douglas Eames in "The MGM Story". *The Screen Guild Theater* broadcast a sixty-minute radio adaptation of the movie on October 12, 1950, with the actress reprising her role.

In real life she was only ten years older than Darryl Hickman. Smith was twenty-seven at the time of filming and he was seventeen. In her book *Long Live The King: A Biography Of Clark Gable*, Lyn Tornabene writes that the actress' pivot tooth got stuck in his moustache during an embrace. This caused the cast and crew to break into uncontrollable giggles. She reported that Gable was a very serious actor and highly disciplined. At the time Smith tended to be late on set and was told that if the leading lady was late for work, Gable went home for the day. Thereafter she was always on time.

The actress told her friend Audrey Totter that M-G-M treated Smith beautifully. The studio was great to work for. She appreciated the more leisurely pace and painstaking efforts everyone at M-G-M took in making their films. Still the actress preferred Warners Bros. Warners was a very congenial lot. There was a very democratic atmosphere, as opposed to Metro, where the star system was so evident. At the time, it seemed so much more exciting to be working at Metro because that's where all the glamorous stars were. But ultimately, Warners was a very progressive studio and did courageous things. They had real human beings and the actors developed as people. Metro was merely a glamour factory where a star was a star.

Smith also described Metro as pretentious. At Warners, Errol Flynn drove in his station wagon with his dogs, and all the actors were made up in the same room. At Metro she had brought over her make-up and hair man from Warners to do the film and to be prepared in the dressing room the actress had been given. A Metro make-up person one time asked where she was and was told Smith's dressing room was in building A. The make-up person replied that they didn't know she was *that* important.

Totter said Smith and Gable got along as any actor and actress would. She loved working with him, but then who wouldn't love working with Clark Gable? Totter also told her about a meeting she once had with Metro boss Louis B. Mayer. He asked if Totter knew whose name on the marquee would draw the most people. She suggested Gable, Joan Crawford, Greer Garson, and Robert Taylor. But Mayer said it was Wallace Beery. Smith concluded from that the film business was really a funny and strange one.

Mary Astor who plays Ada writes in her book *A Life on Film* that the M-G-M wardrobe department had a dressmaker's dummy for Smith, although she only worked that one time at the studio. They made a dummy to be kept on file at all the studios where the actresses worked and might work again. Measurements were checked at the beginning of fittings and time and strength were saved. Those headless forms looked very odd, standing in one part of the huge workrooms, with the names of the famous ones stamped on their chests.

Poster for *Any Number Can Play* (1949)

A February 5 article in *The New York Times* about The Treasury's final listing of salaries paid in the calendar year 1946 and fiscal years which ended in 1947 mentioned Smith. She was said to have earned $120,000. This was opposed to the biggest star, Bette Davis, who earned $328,000, making her the highest paid woman of the year.

The actress is in the group photograph celebrating M-G-M's twenty-fifth silver jubilee in February. This was presumably because she was making *Any Number Can Play* at the studio at the time.

Smith is not in the black and white footage of the stars entering the soundstage individually alphabetically but she can be seen seated for lunch. Louis B Mayer gathered all his fifty-eight stars under contract together on the studio's biggest soundstage with executives and exhibitors for the gigantic lunch.

On March 29 she and Randolph Scott were named for the leading roles in the Warners "Colt. 45", a photoplay by Seton I. Miller. The property had been on the studios schedule since 1947.

On April 11 it was reported that the actress had refused the assignment of the leading feminine role in Warners "The Return of the Frontiersman". She was therefore put on suspension from salary. The film was scheduled to start shooting later in the week. Julie London was cast as the female lead in the western. The film's running time suggests it was a B movie, but Smith described it as a D western with an awful script. But while she refused the part, the studio made her test for it. The actress claimed to be sufficiently naïve to believe that if she made a lousy test, they would think her wrong for the part.

Smith was to test with four leading men and planned to do something with each to sabotage herself. The first was with Gordon MacRae, who was only five foot eight inches. She ran to wardrobe and got boots with very high heels to be ridiculously tall. Another was Rock Hudson in his first screen test. He was very tall, very shy, and very frightened. The actress had never seen an actor so frightened in her whole life. She just couldn't do anything awful to him and played the role to the best of her ability. He didn't get the part and Smith was put on suspension.

On September 21 it was announced that Edwin Marin had been engaged to direct "Colt. 45" to be produced by Saul Elkins and to star her and Randolph Scott. However, when the film went into production in November Ruth Roman played opposite Scott.

She was back on the *Command Performance* radio show that was broadcast on October 18, a program assembled from other broadcasts. The actress was the co-host of the show with Marvin Miller. It is said G. I's had voted her the gal they'd most like to be with after seeing *Any Number Can Play*. She good-naturedly returns the flirting of Dean Martin and Jerry Lewis and is one of the wives of "The Sheik of Araby" in a skit with Martin and Lewis.

It was reported on October 23 that Smith was again on suspension for refusing to be lent to Universal-International for "The Shoplifter". She was replaced by Andrea King. The melodrama about organized crime was to be Smith's first time playing a heavy. The character was the principal in a shoplifting ring, a part the actress felt she was totally unsuited for. The film was released as *I Was a Shoplifter* (1950).

On October 29 she was granted a release from her Warners contract. On July 15, 1946, Smith had entered into a four-year agreement which provided for extension into 1953 if the studio desired. But after turning down the part in "Shoplifter" and given the threat of suspension, she decided to end her contract early.

The actress gave two opinions. She and Warners had parted amicably, but also, they had fired her. Craig Stevens was equally ambiguous. He said Smith left without any ill feelings, and that the decision to leave was influenced by how she had been offered several things which were different. One was the Paramount musical comedy *Here Comes the Groom* which had been announced in August. However, the studio didn't want to pay her gain in the contract.

On December 31 it was reported that Warners asked the actress for recovery of $40,000 in a suit filed in Superior Court. The suit also asked for the cancellation of the signed agreement, which had called for her services for a minimum of three films a year for an annual salary of $120,000. Warners had paid her $40, 000 under the agreement the day before she asserted her refusal of an assignment for a loan-out to Universal-International.

Smith said it was a time when she had integrity about the work. Now the actress had her integrity and no income. She was sure there would be a great rush to pick up her contract, but it was a rude awakening.

Ironically, Smith ended up at Universal-International anyway. On April 16, 1950, it was reported that she had been signed by Universal-International to appear in "Wyoming Male". The Technicolor western *Wyoming Mail* (1950) was shot from May 4 to June 5 on locations in California and at the Universal studios. The screenplay was by Harry Essex and Leonard Lee from a story by Robert Hardy Andrews. The director was Reginald LeBorg. Set in 1869 it centred on boxer Steve Davis (Stephen McNally), who is hired by the government to infiltrate a gang of bandits who attack the railroad mail service.

The actress is second billed above the title and plays the supporting part of music hall singer Mary Williams with the stage name Denise La Verne. She is also involved in the gang of bandits until the murder of Indian Joe (Armando Silvestre). Hair by Joan Van St. Oegger is longer though perhaps a wig and has period ringlets.

Mary sings one song, "Endlessly" with music by Lester Lee and lyrics by Dan Shapiro, though Smith is seemingly dubbed. During her performance on stage, director LeBorg has foreground audience, cutaways to Steve and dialogue between him and a waiter (actor unknown), and a foreground accompanying violinist. However, Steve talking as she sings is used as a plot point, since Mary confronts him about it. She gets a funny exchange. When Mary asks Steve if he loves her, the man replies. "Very much. A little too much". Mary then tells him, "That's what I wanted to hear."

Costumes by Bill Thomas are in pastel colors and include bustles, Mary in her underwear, and an arm sling. The role sees her ride a horse, treat Steve's injuries with whisky, be kissed by Steve, handle a gun, get her hand caught in a drawer by Cavanaugh (Howard da Silva), scream, be off-screen slapped and be shot by Charles De Haven (Roy Roberts). LeBorg gives the actress a few close-ups.

The film was released on October 10, 1950, with taglines that included "The West's Most Daring Train Robbery!" It received a mixed reaction from A.W. in *The New York Times* who wrote that Smith was pretty and fetching in period gowns and even sat a horse well. There was also a mixed reaction from Clive Hirschhorn in "The Universal Story".

On June 27 it was reported that Universal-International had signed her to play the title role in "Under-cover Girl". The story by Frances Rosenwald was about a woman who joins the New York police force to avenge the murder of her policeman father. Joseph Pevney would direct the film from a scenario by Harry Essex. Aubrey Schenck would produce.

The black and white crime drama now titled *Undercover Girl* (1950) was shot from early July to early August at the Universal studios. Smith is top-billed above the title and plays the leading role of Christine Miller – her first and only real leading film role. Hair by Joan Van St. Oegger is back to being short and the clothes by Bill Thomas include shorts and a two-piece bathing suit. Christine gets a funny line about Liz (Gladys George), "She reminds me of everything's that rotten. Everything I want to step on."

The role sees her do ju-jitsu on Jess Taylor (Richard Egan) and Babe (Angela Clarke), laugh, fire a gun, smoke, be kissed by Lt. Mike Trent (Scott Brady), taste narcotics, and cry. The actress is funny rehearsing to play the seductress and is fearful standing close to a furnace fire and menaced by Moocher (Royal Dano). Her best scene is perhaps when Christine admits her real identity to Doc Holmes (Edmon Ryan). Director Pevney does a camera tilt up and down Smith when Christine appears dressed sexily for her undercover assignment and gives her some close-ups.

The film was released on November 2 with taglines that included "The Inside Story of America's Daring Police Women!" and "Beautiful Bait for a dangerous game!" It received a mixed reaction from *Variety* who wrote that Smith made the most of her routine role, and T.M.P. in *The New York Times* who said she was both pretty and admirably daring.

In the film's pressbook the actress said she was delighted with the policewoman role. Smith had been trying to be herself for ten years but until now had not succeeded. Each year she had been in films the actress realized more and more that she had been living a lie and had wanted to do something about it. Smith had played a sneering heel so many times that she began to feel that the world's worst villain wouldn't be caught alive with her. On the other extreme the actress had played such a sweet-sweet person that she almost became unbelievable. Reality is what Smith wanted to play just once. A little bad, a little good, a little sugar, a little vinegar, a couple of laughs and a few tears. That was a human being and that was her. Later Smith commented that she felt this film was the nadir of her Hollywood career.

Poster for *Undercover Girl* (1950)

Next was the Paramount black and white musical comedy *Frank Capra's Here Comes the Groom* (1951) which was shot from late November to January 29, 1951, at the Paramount Hollywood studios. The screenplay was by Virginia Van Up, Liam O'Brien, and Myles Connolly from a story by Robert Riskin and O'Brien. It was produced and directed by Capra. The story centred on foreign correspondent Pete Garvey (Bing Crosby) who has five days to win back his former fiancée Emmadel Jones (Jane Wyman), or he'll lose the orphans he adopted. Smith is third billed above the title and plays the supporting role of Winifred Stanley, the cousin of Wilbur Stanley (Franchot Tone) who is engaged to Emmadel.

We wait 68 out of the 113 minutes to see her and the role of a snooty heiress is a call back to the actress' old roles with Winifred exclaiming, "Well, really" in reaction to Emmadel appearing at breakfast in a party dress. There is a plot point of how tall Winifred is which explains her lack of success with men. She undergoes a change in dress, speech, and behavior to win Wilbur with whom the woman is in love. Under the tutelage of Pete, Winifred must become more like a Jones than a Stanley, which sees her wear men's pajamas, laugh, walk slinkily, and wrestle. This tutelage is paid off in the wedding rehearsal where Winifred and Emmadel have a catfight, though the outcome is expected given that Emmadel is the original Jones and the superior streetfighter.

Smith's short hair reads as brunette although it is referenced as being blonde, and it is seen wet after Winifred is caught in a sprinkler. Costumes by Edith Head include a conversative suit which is replaced by Pete's pajamas. A sheer white-colored polka-dot patterned dress with black sheer skirt, black gloves and black hat is an outfit which demonstrates the change in Winifred. She also sings and dances to Pete's theme song "In The Cool, Cool, Cool of the Evening" with music by Hoagy Carmichael and lyrics by Johnny Mercer.

The role sees Winifred get her hair dried by Pete with a towel, be head-locked by and wrestle Pete, kiss and be kissed by Pete, kiss Wilbur, put Wilbur in a head-lock, and knock down Cusick (Charles Halton). The cat fight has obvious use of stunt doubles for Smith and Jane Wyman, and director Capra has repeated shots of the actress' legs as Pete's point of view to show she is attractive. Winifred gets a funny line about wanting to land Wilbur, "I'll do anything short of murder". Smith makes Winifred funny, especially laughing at how silly batting her eyes is as part of Pete's lessons.

The film's release was delayed until 1951, with the first preview screening held on June 29 in Hollywood. It was given a wide release on September 20, 1951, with taglines that included "Here's The Biggest Package Of Entertainment Ever To Brighten A Movie Screen!" The film was a box office success and won the Academy Award for Best Music Original Song for "In the Cool, Cool, Cool of the Evening", and was nominated for Best Writing, Motion Picture Story. It was praised by *Variety* and John Douglas Eames in "The Paramount Story" but received a mixed reaction from Bosley Crowther in *The New York Times*. *Lux Radio Theater* broadcast a sixty-minute radio adaptation on September 15, 1952, however it appears Smith did not reprise her role.

The actress said she liked the film. Capra was lovely to work with and an exceedingly imaginative and creative director.

In Capra's autobiography *The Name Above The Title* he calls her 'Axle' and writes that she was the most beautiful stately woman. But because the actress was so tall she was condemned to play only villainous roles. Capra describes her as a six-footer and many of Plaster City's romantic heroes as half-pints. The more sympathetic parts went to the less beautiful but more petite clinging vines, and he believed men didn't even waste sympathy on six-foot Minervas. But Capra thought Smith would be a fine as a comedienne and included having Pete saying Winifred should be proud of her height.

She said the height used to worry her terribly. The actress could stand up straight in long shots. But as she walked towards the camera Smith would throw out her right hip and slump. This took inches off the height. For close-ups of love scenes she always had to take off her shoes and it got so that the actress couldn't perform with her shoes on. All the directors would say to scrouch down a bit to look shorter. But she was never able to do that wonderful angle of a throat when the woman looked up into the leading man's eyes, that is until Smith made *"South Of St. Louis"* with Joel McCrea.

With shorties like Charles Boyer and Humphrey Bogart, the actress worried if she took a deep breath they would be tucked under her chin. But Capra tried a switch. By having Pete commenting on her height, they didn't have to fuss about it. After that Smith didn't worry about her tallness. To her it wasn't that she was too tall. It was that the leading men were too short.

In his book, *Frank Capra: The Catastrophe Of Success* Joseph McBride quotes Smith who reported that Capra seemed to enjoy himself so much on the set. But the pressure that came from the schedule and money drove him crazy. This was at a time when the banks were moving into a position of creative control in the movies. She was very disturbed by the idea that Capra would walk away from movies because they weren't fun anymore.

From left Frank Capra with Smith on right on the
set of *Frank Capra's Here Comes the Groom* (1951)

On March 7, 1951, it was reported that the actress was to play opposite Macdonald Carey in Universal-International's "The Cave". The melodrama was about the recovery of stolen treasure and would be photographed on location at the Carlsbad Caverns in New Mexico the next month in Technicolor. Retitled *Cave Of Outlaws* (1951) the western was shot from March 27 to late April on locations in New Mexico, Arizona, California and at the Universal studios. The screenplay and story were by Elizabeth Wilson and the director was William Castle. It was set in Arizona in 1895 and centred on ex-con Pete Carver (Carey) who goes looking for train robbery loot in the caves where it was hidden.

Smith is second billed after the title and plays the supporting role of widow Elizabeth 'Liz' Trent, who wants Pete to use his money to invest in her newspaper. The actress' hair is longer here presumably a wig by Joan Van St. Oegger and the Bill Thomas period clothes include dresses with bustles. The role sees her operating printing equipment, be kissed by Pete, slap Pete, scream, and she gets to appear in the titular cave or a studio mock-up of the same in the climax. Smith makes Liz funny.

The film was released on November with taglines that included "THE MYSTERY OF THE GREAT WELLS FARGO ROBBERY!"

She reportedly spent several hours in wardrobe being fitted for a pair of asbestos pants, as the film called for Liz to be spanked by Pete. However, this scene does not appear in the film.

On September 13 it was reported that the actress would be the girl who helps William Holden's crusading reporter to uncover the activities of a crime syndicate operating in a big city in Paramount's "This Is Dynamite". She would also be the centre of a love triangle between Holden and a state special investigator that had yet to be cast.

On September 22 Smith was a guest on the radio show *Twenty Questions.* On the same date she was inducted as an honorary colonel and honorary commander of the 912th Air Force Reserve Training Wing. This happened at a ceremony at Floyd Bennett Field in Brooklyn.

"This Is Dynamite" was renamed *The Turning Point* (1952) and the black and white crime drama was shot from early October to mid-November on locations in California and at the Paramount studios. The screenplay was by Warren Duff based on a story by Horace McCoy and the director was William Dieterle. The central character is Jerry McKibbon (Holden).

Smith is third billed above the title and plays the supporting part of Amanda 'Mandy' Waycross, writer and secretary to special prosecutor John 'Johnny' Conroy (Edmond O'Brien). She is back to having short hair and her costumes are by Edith Head. The role sees Mandy kissed by Johnny, smoke, drive a car, kiss Jerry, and get jostled by an exiting crowd at the fights. The actress' best scene is perhaps when Mandy gives a speech to Johnny asking him not to give up on his work despite his disappointment in her.

The film's release was delayed until November 14, 1952, with taglines that included "Today's most sensational story of racket-busting!" and ""What's a nice girl like me in a setup like this . . . ? For thrills of course!" It was praised by John Douglas Eames in "The Paramount Story" but received mixed reactions from *Variety*, and Howard Thompson in *The New York Times*. A thirty-minute radio adaptation was done by *Broadway Playhouse* and broadcast on May 13, 1953, but Smith was not in the cast. There was also a *Lux Radio Theatre* radio adaptation broadcast on October 5, 1954, but again without her in the cast.

On November 21 she was a guest on the *Bing Crosby Chesterfield Show* radio show. Crosby introduces her as someone he just had the pleasure of working with in *Here Comes The Groom*. He describes Smith as a fine actress, a clever young lady and really a delightful person, and one he was sure would bring a lot of quality and dignity to the show. The actress tells him she enjoyed working with him too. Crosby says the one thing he regretted was that the man didn't get her at the finish. Smith replies, "Well as long as you tried."

Crosby asks how he compared to Errol Flynn as a leading man. She says as it is her first time on his show, and everyone is having such a wonderful time, the actress hates to throw cold water on things. She says Crosby was a dear, sweet, harmless boy. Crosby points out he can sing, and Flynn can't, and Smith says Flynn doesn't have to. She also plays Daphne in the movie as shown on television skit "Tess Of The Potato Patch." At one point the actress breaks character to introduce herself to co-star Bert Wheeler.

She was the hostess for the radio show *Family Theater* episode entitled "Grandpa's Marvelous X-Ray" broadcast on November 28 on the Mutual Broadcasting System. The twenty-five-minute drama was written by Roderick Petersen and directed by Joseph F. Mansfield. The story centred on Grandpa (Ralph Moody) who finds a dog that barks with x-ray vision.

On December Smith boarded a plane in Los Angeles for Mexico as part of a group of Hollywood stars invited to attend a week of festivities as guests of the Mexican government. This was to celebrate the twentieth anniversary of Mexico's first talking picture. The festivities included receptions, dinner, presentation of medallions by President Aleman of Mexico, and side trips to Acapulco, Cuernavaca and Xochimilco. There was also a dedication of prize bulls at the biggest bullfight of the year, and tours of theatres and special performances by leading Mexican stars.

She was back again on the *Bing Crosby Chesterfield Show* for the episode broadcast on December 12. The actress comments on enjoying the previous skit they did about a movie on television and reports she just bought a six-by-ten-foot screen for *in front of* her television set. Together they do another movie done for television set in The Roaring Twenties. When Crosby initially states he wasn't born at the time - though he was born in 1903 – Smith jokes that his research on the era was reading his diary. The new skit is called

"Ding Dong Daughters" and the drama is repeatedly interrupted by commercials and a broadcast from another station. She plays Leona opposite Bert Wheeler and joins Wheeler and Crosby singing a Chesterfield pitch song.

The actress appeared on the radio show *The Dean Martin And Jerry Lewis Show* that was broadcast on January 25, 1952, on NBC. It was written by Ed Simmons and Norman Lear and produced and directed by Dick Mack. She jokes with Martin and Lewis, believing Martin is the studio cleaner and Lewis his broom. Smith flirts with Lewis who she finds to be cute. The three do a skit about Lewis visiting the dentist, where Martin is the dentist, and the actress is the nurse. Smith interrupts the skit asking if she has to do the same stocking joke where men wear stockings that hang loose.

In the summer the actress augmented her film work with summer theatre for several months for producer John Kenley. She performed in *Private Lives* at venues that included the York and Lakewood Park Theatre in Barnesville, Pennsylvania.

On July 25 it was reported that Smith would play the female lead in Universal-International "Sioux Uprising". This was a Technicolor western set in the Civil War. Albert J. Cohen was named as the producer and filming was to start late in August, probably on location in Arizona. However, Faith Domergue was cast as the female lead instead and the film released as *The Great Sioux Uprising* (1953).

Chapter 7. *Split Second*

Her next film was the RKO black and white crime drama *Split Second* (1953) shot from October 27 to late November on location in Nevada and California and at the RKO Encino Ranch in Los Angeles. Production had been announced in May but was then postponed because of casting problems. The screenplay was by William Bowers and Irving Wallace from a story by Chester Erskine and Wallace. The director was Dick Powell. It centred on escaped convict Sam Hurley (Stephen McNally) and his associates who take hostages and hide in a Nevada mining ghost town where an atom bomb is to be tested the next day.

Smith is billed second after the title and plays the supporting role of Kay Garven, a Pasadena wife divorcing her doctor husband Neal (Richard Egan) who is summoned to treat the injured Bart Moore (Paul Kelly). Her hair is by Larry Germain and costumes by Michael Woulfe which include a fur stole that a symbol of Kay's wealth as a doctor's wife. Kay has a new partner in Arthur Ashton (Robert Paige) whose main attraction has been his availability compared to Neal always working. Arthur's lack of obvious sex appeal, compared to the hunky Neal, is leavened by his defence of Kay which ultimately kills him. Kay's fascination with Sam is perhaps naïve, since he is a psychopath who teases and ultimately rejects her.

Kay is contrasted with the other female hostage, dancer Dorothy 'Dottie' Vail (Jan Sterling). Sam makes advances to both women, but Dottie is streetwise enough to know he cannot be trusted. When Sam asks if she wants to go with him, Dottie tells him, "I'd stick a knife in your back the first chance I got." Another difference between the women is how Dottie is prepared to try to help Neal operate on Bart, whereas Kay tells Sam she can't help because "I'm no good at that."

Smith in portrait for *Split Second* (1953).

Poor Kay is rejected by both Sam and Neal, the latter telling her "I understand the basic weakness in you that makes you do the things you do. But just because I understand it, doesn't mean I want to put up with it anymore." In the climax Kay runs after Sam and joins him and Bart in a car but they are presumably killed in the nuclear explosion. Neal and Dottie survive in in a mine.

Kay is funny when Larry Fleming (Keith Andes) comments, "Lots of men seem to be crazy about you", and she replies, "Shut up." The role sees her drive a car, kiss Arthur, laugh, smoke, be man-handled by Dummy (Frank de Kova), scream and cry, and be kissed by Sam. The actress makes Kay likeable despite her pitiable character. Director Powell provides a shot of Smith's legs as Kay exits the car, as Sam's point of view, and some close-ups.

The film was released on May 2, 1953, with taglines that included "Steel Your Nerves! Here's excitement that will smash them!" and "Six people face-to-face with utter destruction! Doctor . . . convict . . . hard-boiled reporter . . . and two "nice" women . . . who fought over a killer's brutal kisses!" It was a box office success. The film was praised by Richard B. Jewell and Vernon Harbin in "The RKO Story" but received a mixed reaction from A. H. Weiler in *The New York Times*.

The actress said she liked this film.

Smith was a guest on the radio show *Stars Over Hollywood* in the twenty-three-minute episode entitled "It's a Man's Game" that was broadcast on November 1 on CBS. The story was by Dorothy Millard Brown and adapted for radio by Millard Brown and Wilson Bauer. The director was Don Clark. She played the part of Susan Douglas, a school history teacher at Littleton High who becomes the new football coach.

Susan gets a funny comment: "Why shouldn't a woman be a good football coach? It's practically all strategy and knowing how to handle men. Why we're practically taught that from the age of two!" Another funny line is "The Garden Club Ladies would never invite an ex-football coach to join their group." However, her last line is a howler. When she accepts a man's invitation to dance, Susan tells him, "If I start to lead, kick me or something."

The actress had a curtain call chat with announcer Art Ballinger, saying this was the kind of role she especially enjoyed. Smith also joined in plugging Carnation Milk which was the show's sponsor, and Ballinger presented her with a bouquet of red and white carnations just like those pictured on the carnation milk can.

She was in a publicity photograph on November 18 in a negligee on a bed. The accompanying text by Bob Thomas reported that the actress saw red when she was referred to as cold and statuesque. Smith hoped the photograph would help dispel this impression. Lately she had been getting sexier roles and the actress thought she was finally going to escape from the cool acquired during her years at Warners.

Smith appeared in the *Lux Radio Theater* production of "Submarine Command" broadcast on November 17 on CBS. This was a sixty minute adaptation of the Paramount 1951 war drama which starred William Holden and Nancy Olson. The new version starred the actress as Carol, the wife of Lieutenant Commander Ken White (Holden), who reminisces about his wartime years aboard submarine USS Tiger Shark. The show was produced by Irving Cummings. We wait 13 of the 49 minutes running time to hear her and she plays a supporting role. Smith also spoke in a post-show chat, reporting how some stars sneaked into their film previews as not wanting to be seen. She and Holden promoted *The Turning Point*.

On February 7, 1953, it was reported that the actress would possibly star in the stage thriller "Murder Mistaken" on Broadway in mid-October after a spring tryout in San Francisco. Producers Edward Choate and George Ross had had a hit with the play in London's West End since October.

She continued with producer John Kenley's summer tour with *Bell, Book and Candle* at the Lakewood Park Theatre, and at the Ogunquit Playhouse in Ogunquit, Maine.

On September 7 it was reported that Smith was one of the actors whose services were being negotiated for by Burt Balaban, the president of Princess Pictures. They would be in productions made for television that later would be made available for theatrical distribution under a joint venture with the Vitapix Corporation, a film syndicate owned by individual television stations.

She was photographed arriving at London Airport on November 27. Her next film was made in England, the independent black and white thriller *The Sleeping Tiger* (1954). It was shot from December to January, 1954, on location in London and at the Nettlefold Studios in Surrey. The screenplay was by Derek Frye based on a novel by Maurice Moiseiwitsch. The producer and director was Victor Hanbury. The story centred on convict Frank Clemmons (Dirk Bogarde), who breaks into the home of English psychotherapist Dr. Clive Esmond (Alexander Knox) and whose American wife Glenda (Smith) becomes infatuated with him.

She is second billed above the title and plays a supporting role. Hair is by Bette Lee and clothes are by Evelyn Gibbs which include horse riding outfits and a black high-necked sweater when Glenda dresses cheaply to go to a cheap nightclub. Glenda is presented as the older woman to Frank, and the actress is photographed to look older than her real age. She was thirty-one and Bogarde thirty-two at the time of filming.

The role sees her smoke, be kissed by Clive, ride a horse, drive a car, interact with a dog, dance with Frank and be man-handled by him, try to hit Frank with a riding crop, be kissed by him, slap Frank, break a car window with a rock, cry, try to scratch Frank, and kill them both by driving their car into a billboard. Glenda gets a funny line. When Frank points out how there is a police car following the car she is driving, Glenda laughs and says, "You bore me."

Smith makes Glenda's desire for Frank believable, with one effective transition from hysterical laughing to hysterical crying. Director Hanbury overuses the music by Malcolm Arnold to underline the sadomasochistic nature of the love affair and Glenda' neuroticism. However, gives the actress some close-ups.

The film was released in England on June 24, 1954, and in the United States on October 8 on with taglines that included "Hidden deep within every woman is a Sleeping Tiger . . . when aroused it can turn a saint into a sinner!" It was a box office success. The film received a mixed reaction from H.H.T. in *The New York Times*.

Victor Hanbury was credited for blacklisted director Joseph Losey, and Victor Frye was a pseudonym for blacklisted writers Harold Buchman and Carl Foreman.

Smith said she liked the film.

In his book *Joseph Losey: A Revenge on Life*, David Caute writes that when she arrived in England the actress was unaware that Losey had been blacklisted. She and the director were dining in the Ship hotel at Shepperton on her first night when in walked Ginger Rogers and her mother Lela. Lela was considered by Losey to be one of the worst, red-baiting terrifying reactionaries in Hollywood. As they all knew each other, it was said that the director and Smith fled through the kitchen, primarily for the sake of her career.

She said that what was astonishing with Losey was that one had the chance of playing one's part at a very high emotional level, without ever having to limit the intensity. Like Raoul Walsh, he generated enormous energy on the set, and it was this energy which really made the film.

In Michael Ciment's book *Conversations With Losey*, the director reported that the actress was brought by the American end of the production. He knew her because Losey had had long conversations with Smith about the thriller *The Prowler* (1951) which he had made in the United States in 1950. However, the director cast Evelyn Keyes in that film instead.

Losey didn't think this was a good beginning for a future collaboration. Without telling her who the director was, Smith was brought to England. She had no particular objection to him but was petrified of the political situation. Losey told the actress she could quit but because he knew there would be no credit for him on the film. Losey didn't think that would hurt her and Smith accepted.

The production housed them both in the same village hotel. It was winter and the hotel had an intimate bar where you could have dinner. Losey said when Ginger Rogers appeared, Smith went green. She called the producers and the next day the director was moved to a hotel in Windsor. But Losey said the actress helped to improve the film as they went along, and he felt the cast all worked very well together.

In his book *Snakes And Ladders*, Dirk Bogarde writes that she took an incredible risk making the film for an American actress in those days of the McCarthy witch hunts.

In John Coldstream's book, *Dirk Bogarde: The Authorised Biography*, he writes that the actor struck up a fast friendship with her, and Smith remained one of the tight circle of regular guests when she was in England. Coldstream also reports that the actress was described in the publicity as the girl with a laugh in her voice. Bogarde added that her fun, total professionalism, energy, loyalty, and above all, courage remained as they always were - first in Smith's life. The days were brighter for knowing her.

Smith on left and Dirk Bogarde on right
in still from *The Sleeping Tiger* (1954).

Her next film was the Republic war biography *The Eternal Sea* (1955) shot from October 7 to late October, 1954, on locations in Asia and at the Republic Hollywood studios. The working title was The Admiral Hoskins Story. The screenplay was by Allen Rivkin based on a story by William Wister Haines. The director was John H. Auer. This is the true story of Rear Admiral John Madison Hoskins (Sterling Hayden) who fights to stay on after losing a leg on an aircraft carrier in World War II.

She is second billed after the title and plays the supporting part of Sue Hoskins, John's wife, and the mother of his children. The role sees her interact with children and a dog, be kissed by John, cry, read letters from John, and dance with John. The strongest impact Sue has on the narrative is that she provides John with the Navy code regulation that stops them from discriminating against him because of his disability. Smith's best scene is perhaps when Sue delivers a speech to Vice-Admin. Thomas L. Semple (Dean Jagger) about how her husband has changed after losing the leg. Director Auer presents her in a profile close-up while giving Jagger the camera focus as he listens.

The film premiered in Providence, Rhode Island on April 20, 1955, and was given a wide release on May 5 with taglines that included "Inspired by the depths of a woman's love!" and "The real-life Naval Hero who defied disaster - to soar his jet to glory!" It received a mixed reaction from Howard Thompson in *The New York Times* who wrote that Smith did nicely on the sidelines.

One evening in 1954, she and Craig Stevens were at the Encore, a jazz nightclub on the Sunset Strip. The table was hosted by William Holden and the other guests included Audrey Hepburn and Mel Ferrer, who were then dating. Hepburn announced that she and Ferrer were engaged.

The actress now entered television. Her first venture was the episode of the drama anthology series *The Star and The Story* aka Star Performance entitled "W. Somerset Maugham's The Back of Beyond". This was shot at the Republic Hollywood studios and broadcast on March 5, 1955. The teleplay was by Frederic Brady based on a story by Maugham. The director was Arthur Ripley. The story was set in Malaya and centred on Roger Saffrey (George Macready), a pompous official who confronts the infidelity of his wife Violet (Smith). She also introduced the show.

The actress plays the leading role which sees her kiss Tom Clark (Robin Hughes), faint, cry, and be man-handled by Roger. She is perhaps best when Violet delivers a speech about not being afraid to die when Roger threatens to kill her.

Next was the drama anthology series *Stage 7* episode entitled "To Kill a Man" broadcast on March 6, 1955. The teleplay was by Hagar Wilde based on a story by Jack London. The director was James Neilson. The story had a dinner party interrupted by an intruder. Smith played the part of Caroline Taylor, the wife of wealthy businessman Phillip (Scott Forbes), who plots with the intruder (Dan Barton).

On June 18 it was reported that she and Craig Stevens had been engaged for the leading roles in the West Coast company of "Plain and Fancy". The part of Ruth Winters had been originated on Broadway by Shirl Conway. The new show would open August 29 at the Los Angeles Philharmonic Auditorium. The musical comedy about an Amish community had a book by Joseph Stein and Will Glickman, lyrics by Arnold Horwitt, and music by Albert Hague. The Broadway production was directed by Morton DaCosta and ran from January 27, 1955, to March 3, 1956. A program for the touring company shows it was also directed by DaCosta, and Ruth gets the solo number, "It's A Helluva Way To Run A Love Affair". The tour continued into San Francisco at the Curran Theatre from October 10.

In February, 1956 *Plain and Fancy* played in Chicago. The tour was said to be a critical and personal success for the actress. However, in his book *One More Kiss: The Broadway Musical In The 1970s*, Ethan Mordden writes that she had more or less talked through her three numbers. Stevens claimed that they did the show for fourteen months.

The next television role was in the sixty-minute episode of the anthology of mini-features *The 20th Century-Fox Hour* entitled "The Hefferan Family" broadcast on June 13 on CBS. These mini-features were retreads of successful Fox movies, and this episode was a remake of the Fox 1949 romantic comedy *Chicken Every Sunday.* That film was an adaptation of the Broadway play by Julius J Epstein and Philip G. Epstein which in turn was based on a book by Rosemary Taylor. The play had run from April 5, 1944, to January 6, 1945. The new television version was originally entitled "Mama's Boarding House" and had a teleplay by Dorothy Cooper. The director was Jules Bricken. The show was shot at the 20th Century Fox Hollywood studios. It centred on Emily Hefferan (Smith), the long-suffering wife of a kindly but not very practical man who takes in boarders to keep the family in food. The role had been originated on stage by Mary Philips and played in the film by Celeste Holm.

She was back in films in the Paramount Technicolor biography *Beau James: The Life and Times of Jimmy Walker* (1957) shot from July 23 to September 14 on locations in New York. The screenplay was by Jack Rose and Mel Shavelson based on the book by Gene Fowler. The director was Shavelson. Walker (Bob Hope) was the flamboyant and somewhat corrupt Mayor of New York City from 1926-1932.

Smith is fourth billed after the title and plays the role of Allie Walker, Jim's estranged wife of eighteen years. Allie is contrasted with the twenty-two-year-old Betty Compton (Vera Miles), who is Jim's mistress. She is younger and passionate while Allie is emotionally distant. In real life Smith was thirty-five and Miles was twenty-six. In their confrontation scene, Smith looks more blonde, presumably to contrast with Miles as a brunette. The younger actress has a bigger part in the narrative and gets a great scene to play – an attempted suicide – that is better than anything Smith gets. Her hair is by Nellie Manley and clothes by Edith Head. The role sees Allie kissed by Chris Nolan (Paul Douglas) and Jim, sing "Will You Love Me in December as You Do in May?" with music by Ernest Ball and lyrics by Walker in a crowd of singers, and dance with Jim.

The film's release was delayed until June 7, 1957, and the taglines included "The Story of Fabulous Jimmy Walker . . . Mayor of New York" and "He took New York for its wildest joyride!" It received a mixed reaction from Land. in *Variety* who wrote that Smith gave a shaded and attractive performance, H.H.T. in *The New York Times* who said she was surprisingly convincing, and John Douglas Eames in "The Paramount Story".

Jack Rose and Mel Shavelson commented on the film in *The New York Times* of June 15, 1957, in an article entitled "On Hailing His Honor". They wrote that the actress was tall and beautiful. If anyone could had played the heartbreak that was Allie Walker's life any better, they hadn't met her.

She was next seen on the thirty-minute episode of the television crime anthology series *The Joseph Cotten Show: On Trial* entitled "We Who Love Her" broadcast on September 21 on NBC. The show was shot at the Republic Hollywood studios. The teleplay was by Don Mankiewicz, and it was directed by Don Weis. The story centred on Libby Wilson (Smith) and her husband Carl (Kevin McCarthy) who want to adopt their niece who has been living with them since her parents were killed in an auto accident.

The actress appeared in the sixty-minute episode of the television anthology series *Robert Montgomery Presents* entitled "September Affair" shot at the NBC studios in New York and broadcast on October 8. This was a remake of the Paramount 1950 film romance which had starred Joan Fontaine and Joseph Cotten. The new teleplay was by Mathilde Ferro and Theodore Ferro, but the director is unknown. The story centred on two survivors of a plane crash in the Atlantic who fall in love, and decide to stay together in Europe, leaving their former lives and responsibilities back home. Smith co-starred with John Newland.

Next was the thirty-minute episode of the *Lux Video Theatre* live television series entitled "The Gay Sisters" shot at the NBC Studios in Hollywood and broadcast on November 22. This was a remake of the Warners 1942 film romance which starred Barbara Stanwyck as Fiona Gaylord. The teleplay was by S.H. Barnett and the director was Norman Morgan. The story centred on Fiona (Smith) who is one of three sisters who are orphaned and must manage their Fifth Avenue mansion by themselves.

She was an intermission guest in the *Lux Video Theatre* episode "To Have and Have Not" broadcast on January 17, 1957.

On April 3 it was reported that the actress would appear as the mother in a new television series "Mother Was a Freshman". However, it appears this show was never made.

She was back on *Lux Video Theatre* for the episode entitled "Death Do Us Part" broadcast on May 16. The teleplay was by S. H. Barnett from a screenplay by Don Martin based on a story by Jo Pagano. The director was David Orrick McDearmon. The story centred on a young detective on the hunt for a killer who almost causes a grave miscarriage of justice. Smith played the part of Lilly.

She was a guest on the episode of the television comedy series *The Steve Allen Plymouth Show* broadcast on June 30 on NBC. The show promoted *Beau James: The Life and Times of Jimmy Walker* and had the actress and Vera Miles perform a scene from the film. The show was directed by Dwight Hemion.

In July she appeared in the stage musical *Wonderful Town* at Paul Winston's Music Theatre Memorial Hall in Dayton, Ohio. The show was staged by Leonard Patrick and Smith played the part of Ruth. The Broadway show with book by Joseph A. Fields and Jerome Chodorov, music by Leonard Bernstein and lyrics by Betty Comden and Adolph Green had run from February 25, 1953, to July 3, 1954. Rosalind Russell had originated the part of Ruth.

She was profiled in the August 17th edition of *Picture Show* magazine. It was said she liked bright happy colors but was not particularly interested in clothes beyond a desire to look well-groomed. Her favorite sports were swimming and horse-back riding.

The actress next appeared in the Universal International Eastman film color comedy *This Happy Feeling* (1958) which was shot from late September to early November at Universal studios. The working title was For Love or Money. The screenplay was by Blake Edwards based on the play "For Love Or Money" by F. Hugh Herbert. The play ran on Broadway from November 4, 1947, to June

19, 1948. Edwards was also the film's director, and the producer was Ross Hunter. The story centred on Janet Blake (Debbie Reynolds), a New York dentists' assistant who takes a job as the secretary to actor and Connecticut horse breeder Preston 'Mitch' Mitchell (Curt Jurgens).

Smith in portrait for *This Happy Feeling* (1958).

Smith is fourth billed after the title and plays the supporting role of Nita Hollaway, the part originated on stage by Vicki Cummings. She is an actress with a romantic interest in Mitch. Her gowns are by Bill Thomas. We see Nita take a curtain call in a play with Mitch but not her acting. She gets some funny lines. Nita tells a seagull – "On a day like this, why aren't you at the beach?" And in response to Mitch's tirade against Method actors in the theatre she asks, "I wonder how Olivier and Evans keep going?"

The role sees her smoke, be kissed by Mitch, interact with the seagull, laugh, stick out her tongue at Janet, and have her bottom slapped by Mitch. Nita is threatened by the younger Janet and Mitch's preference for her, though the sensual Nita is far more appealing than the dull, sexless Janet. Smith makes Nita funny.

The film was released on June 18, 1958, with taglines that included ""So he lent me his pajamas with no strings attached! . . . and now I'm his very private secretary!" and "Another spicy look at Love by the Author of "THE MOON IS BLUE""" It was not a box office success. The film was praised by Powe in *Variety* who wrote that Smith rendered strong support but received a mixed reaction from Clive Hirschhorn in "The Universal Story". It was lambasted by Bosley Crowther in *The New York Times*.

When Errol Flynn was making the Warners biographical romance *Too Much, Too Soon* (1958) in October he finally admitted to his true feelings about his former co-star. After sixteen years and only a few months Flynn telephoned and wanted to have lunch with the actress at Warners. She agreed. Craig Stevens said his wife had tears in her eyes when she came home from the reunion. Flynn knew he didn't have much longer to live and wanted Smith to know how much he enjoyed working with her, and that Flynn loved the woman. She never forgot that.

The actress returned to television for the thirty-minute black and white episode of the *Schlitz Playhouse* aka Schlitz Playhouse of Stars entitled "I Shot A Prowler". This was shot at the Republic Hollywood studios and broadcast on March 28, 1958, on CBS. The teleplay was by Arthur Sheekman and the director was Arthur Hiller. The story centred on Vivian Braxton (Smith), a lonely married Connecticut woman who becomes infatuated with conman Andre Merrick (Helmut Dantine).

She is top-billed above the title and plays the leading role. Hair is by Florence Bush and her costumes include reading glasses. Vivian's age is a plot point. Andre seduces the woman by saying her face has character which comes from living and experience. Later he calls her "old girl" and asks, "Do you think it's a treat for me to kiss a frustrated housewife?" Vivian has a funny line to geologist husband

Ralph (Craig Stevens). "If you knew as much about women as you did about oil, you'd know the one thing worse than jealousy is no jealousy." The role sees her handle a gun, faint, smoke, be kissed by and dance with Andre. Director Hiller gives the actress some unflattering close-ups.

Chapter 8. *The Young Philadelphians*

She returned to films in the Warners drama *The Young Philadel-phians* aka The City Jungle (1959) shot from mid-September to mid-December on locations in California and at the Warners studios. The working title was The Philadelphian. The screenplay was by James Gunn from the novel "The Philadelphian" by Richard Powell and the director was Vincent Sherman. The story centred on Anthony 'Tony' Judson Lawrence (Paul Newman). He is a promising lawyer who tries to handle his social and professional problems while climbing the ranks in Philadelphia.

Smith is billed third after the title and plays the supporting role of Carol Wharton, the wife of a wealthy older lawyer. Costumes by Howard Shoup include a sleeveless and backless evening gown and a black negligee which seem rather shocking as worn by a middle-aged woman. The thirty-seven-year-old actress also appears to be wearing less make-up to make herself look older.

We wait 47 out of the 136 minutes running time to see her and she only appears in nine minutes. Carol is first viewed objectified as a pair of legs as she stands on a ladder. Carol's being married to an older man has her sexually frustrated so the attraction to the younger Tony is not a surprise. The inevitable scene where she goes to him for sex has her saddled with some howlers Carol tells Tony. "I'd forgotten how it feels to be with someone". "Thank you for not laughing at me". "Let's give ourselves something to remember". And "I'm leaving here with something so much better than I'd hoped to find."

It is an interesting twist that Tony won't have sex with her unless they marry. While she can't leave her comfortable life, Carol is grateful for his sexual interest and proposal. The role sees her ride a horse, dance alone and dance with Tony, be kissed by Joan Dickinson (Barbara Rush), and Tony. Smith retains her dignity in Carol's love scene with Tony.

The film premiered in Philadelphia on May 19, 1959, and was given a wide release on May 21 with taglines that included "You may recognize yourself in this BLAZING STORY OF TODAY'S "MODERNS"!" and "Guilty secrets. Shocking scandals. All in a day's work for one Philadelphian lawyer." It was a box office success. The film received Academy Award nominations for Best Actor in a Supporting Role for Robert Vaughn who plays Chester A. Gwynn, Best Cinematography, Black-and-White, and Best Costume Design, Black-and-White. It was praised by Clive Hirschhorn in "The Warners Bros. Story" but received a mixed reaction from A.H. Weiler in *The New York Times* who wrote that Smith was momentarily effective.

It was reported that she was cast in the film on October 13. However, in November *The Hollywood Reporter* wrote that the actress fell off a horse during shooting. When director Vincent Sherman had yelled 'Action' the horse bolted and threw her to the ground. She fractured several vertebrae. Smith was said to have been out of commission for three to seven weeks. Sherman was able to shoot around her, but the accident did delay production and made the film go overbudget.

She considered this to be her best screen performance. Smith said she was more mature, both as a person and as an actress. She found going back to Warners an eerie experience. Most of the people Smith had worked with for years before were still there - all except the actors.

She knew how to ride a horse a little as the actress had been taught back in her Warners days by Poodles Hanneford who taught anybody who was anybody. He had a ranch out in the San Fernando Valley and would set you down on a gentle old horse. With a rope around your waist that was attached to a pole in the centre of the riding ring you would go round and round. Smith managed to stay on but wondered what would happen if she had to ride in a straight line. Sure enough, this is what was required for the new film. Playing an Eastern society woman, the actress had to use an Eastern saddle and not the Western saddle she had learned on. The Eastern saddle did not have the pommel you could hang onto if you were in trouble, like the Western saddle, which is why Smith fell.

Paul Newman on left and Smith on right in still for *The Young Philadelphians* aka The City Jungle (1959)

Sherman said she was grand to work with and a much better actress than people gave her credit for. He felt this was because for a long time all Smith did was play the love interest in Errol Flynn's actioners. Sherman noted that while it didn't make for news, she was never involved in a scandal, always behaved in a dignified manner and was charming to be around.

In his book, *Paul Newman, The Man Behind the Baby Blues: His Secret Life Exposed*, Darwin Porter quotes the actor on Smith. He says she was about as attracted to him as Eleanor Roosevelt was to Jerry Lewis.

At this time Craig Stevens enjoyed fame as the title character in the television series *Peter Gunn* which debuted on September 22 on

NBC. Stevens reported that it was his wife who first read the script and arranged for him to meet with Blake Edwards. Edwards had created the show, and the actress knew him from working on *This Happy Feeling*.

She seemed no longer interested in making movies. Her husband felt if she had continued to work, Smith would have never gotten to see him, since the television show took up all his time. She now ran their house and was happy not working. When they had first married, the actress could not cook but Stevens was never demanding about it because he knew this was not the way to handle her. If he had been demanding his wife would have done just the opposite. As time went on, she fiddled around in the kitchen and experimented, but mostly since Smith was working, they hired a cook.

Now she had the time to learn, and became a gourmet cook, with many cookbooks. In a 1971 interview it said the number of cookbooks was 300 but at the time of her death it would be 680. The more exotic the recipe the better. The actress would make it once and then move on to something new. That was her nature.

When his television series was on hiatus between seasons Stevens and his wife travelled to Europe.

She was back on television doing a sixty-minute episode of the live anthology series *The United States Steel Hour* entitled "The Last Autumn" shot in New York and broadcast on November 18, 1959, on CBS. It was written by Arthur Heinemann and adapted from the novel by Herbert Gutterman. The story was set in a New England boarding school where a boy is killed in a fall during a geology field trip. Smith played the part of Barbara Welch, the fiancé of Roger Conway (Pat Hingle), whose son has been killed. The show received a mixed reaction from John P. Shanley in *The New York Times* who wrote that her performance was competent.

Next was a guest appearance in the black and white television adventure series *James A. Michener's Adventures in Paradise* in the sixty-minute episode "Somewhere South of Suva" broadcast on December 28 on ABC. It was shot at the 20th Century Fox studios in Hollywood. The teleplay was by Harry Miles Muheim and the director was Gerald Mayer. The series told the adventures of the Tiki III and crew as they sailed from island to island through the South Pacific. The episode saw Adam Troy (Gardner McKay) contracted to search for a large diamond.

Smith is top-billed among the guest stars and plays the part of Loraine Lucas aka Loraine Nichols, the aviatrix daughter of deceased Hawaiian merchant Lucky (John Gallaudet). The role sees her handle a gun, laugh, cry, receive an off-screen beating, and pilot a plane. She gets a switcheroo scene with the gun – aiming it at Adam, he taking it from her and throwing it away, and she getting it back to again aim at him. Loraine has a monologue about carrying Japanese heroine on her plane.

She and Craig Stevens were guests on the episode of the television documentary news talk-show *Person to Person* broadcast on May 20, 1960, on CBS.

The actress was a guest on the episode of the black and white crime drama television series *Michael Shayne* entitled "A Night with Nora" broadcast on October 7 on NBC. The show was shot at the Republic Hollywood studios. The series centred on the titular private detective (Richard Denning) in Miami, Florida. The episode's teleplay was by Brett Halliday and the director was Paul Stewart. Smith played the part of Nora Carroll.

After *Peter Gunn* was cancelled in September, 1961, she and Craig Stevens acted together in Ira Levin's play, *Critic's Choice* in a thirteen-week run that toured the country.

When her husband was offered a musical in London, Smith accompanied him and stayed in Britain for the next two years. With Stevens working on the show and then the television crime drama series *Man of the World*, she occupied her time by studying Italian, French, and yoga. The actress got a realtor's license, learned speed reading, and read works of psychology and philosophy. She was said to have also travelled alone.

In 1963 the couple returned to the United States where he starred in the Broadway musical *Here's Love* which ran from October 3 to July 25, 1964.

Smith was a guest panelist on the television family game-show *To Tell the Truth* for the episodes shot in Hollywood and broadcast from September 21 to 25, 1964, on CBS.

She was a guest on the crime drama television series *The Defenders* in the episode entitled "Impeachment" which was shot in New York and broadcast on March 18, 1965, on CBS. The show centred on Lawrence Preston (E.G. Marshall) and Kenneth Preston (Robert Reed), a father and son lawyer duo who took on a variety of cases that often dealt with the important issues of the day. The sixty-minute episode teleplay was by Stanley R. Greenberg and the director was Paul Bogart. In it, Lawrence defends old college buddy Governor William Defoe (Dan O'Herlihy) on a charge of malfeasance. Smith played the part of Carol Defoe.

The actress was back as a panelist on *To Tell the Truth* for the episodes broadcast from March 29 to April 2.

In the summer she and Stevens co-starred in the Jean Kerr play, *Mary, Mary* for John Kenley at the Veterans Memorial Theatre in Columbus and the Packard Music Hall Theatre in Warren, Ohio. The show was directed by Fred Baker. Smith played the part of Mary McKellaway that had been originated on Broadway by Barbara Bel Geddes. The Broadway production had run from March 8, 1961, to December 12, 1964.

The couple appeared on the episode of the television talk-show *Gypsy* that was shot in San Francisco and broadcast on July 2 on ABC. Hostess Gypsy Rose Lee interviewed them about man-wife acting teams.

On June 5, 1966, it was reported that she would make her Broadway debut in the comedy "The Coffee Lover" by Stefan Kaner and Jess Korman. Morton da Costa was to direct. Five weeks in the summer circuit were planned before the Broadway opening in late September. The show ran at venues including Westport Country Playhouse in Connecticut from August 8 to 13, the Falmouth Playhouse in Massachusetts from August 22 to 27, and the Ogunquit Playhouse in Maine from August 29 to September 3. However, it appears this show didn't make it to Broadway.

On May 30, 1968, it was reported that the actress and Craig Stevens would co-star in a Broadway hit comedy for the summer circuit by the Producing Managers Company. The comedy was unable to be announced at this time. However, this presumably turned out to be Abe Burrow's play *Cactus Flower*, which the couple played in August at the Ogunquit Playhouse in Maine. She performed the part of Stephanie which had been originated on Broadway by Lauren Bacall in a run that went from December 8, 1965, to November 23, 1968. The couple then did the national tour of the show from September 23 until March 1, 1969. The show was also directed by Burrows. The tour included a show at the O'Keefe Centre for the performing arts in Toronto from December 2 to 14.

Stevens said the tour was another fourteen months. He said working with his wife on stage was a joy. Sometimes married people didn't get along too well but they were the opposite. They complemented one another and were very supportive and very critical which was good. It was terribly tiring to do the same show eight times a week for such a long time, but every audience was different and a challenge. They would find new things all the time, and the couple discussed them and worked on them. This made the show a constant challenge and fresh all the time.

They had made a guest appearance on the episode of the television comedy music talk-show *The Mike Douglas Show* that was broadcast on February 26, 1969.

After the tour the couple then moved back to California. She did a guest spot on the color television comedy series *The Governor &*

J.J. entitled "State of Reunion" shot in Hollywood and broadcast on December 9, 1969, on CBS. The show centred on the relationship between widowed state Governor William Drinkwater (Dan Dailey) and his hip daughter Jennifer Jo (Julie Sommars). The episode had a teleplay by Barbara Avedon and the director was Jay Sandrich. Smith played the role of Leslie Carroll, a woman from the Governor's past.

Smith in still for *The Governor & J.J.*

She returned for her second appearance as Leslie in the episode "Once Upon a War" broadcast on January 6, 1970. This was written by Earl Barret and directed by Alan Rafkin.

The actress was said to be anxious to do more stage work, especially a musical. To this end she studied with vocal coach David Craig. He was known as the guru of singing coaches for non-singing actors, giving a course called The Actor as Singer. Smith said Craig was extraordinary and his course specialized in preparing people for auditions. The result was that you gave the best performance possible and if you were unsuccessful, you were satisfied. Someone would not go off and cry that they could have done better.

In the fall she heard that producer Hal Prince was preparing a new musical. *Follies* was about three former showgirls who reunite twenty-five years later at the theatre where they had appeared. Auditions were being held and the actress was interested in the role of Phyllis Rogers Stone, one of the former showgirls who is now an unhappily married society matron.

She auditioned three times for Prince before winning the role. It was said that at her first audition Smith looked less than glamorous. For the second she was put in the hands of the production supervisor Ruth Mitchell and the show's hair designer, Joe Tubens. They turned her into the movie star the actress had formerly been. Smith reported that the second audition took place five months after the first. She said David Craig taught her to know exactly what to do from the moment the actress came on stage. She had to have it down perfectly but make it look spontaneous despite the calculation.

In *One More Kiss: The Broadway Musical In The 1970s*, Ethan Mordden writes that Smith only studied with David Craig after the disastrous first audition. Craig taught her not only how to vocalize but also how to present herself in every moment in the audition. She chitchatted with the team, related to the accompanist, and used her stance and eyes and teeth. The whole sequence was placed and timed to demonstrate the character of Phyllis with her ruthless self-confidence.

Craig predicted that the only problem would be if they asked Smith to do a song twice – which was rarely done. If it occurred, she could not make the same moves at the same time. At the audition when the actress finished the song, they asked her to sing it again and take it down a half tone. She panicked and almost said that they didn't know how to audition right because David promised Smith wouldn't be asked to do it twice.

In her book *Stephen Sondheim: a life* Meryle Secrest writes that the actress made a special study of the song "Could I Leave You?

before her audition. This was Phyllis' big solo, and generally agreed to be the most difficult of the score.

In his book *Sondheim & Co* Craig Zadan says that in her first audition in California she sang so badly that Smith was eliminated from consideration. She later called and asked for a second chance which Hal Prince agreed to. The actress flew out to New York and was terrific the second time, after having worked on her voice and feeling more confident. It was also thought that Smith's casting was helped by the idea that her past embodied the point of the show. She was known from the beauty of her youth and now the actress had aged.

Hal Prince reported that she was the first person he and co-director Michael Bennett saw for the show. Prince knew David Craig and that Smith was working with him after the failed first audition. Prince also said that it was Craig who asked that she be seen a second time. They said yes. The actress was now better but they were still unconvinced. She was given "Could I Leave You?" and told to study it with Craig. When Smith was ready, she could come and sing it for them. At the third audition her singing of the song was marvellous, and the actress looked perfect and delicious, so she got the part.

Prince said Smith was told the news at a party she attended for the show. The actress was told by costume Designer Florence Klotz who thought she was a designer's dream to dress. Smith said she was surprised to be informed this way and not by Prince or Michael Bennett.

In her book *Harold Prince: A Director's Journey* Carol Ilson quotes Prince on the casting of the actress. He thought she would lend the role of Phyllis a permanent radiance. Ilson also quotes Smith on Prince. She said he knew exactly what he wanted. There was no uncertainty or time wasting.

Those considered for the parts in the show were other old Hollywood stars regardless of whether they could sing. Among the females were Rhonda Fleming, Joan Bennett, Kitty Carlisle, Barbara Cook, Gloria DeHaven, and Jane Wyman. Yvonne De Carlo, who would be cast as Carlotta Campion, said she initially auditioned for Phyllis. However, De Carlo decided the brilliant society woman was not somebody she could identify with.

In his book, *Everything Was Possible: The Birth of the Musical Follies*, Ted Chapin writes that DeCarlo audition showed she didn't seem to have the right style for Phyllis. But the song the actress had prepared, "Ten Cents a Dance", made everyone think she embodied Carlotta.

On December 6 it was reported that Smith was to make her Broadway debut in "Follies" coming to the Winter Garden on April 4. The musical would have a book by James Goldman and a score by Stephen Sondheim. Co-director Michael Bennett was also the choreographer. She would make $1,500 a week. This was the second highest salary of the leading actors, with Gene Nelson getting $2,000.

Rehearsals for the show were to be held at the American Theatre Lab in Nineteenth Street from January 11, 1971. However, the leads were called in a week early, with Bennett especially anxious about how well the women would be able to dance.

The actress flew in from California and appeared wearing red knickers, white shirt and a blue sweater wrapped around her shoulders. She was said to look quite smashing at the age of forty-nine and her infectious good-natured laugh echoed down the hall. Smith had a straight-forward manner which was very helpful, if at times a bit harsh. When asked if she wanted coffee, the reply was "I'm not a coffee drinker, so you never have to ask me again." When the actress was brought buttermilk, she was grateful and gracious.

Sondheim originally had the idea that the song "Losing My Mind" be sung by both Phyllis and Sally (Dorothy Collins). Smith was ushered in first to learn the song with the musical director Hal Hastings. Then it was decided that only Phyllis would sing it. Another song, "The World's Full of Boys (Girls), was being played around for her as well but this song would be dropped before the Broadway run. The actress struggled her way through "Losing My Mind" but at one point she turned to Hastings and asked pointed questions. "Are you helping me? Aren't you playing a little something extra for me – like the tune?" Before too long the song emerged as a mistake for Phyllis.

In the first week of rehearsal nicknames were established for the stars of the show: "the big four" for Smith, Gene Nelson who played Buddy Plummer, Dorothy Collins, and John McMartin who played Benjamin Stone. De Carlo was "the big one". When the creative staff huddled in the stage manager's office for a pep talk, Smith quipped to Ruth Mitchell, "This feels like a lousy cocktail party". Mitchell shot back, "Without the booze."

There was six weeks before the show had its first preview in Boston. The actress and her co-stars were a little nervous. Their comfortable routine was now invaded by what seemed like an enormous group of strangers. These were the four actors playing the younger versions of the leads. They may not have looked physically similar, but their personalities matched. The young Phyllis was played by Virginia Sandifur who was tall, dark-haired, and slightly removed from the fray.

By the second week of rehearsal, the cast's behavior was notable. Smith was never very social. She would linger but not for long and sometimes paused for a quip. An article about the show was pinned to the bulletin board which referred to her as tall and striking. The actress commented that she wished someday to play someone short and fat.

Smith quietly worked away. No one was aware of it, but she worked harder and pushed herself further than anyone else. The actress seemed cool and relaxed and funny. She happened to see one of the dancers in the hall with whom Phyllis is caught necking and he was crocheting. Smith looked slightly bemused and asked what he was making. When the dancer said it was a pair of pants she responded with "Oh" and muttered under her breath, "That was not exactly the kind of young lover I had in mind."

The actress had rehearsed her solo song "Could I Leave You?" behind closed doors. When she first performed it in front of the company Smith gave a stunning performance. When she finished there was a moment of silence and then the entire group burst into applause. The actress giggled and smiled.

From January 30, the company moved to Feller's Scenic Studio in the South Bronx where the show's set had been constructed. When Smith emerged from her car on the first day, she looked around said "Well this is certainly a curious place to be." Exploring the multi-dimensional set, the actress climbed up one of the two downstage towers. Looking down over the main stage a slightly seasick expression came onto her face.

She asked Michael Bennett to restage "Could I Leave You?". Smith had the idea that this would be her only solo, knowing that she couldn't really do "Losing My Mind" justice. Bennett decided to have Phyllis perform the number as a drunken rampage. Although the actress threw herself into it with full force the general feeling was that this approach was a mistake. After the song there was polite applause and then Bennett yelled, "This is a work in progress!" Hal Prince decided to restage the number.

Later she went to Sondheim's house to talk. Smith was worried about "Losing My Mind" which she believed Dorothy Collins could sing better. Why not give it to her as a solo? Since Smith had good legs and could move well, she suggested a dance number for Phyllis. Sondheim was intrigued and agreed to write a new one. Finally, the decision was made that Collins would perform "Losing My Mind" alone. It had taken three and a half weeks of rehearsal to realize that the song made more sense for Sally than Phyllis.

The final week of rehearsal was from February 6 to 15. The actress was concerned that she had yet to be given her new dance number. There was a limited amount of time to learn it before the first preview. Sondheim had nearly finished the number by Thursday. It was called "Uptown, Downtown". Michael Bennett worked on the staging, but Smith seemed to be the only one with a copy of the song's lyrics. When the stage manager's assistant peered over her shoulder to get them, she gave a quizzical glance. By Friday Sondheim had finished the song. The actress learned it with Hal Hastings and, when she felt confident, joined the dancers.

With only three days left before the first preview Smith arrived early on Saturday to work through the number. After having worked on Friday, she was entitled to have Saturday off, but the actress wanted to master the number. Bennett liked the song but wasn't sure how to get her to dance. She was tall and had great legs which he wanted to utilize as much as possible. But figuring out how to point up the difference between the two sides of her character in a decidedly lowdown dance was a challenge.

New dialogue was given to Phyllis. Smith scored a laugh in a new read through on "Who's in love with you, Ben, your editor at Random House?" She quipped, "My God. A laugh!"

Poster for *Follies*

Chapter 9. *Follies*

The company moved to the Colonial Theatre in Boston on February 16. The leading actors stayed at the Statler-Hilton hotel. Hal Prince invited them to the orchestra reading which the actress attended. She was thrilled and admitted to checking out the marquee, venturing into the dark auditorium and asking the box office how ticket sales were going.

"Uptown, Downtown" had only been staged in the rehearsal room so Bennett used the theatre's stage for one hour during the tech crew's dinner time. Bennett occasionally snapped at Smith from nerves, and she was equally nervous, performing on the various raked levels. The actress messed up a lot of the movement and lyrics. The observers suggested they cut the number from the first preview. However, Bennett disagreed.

She was given a star dressing room at stage level and an individual dresser. Smith was to wear a wig for "Uptown, Downtown" – long dark red Rita Hayworth hair, falling on one side to the shoulder. She wore it in a run-through.

Technical rehearsals were held from February 17 to 20. There was a playing around with the lights on "Could I Leave You?". Suddenly a blue wash came from stage left and then a white pin-spot backlight found John McMartin standing to one side. The two follow spots focused tighter and tighter on the actress as she sang, sitting on the downstage corner of the second platform. Smith had an occasional look around as she carried on, curious about what was going on. The song finished, the actress stood up and continued with the dialogue The curtain call was staged with her coming on stage last.

Previews ran from February 20 to 24. Craig Stevens flew in for the first performance. She got the best laughs of the night, including one on her seductive line to the waiter: "…And I have thirty thousand dollars' worth of Georgian silver in my dining room."

Before the Tuesday performance of the 23rd Smith commented how she disagreed with what Mary McCarty, who played Stella Deems, was doing. Deems had suggested changing her lines to get bigger laughs. Smith was happy that Phyllis' first line had been changed because now it suggested this lady was going to say funny things. However, there was a difference between asking for one's lines to be changed and finding the right way to say a line. She wasn't complaining about the competition, but rather just seemed to be an aware performer.

The actress was getting good reactions from the audience. She also had a sense of humor. When Smith and Gene Nelson had gotten a cab to come to the theatre the driver didn't know where it was. After they described it, he said "Oh yeah. That's where the Yvonne DeCarlo show is playing." The actress let out a guttural laugh in response.

On Wednesday night the Boston critics attended. The reviews were mixed but Elliot Norton of the *Boston Record American* wrote that Smith was a revelation. Coolly beautiful, entirely at home with the barbed lines, bitter but believable – and wonderful in the song-and-dance numbers.

The Boston run proper was from February 25 to March 20. Before the show she preferred to stay in her dressing room until right before entering. The actress preferred everyone to be quiet around her. One time she scared one of the showgirls to death by turning around and telling her to shut up.

At the first matinee Smith got to the interlude release in "Uptown, Downtown" and was completely lost in the tongue-twisting lyrics. She just kept dancing away, throwing her head back and laughed till the second chorus, where the actress found her way back.

On Monday March 1 she slipped and fell in the dance section of "Who's That Woman? which was performed by Stella and the Company. Smith picked herself up, kept smiling and went on dancing.

She explained it was vitally important for a performer to get right up if something happened on stage that might make the audience uncomfortable. Only once you were off could you look to see if you were hurt. The actress seemed to be uninjured but admitted to not feeling well in general which may have made her concentration less than the best.

On Wednesday March 3 she was in great spirits but had no idea what her singing would be like. Smith had been fighting a cold all week and it was beginning to affect her voice. When the show began and she spoke the first line, it was apparent there was a problem. The actress tried to sing her part in "Waiting for the Girls Upstairs" which was performed by Ben, Sally, Phyllis and Buddy, and their young counterparts. However, there was no pitch, so she simply recited the following lines.

Smith barrelled through to intermission, but it was obvious she would never make it through "Could I Leave You? Hal Prince decided it was best to cut the number for the night and told her. They made the special announcement backstage that the song would not be performed. The audience would have to take the show as it was. In the second act the actress sounded pretty grim in "Uptown, Downtown". When she came out for her curtain call the entire company applauded. After the final curtain came down, they applauded her again.

The company doctor John Caruso phoned for a town doctor. As soon as Smith was out of her costume and in street clothes, she was taken to see a specialist. The actress was amused that no one had paid any attention earlier in the week when she admitted to not feeling well. But now that Smith had lost her voice it was considered a crisis. Hal Prince told Sheila Smith to start learning the role of Phyllis, as there was no understudy. Sheila was the Standby for Carlotta and Solange LaFitte played by Fifi D'Orsay. There was an idea for Yvonne DeCarlo to cover Phyllis but that began to fade once the show's rehearsals had started.

On Thursday March 4 there was the strong possibility that she would have to miss some performances. At 10:30 a.m. Sheila Smith was called in to go through Phyllis's material. Sheila was concerned how contractually it still stipulated DeCarlo should cover the role. However, DeCarlo did not want to. The decision for Sheila to officially fill in for Alexis was not yet made but everyone knew to be prepared for the possibility. The actress played the matinee using a speak-sing style with her reduced voice though not attempting "Could I Leave You?"

She got through the Friday March 5 performance, but her state of health was still a major concern. Smith still couldn't do "Could I Leave You?" so Sheila learned Phyllis' blocking and the musical staging.

The Stage Manager prepared a notice for the lobby that Sheila would play Phyllis for the Saturday March 6 matinee. However, as the company was reluctant to replace Smith because of her box office appeal, they allowed her to perform. She croaked her way through "Uptown, Downtown" and got through the rest of the show. When the performance was over, she burst into tears and said, "You'll be lucky if you see me tonight". The actress then retreated to her dressing room.

Meanwhile a new costume was constructed for "Uptown, Downtown". The existing one was revealing and sexy but not particularly flattering to Smith or the choreography. It was a surprise and a delight to see the repressed Phyllis appear with shoulders exposed and great long legs. Her entrance usually got audience gasps. But though the number appeared to be working, fine-tuning could still be done. The actress had broad shoulders and the dress' spaghetti straps made them look even broader. In addition, the strips hanging from the waist moved when she danced, but they weren't very graceful.

Smith needed a fitting before the new dress could be completed. But as she was sick and surrounded by attendants, there was no opportunity. The actress was asked to try the dress on. With her raspy cold voice she said, "What do you want, a performance or a dress?" Later Smith apologized, stating she often said things that made no sense when stressed. That evening the actress went on, but again without doing "Could I Leave You?" She had learned how to make her way through "Uptown, Downtown".

On Sunday March 7 Smith went in for her costume fitting. The new dress was a red and pink floor-length form-fitting Marlene Dietrich evening gown with a high collar and long sleeves. The skirt had an overlapping long fringe going to the floor and was slit all the way up the right side. The outfit looked heavy. She looked quite unhappy. When asked to execute some of the dance steps it was immediately evident that the skirt hindered the choreography. At one moment a large red bead flew off the dress and rolled off the stage. Michael Bennett thought he would have to redo the choreography for the number. The actress remained quiet. It was decided that this outfit would not do and new one was needed.

On Thursday March 11 Sondheim brought in a new song to replace "Uptown, Downtown" which Bennett had requested. It paid homage to the song from *Lady in the Dark*, "The Saga of Jenny", and was called "The Story of Lucy and Jessie". It was felt to cover the same territory as "Uptown, Downtown" but was faster and more sassy. The new song needed a new dance arrangement, but Bennett intended to stage it in the same manner.

On Friday March 12 Bennett hoped to include the song in the show's next performance but this would not happen. Smith liked the song but was concerned about its pace, saying *this* Lucy and Jessie were certainly faster than her Lucy and Jessie. She hoped to be given enough rehearsal time before the song went into the show.

By Saturday March 13 the actress had been nursing her cold all week and hadn't missed a performance. But she hadn't sung "Could I Leave You?" at any of them. Smith now felt her voice was back enough to try for the matinee but wanted to go through it once with the orchestra first. When she did this it was apparent the actress had trouble with the high notes. She asked Sondheim permission to just punch the notes and he agreed, under the circumstances. At the matinee Smith performed "Could I Leave You?" with enormous emotional conviction, reminding everyone how it been missed from the show.

For the last week in Boston "The Story of Lucy and Jessie" was planned to be put into the show. The actress had been promised a new costume for the number, but it had not emerged. She had apparently made her feeling about the dropped Dietrich dress to Joe Tubens. He was her confidante, and hair and wig designer, and decided to play a joke on Smith. Tubens went to a Goodwill thrift shop. He bought an awful red dress and attached odd pieces of fringe and stray beads. Tubens then wrapped the dress in fresh tissue paper in a box. He had Michael Bennett help with the joke since he knew Bennett hated the Dietrich dress as much as the actress did.

At the evening show's intermission Bennett told her the new dress had arrived. She opened the box and shrieked with laughter. Being game, Smith then went in and put the dress on and paraded around the stage. Because it fit well Bennett suggested she wear it for the first technical rehearsal in New York.

On Monday March 15 Bennett worked on the "The Story of Lucy and Jessie" with the orchestra and the dancers. The plan was to place it in the show on Thursday night.

On Tuesday March 16 there was a party at the Statler-Hilton Hotel after the show. The actress attended with Craig Stevens, who had joined her in Boston, and Joe Tubens. She assumed the role of hostess with delight and regaled the company with stories about Ann Miller and other Hollywood ladies.

On Thursday March 18 when "The Story of Lucy and Jessie" was going into the show Smith was especially nervous. She had lots of tongue-twisting lyrics and a new dance that was similar to that of "Uptown, Downtown" but different. The actress had performed that song the previous night for the last time, and she was feeling under-rehearsed and tense. But the performance this night was flawless and brilliant. There were bravos and cheers in the middle of the song and a roar at the end. At the curtain call Smith hugged DeCarlo who herself performed a new staging of "I'm Still Here". Smith said to her co-star, "Well we both got through it" which was a nice gesture after she had long kept her distance.

On Friday March 19 the actress was critical of the use of white gloves for the dancers in the number, because it muffled their hand clapping. However, they stayed.

She had been interviewed in Boston by Guy Flatley for an article that would appear in *The New York Times* of April 4 entitled "Three Show-Biz Girls and How They Grew". Smith had no nostalgia for her heydays. She felt there were many more interesting things to think about than Warners and whether Jane Wyman or Ida Lupino got the roles the actress should have gotten. When friends would call to say one of her movies was on television, she didn't look at all. Asked what the high points of her life were, Smith said it was her personal life with Craig Stevens. That had been a continuous series of high points.

What was now of more concern to the actress was pollution, travelling to the moon, and the war. She was shocked to ask to compare World War II and Vietnam. Smith felt no war was justifiable, despite some Americans feeling that World War II was. People couldn't settle differences that way and it was a terrible comment on the times that so many were frightened of each other. This fear extended to her new search for an apartment in New York in anticipation of *Follies* coming to Broadway. Everyone kept warning the actress to get one with a doorman. She was also warned not to walk to work because New York was much too dangerous. But Smith felt she could talk to people and not to be mugged.

While she hoped *Follies* would a hit, if it was not, the actress would not be crushed. She admitted not having pursued a career in years and not wanting to now. Smith liked to act but not all the things that went with it, like autographs, and interviews. The article also included an Al Hirschfeld caricature of the show's cast.

The matinee on Saturday March 20 was the last performance in Boston. After this the company moved to the Winter Garden Theatre in New York for the first preview on March 24. She reported being told by people that Broadway was dying but the actress bemoaned, "It can't. I just got here."

In the meantime, a television guest appearance she had done was broadcast. This was in the drama *Marcus Welby, M.D.* in the episode entitled "The Windfall" shot at Universal studios in Hollywood and broadcast on March 23 on ABC. The series centred on Welby (Robert Young) and his assistant Steven Kiley (James Brolin) who tried to treat people as individuals in an age of specialized medicine and uncaring doctors. The episode was written by Paul West and directed by Herschel Daugherty. It saw a young girl develop an ulcer because she felt her rich parents don't love her. Smith played the role of Evie Craig.

Craig Stevens on left and Smith on right in still for *Marcus Welby, M.D.*

Previews for *Follies* were scheduled until April 3. In New York rehearsals were held at the Broadway Arts Studios. At the first preview she received bravos and a hand from the audience when the actress appeared at the top of the stairs for "Beautiful Girls", which featured the entire company. This had never happened in Boston. She scored a big laugh on some of Phyllis' more campy lines likes "Let's dish" said to Sally. There was a long and loud response for each principal at the curtain call. But in the subsequent previews Smith received the biggest hand.

The issue of the dress for "The Story of Lucy and Jessie" was still unresolved. It finally arrived at the theatre for her last fitting and when she appeared from wardrobe and walked out onto the stage in it, the actress looked happy. It was a fire-engine red with a flattering square neckline and loose ruffles around the back. There were mid-length sleeves with ruffles from the elbows and large beaded stripes making an X across the front. Three layers of long fringe started at the hip line above the left leg, each a slightly different shade of red, and hung from the waist down to the right knee, angling slightly upward. After showing the dress she went through the staging of the song to everyone's delight. The dress was sexy, flattering, surprising and utterly suitable to the choreography.

The arrival of the dress had another unexpected result. When the frumpy Sally discarded her pink party dress and appeared in a floor-length clingy beaded gown to sing a torch song it was dramatically stunning. But when the cold regal Phyllis who spat out acid remarks all night appeared in red fringe, revealing a terrific pair of legs and danced, it was a revelation. The actress also demonstrated she had range. Smith was able to get laughs, be hard for "Could I Leave You", and then funny in "The Story of Lucy and Jessie". In terms of pure showbusiness the sexy movie lady stole the show.

On matinee days she would nap in between shows. Before the Friday show on April 2 Dorothy Collins had a blow-up with her. Collins felt Smith was being bossy during one of Hal Prince's notes sessions.

Follies opened on Sunday April 4 and would run till July 1, 1972, with the actress never missing a performance. Before the opening night show she gave copies of Brook Atkinson's book *Broadway* to her fellow performers. Smith also sent a telegram to the company, writing "Enjoy our farewell opening." The opening night party was held at The Rainbow Row where Elaine Stritch was heard to say to Ethel Merman, "Isn't it too bad that Alexis Smith has gotten so fat and ugly." To which Merman replied, "She looks like a microphone."

The show was not a box office success but won the Tony Awards for Smith for Best Performance by a Leading Actress in a Musical, as well as Best Original Score, Best Direction of a Musical, Best Choreography, Best Scenic Design. Best Costume Design, and Best Lighting Design. The original Broadway cast album was recorded on April 11 and released on May 16.

It was praised by Clive Barnes in *The New York Times* who said that she still looked wonderful and had a mixture of ice and vitality that was tantalizingly amusing. Smith sang and danced with style and acted with commanding serenity. In his review of the cast album recording in the *Times* John S. Wilson wrote that "The Story of Lucy and Jessie" revealed her attractive and serviceable voice.

The poster art for the show was designed by David Edward Byrd. He used a photo of Marlene Dietrich though Smith believed the face was hers. Byrd never corrected her.

She was on the cover of *Time* magazine for the May 3 issue. The actress was seen in the *Follies* fringe dress kicking up her heels, with the caption, "That Old Magic Relights Broadway." Originally it was planned that the cover shot would be showgirl Suzanne Briggs in a large butterfly costume on a high stage level with Smith, Collins and DeCarlo seated below in their Follies dresses.

The article by Peter De Vries said the actress' experience was the repudiation of F. Scott Fitzgerald's axiom that there were no second acts in American lives. At forty-nine she was in the best second act of her life. De Vries describes her persona at Warners as their snow queen though in reality Smith played other warmer roles. He also quips that when she stopped working and Craig Stevens had financial success from the *Peter Gunn* television series, the actress was never successfully cast as Mrs. Front Porch. She said the acclaim for *Follies* was not that important. One could only really respect the opinion of a few people. More than that was just pleasantry.

Newsweek had also planned on doing a story on the show, but they cancelled.

In an article by Judy Klemesrud in the *Times* about happy marriages dated June 1 she mentioned the Smith and Craig Stevens union. Stevens was now back in their home in West Hollywood. On June 18 they would celebrate their twenty-seventh wedding anniversary. She said that her husband got so tired of people asking about the longevity of the couple. So, he now said it was only twelve years which stopped any argument.

The actress credited Steven's extraordinary disposition for their happiness. He didn't believe in arguing and she agreed. It was a waste of time. Smith could go on and on for twenty minutes and, when there was no retaliation, she pretty soon found the whole thing funny. Stevens believed the success of their marriage was due to the fact that neither of them had a jealous nature and his wife was very healthy mentally. She also looked as good as the actress did when they married and was a marvellous cook. Klemesrud reported that the value of Smith's autograph had shot up from $2 to $6 after *Follies*.

She was a guest on the episode of the television comedy talk-show *The Tonight Show Starring Johnny Carson* shot in New York broadcast on June 11 on NBC.

The actress was a guest on the episode of the television talk-show *The David Frost Show* that was shot in New York and broadcast on June 23. The ninety-minute show was dedicated to *Follies*. She reported having read the script of the show two years prior. Smith was surprised at being cast as she had not pursued a career actively for quite some time. The actress wanted to do it because she was so impressed with the script and the role of Phyllis.

Smith described Phyllis as a wealthy woman who travelled extensively and had a superficial life. Other people admired her for the clothes and the wealth, but the marriage was very empty. She was not fulfilled by material things because, though very deeply in love with her husband, the feeling was not reciprocated. Of all the characters, Phyllis was one most likely to find a life for herself. She was the most positive of the characters. Through her strength there could a future of some worth, and in finding a life with her husband, Phyllis could be a happy woman.

On the show they screened a clip of the dance from *Thank Your Lucky Stars* which she talked about. Smith said possibly her favorite film to make was *Frank Capra's Here Comes the Groom*. This was because it was one of the few opportunities she had to play comedy. The actress talked about some of her film leading men, like Clark Gable.

Many of the photographs taken for the cancelled *Newsweek* story appeared in the July edition of *Show* magazine. The cover shot of Smith was credited to Lawrence Fried and the article inside the magazine was entitled "The Pedigree of a SMASH: Sondheim plus Prince = FOLLIES."

She was a guest on the ninety-minute episode of the music talk-show *The Dick Cavett Show* that was broadcast on August 5 on ABC. The actress talked about *Follies* being able to be appreciated on various levels by audiences because it had entertainment value and was haunting. She herself would have loved to see it but didn't think the producer would be too pleased to have someone go on so Smith could be in the audience. The actress reported having fallen on stage one night. Things were going along nicely in "The Story of Lucy and Jessie" and suddenly she did a pratfall and found herself sitting in the middle of the stage. Smith laughed a lot to show the audience she had not hurt herself. They applauded and the actress acknowledged the applause. But since it was a musical number, she had to catch up with the orchestra, which kept going. The number had sixteen dancers behind her looking upstage who couldn't turn around to see what had happened after hearing the awful thud.

Smith thought it was fairer to say that Hollywood quit her rather than she quit Hollywood. The actress didn't make any more movies because nobody asked her to. She didn't like to look at her films because Smith had no association with that lady on screen. She didn't really believe that it was her. The actress had forgotten a lot of her films. Ironically, in her early years in Hollywood she had been told by a well-known actor that he too had forgotten his films. At the time Smith was appalled because she thought if you were ever fortunate enough to do something as wonderfully exciting as a film you certainly wouldn't forget it.

The actress didn't care too much about pursuing a career, but she did care about working when Smith did work. She would like to do a new film if it was a stimulating and interesting experience. The actress had just seen *Panic in Needle Park* and was very impressed. She was a big fan of Al Pacino and would love to work with the brilliant director Jerry Schatzberg.

Smith was back *The Tonight Show Starring Johnny Carson* for the episode broadcast on December 28.

She was back on *The Dick Cavett Show* for the episode broadcast on January 6, 1972. On January 25 the actress was one of the winners of the Prince Matchabelli Awards for having achieved new heights in their careers during 1971.

On February 13 she attended the premiere of the musical film *Cabaret* (1972) at the Zeigfeld Theatre in New York City.

The February issue of *After Dark* magazine had Smith on the cover. Photographed by Kenn Duncan she wore a Halston black rayon and silk dolman sleeve evening dress piled high with black and white fox skins. Inside was an article by Craig Zadan entitled

"One Last Look at Where It All Began" with another photo by Duncan. There was also a photo spread of "Alexis Smith is Back – In Style" by Roberta Burrows. The photos were again by Duncan and saw her dressed in the designs of Saint Angelo and Halston.

She commented that it was just marvellous in the theatre when people said you were absolutely brilliant, and you could live in that lovely world of make-believe. In the movies you had to sit there and see yourself on that screen and somehow you knew better. The actress never really believed that she was a glamorous movie star. The whole idea of it made her laugh a lot.

Smith talked about the difference for actors in the studio system and now. It had to be very difficult today for young actors where there was no studio grooming or protection. Now you could make a big splash in a film and never be heard from again. But she had more respect for today's films which the actress said were really coming into their own as an art form. They were more in the hands of the creative people. They were no longer controlled by five or six powerful men, and there was no longer a star system. Today the directors were the stars which was right because film was a director's medium.

She preferred playing on the stage in New York to being on the road which held little enchantment for her. This was mainly because there were not that many interesting cities in the country and plenty of dreary ones. The great heartland of America was not a great source of theatre revenue.

There was talk that Smith would be a leading contender for next year's Tony Award and that an announcement would be made that she would star in the west coast production of *Follies*. This was to open at the Shubert Theatre in Los Angeles late in spring. The actress said it would be exciting opening in California for about a week or so and then it would settle down to What does one do after the theatre? She preferred living in New York which was the most important city in the world.

Smith had been sent a multitude of film scripts and stage properties to sort through in her spare time when she wasn't attending classes in voice, dance, and Spanish. During the day the actress toured the city's art museums and after the show usually headed for any of its liveliest discos. With all this great fortune that had come to her, people told Smith she had worked for it. But the actress thought that was nonsense. It was being at the right place at the right time with all things falling together. It had little to do with one's ability. It could have happened to someone else just as likely.

She felt there were many things to learn and so many things to do in New York. Smith had never been a lady who lunched. There was no time to stop learning and be satisfied with past accomplishments. There was no limit to what one could do when they put their mind to it. Besides, it was too much of a challenge to keep up with the future.

On March 2 she attended a Bobby Short concert. On March 15 the actress attended the opening night of the Broadway play *The Country Girl* at the Billy Rose Theatre and the after-show party held at Raffles in New York City.

She was back on *The Tonight Show Starring Johnny Carson* for the episode broadcast on April 4.

Smith was back again on *The Dick Cavett Show* for the episode broadcast on April 17. She talked about the Tony Award nominations for *Follies* and herself. The actress listed many legendary theatre people who had never won Tonys. She wanted to win because there was never anyone who wanted to lose. But it was a peculiar thing to be in competition involuntarily for the award with Dorothy Collins. This week Smith was involved with fittings and appearances, so she had postponed her studies. But the actress would then go back to studying dancing and singing, specifically solfege, and Spanish. She talked about being tall in Hollywood and of the leading men who had to stand on apple boxes.

Fellow guest Gloria Swanson said how she admired Smith tremendously because Swanson always wanted to be her height. Swanson was four feet nine inches. She replied that it was so admirable to have had the extraordinary career in films that Swanson did and then have the courage to go to the theatre.

Chapter 10. *The 26th Annual Tony Awards*

The actress attended *The 26th Annual Tony Awards* aka 1972 Tony Awards which were held at the Broadway Theatre in New York on April 23 and broadcast as a television special on ABC. The show was directed by Clark Jones. She accepted her award by saying one of the nicest things about winning was that you didn't have to be a good loser. Smith thanked the very talented people with whom she worked and studied who helped her get it together so the actress could be there at that moment. She shared the award with them. Craig Stevens reported that this was a big thrill for her. Smith had never won anything before, and he believed the luckiest thing the show ever did was get her. She also attended the after-show party held at the American Hotel.

On May 29 it was reported that the actress would stay with *Follies* after it closed on Broadway on July 1 and re-opened on July 2 at the St. Louis Municipal Opera House in Missouri. After playing for one week the show would then open at the new Shubert Theatre in Century City, Los Angeles on July 22. It would run until October 1.

On June 4 or 5 she attended a benefit for Phoenix House held at Roselands dubbed "The Fabulous Forties". Smith was reported to have done a jitterbug as one of the acts to raise money for drug addiction and performed wearing a gorilla mask. She was also said to have judged jitterbug and Lindy contests.

The actress was back on *The Dick Cavett Show* for the episode broadcast on June 22. In regards to the petition sent by actors to move the red light district away from Broadway, she commented on talking to the Mayor about it. Smith joked she would sign the petition if the actress could have some of the profits. She ultimately didn't sign. Smith had not had any problem with the sex workers near Wintergarden Theatre that she saw as the actress walked alone there. Though she had heard that others had. She swore that some of the cast missed their cues to appear on stage because they were hanging out the windows watching the action on the street.

One day traffic was backed up solidly for blocks. What was causing the delay was not a visit by the President or the Vice-President but a policeman chasing a fifteen-year-old hooker up the street. The girl did the movie trick of getting into one side of a taxi and out the other when being chased. When she got caught people were booing and saying Let Her Go. On a serious note, Smith was concerned that experiences with the red light may discourage people from going to the city.

She spoke about going to California and how it was different to have the Broadway company, intact, move to another state. In addition, the actress did not agree that she had been wasted in the movies. Perhaps it was not possible that she could have performed in musicals then the way Smith could now. She also reported that Michael Bennett had decided to restage "The Story of Lucy and Jessie" so now the actress had to rehearse the new version. This was because Bennett thought it could be better.

Smith also spoke about winning the Tony award. She realized it was when the announcer said the first syllable that the actress knew who won since it wasn't an M or G or D. She compared it to any time Smith had been under a great tension like an opening night. She got through it somehow but couldn't remember anything about it. But with that night the actress remembered every detail perhaps because she really wanted to relish the experience.

The real award was delivered to the theatre and then the next night Smith messed up her first speech. She was afraid they would come and take the award back. There was also another incident. One performance the actress thought she had been just dandy and God punished her. Smith read an exit line awfully well and got a good reaction. But when she turned around to make the exit the actress walked right into a pole. It got a laugh, and she was glad Hal Prince wasn't there to see it in case he would have wanted her to keep the pole crash in the show. The actress didn't hurt herself but was embarrassed.

Paul Gardner in *The New York Times* of July 23 reported on the opening of *Follies* in Los Angeles on July 21. She was quoted as saying the new Shubert Theatre was not an auditorium, it was a legitimate theatre. Smith had been housed in a three-room backstage suite. The article was accompanied by a photo of her in the show. *Follies* ran in Los Angeles till October 1 but a proposed national tour of the show was scrapped. After the run ended the actress maintained a strong friendship with Michael Bennett.

While in Los Angeles doing *Follies*, she was back on *The Tonight Show Starring Johnny Carson* for the episode broadcast on July 28.

Smith was a guest on the episode of the comedy family music television series *The Merv Griffin Show* entitled "Salute to the Musical" that was broadcast on July 31. This was a salute to *Follies*. Griffin complained that her outfit for his show covered up her legs, which were one of the thrills in the stage show when she came out showing them. The actress said it was a new and wonderful experience to follow a show from the first day of rehearsal and to create a role. She praised Hal Prince in producing the most expensive musical to have ever been done and one that was not the standard type of musical. Of the costumes Smith didn't think there was a bugle bead left in the country because they were all in the show.

Not making movies regularly as she had done in the past was compensated by the many other things in the world to explore which were just as interesting. To have the time to enjoy them was a luxury. When the actress had done summer stock in the past it was like preparation for a Broadway show she hoped would someday come to her. And it did. To keep in shape Smith danced and studied yoga exercises every day, had a high protein diet and she was not particularly fond of sweets which was helpful.

The actress was not tired of doing the show because there was such depth in the material that she was constantly making new discoveries. An example was how Smith found a new laugh in the Los Angeles show, after playing it for a year and a half. The Los Angeles' audience thus forth had been as equally enthusiastic as those in New York. On opening night in Los Angeles, she wanted to go out and look at the movie stars in the audience but had to stay backstage. Smith hoped to do another Broadway show or a film, but it depended mostly on the role. The medium didn't matter though she certainly enjoyed the theatre because it had been so good to her.

The actress was the subject of the biographical television series *This Is Your Life* broadcast on September 24 on NBC. The show was recorded at the Shubert Theatre in Los Angeles where she was performing in *Follies*. Host Ralph Edwards surprised her after the stage show's performance that night. The television episode was directed by Jim Washburn. Guests included Helen Hayes, Frances Rafferty, Nanette Fabray, Lloyd Nolan, Craig Stevens, her housekeeper Julia Green, Hal Prince, Florence Klotz, Jerry Blunt, her eighty-eight-year old father Alexander, and Stevens' parents. There was also a filmed message from Dirk Bogarde.

When Ralph Edwards tells Smith that this is your life, she replies amusingly, "Why?" Hayes presented her with an award from the Actor's Fund of America. When the actress tells Nolan that she is so happy to see him, he quips it is because Smith thought he was dead. Edwards also presented her with a Marchal Jewelers charm bracelet.

She was a guest on the episode of the musical comedy television series *Rowan & Martin's Laugh-In* that was broadcast on September 25 on NBC. The show had multiple writers and was directed by Bill Foster.

The actress was a guest on the television special *The Bob Hope Special* broadcast on October 5 on NBC. This had multiple writers and was directed by Kip Walton. Although the show is unavailable for viewing it is believed that a snippet appears in the television special *Bob Hope's Women I Love: Beautiful and Funny* broadcast on February 28, 1982, on NBC. She is seen in the collection of skits where women play Hope's wife, with he introducing her as the lady who invented the fountain of youth.

In the skit the wife tells him she has been chosen by the reform party to run for Governor. Hope asks her to think of all the wonderful times they had together in Acapulco and Hawaii, but she replies, "I've never been to Acapulco or Hawaii." He says the wife will never make it in politics because she doesn't know how to lie, cheat, or connive. The wife replies, "You can teach me." Smith stands in a way to make herself look shorter, which is odd since Hope was supposedly taller than she at five foot eleven inches. But the skit shows the actress is good at playing comedy.

On October 8 it was reported that she would be in the cast of a new stage production of the Clare Boothe Luce comedy *The Women*. Director Ellis Rabb expected to start rehearsals November 27 with a January 18, 1973, opening date on Broadway.

On October 31 Smith attended a party in Beverly Hills, California, celebrating the release of Ann Miller's book *Miller's High Life*. On November 15 she attended the opening of an exhibition celebrating the life of Tallulah Bankhead (1902-1968) in New York City. The actress was back on *The Tonight Show Starring Johnny Carson* for the episode broadcast on November 30. She was among the ten best coiffed women of the year as selected by the Helene Curtis Guild of Professional Beauticians.

On February 25, 1973, Smith attended the Broadway opening night of *A Little Night Music* at the Schubert Theatre in New York. This was the new musical by Stephen Sondheim directed by Hal Prince.

On March 10 she appeared in a "Party Musical" aka "Sondheim" and "Sondheim: A Musical Tribute", a Burt Shrevelove production to hail Sondheim at the Shubert Theatre. This was followed by a supper party in the Pub Theatrical. The event was a benefit for the American Musical and Dramatic Academy and the National Hemophilia Foundation. The show was said to have only had one rehearsal and was captured in a cast album where the actress sang "Could I Leave You?"

On March 11 it was reported that the revival of *The Women* had overcome funding problems and was in rehearsal for an April 25 opening at the 46th Street Theatre. Elliot Rabb had withdrawn from the show and Morton DaCosta was the new director.

On March 18 she attended the opening of the musical *Seesaw* at the Uris Theatre in New York.

Smith was a presenter at *The 27th Annual Tony Awards* aka the 1973 Tony Awards which was held at the Imperial Theatre in New York on March 25 and broadcast as a television special. The show was written by Hildy Parks and directed by Clark Jones. She presented Best Actor in a Musical to Ben Vereen for *Pippin* who hugged her when he accepted the award.

On April 15 it was reported that *Follies* was to be made into a film. 20th Century Fox had hired Hal Prince to direct and most, if not all, of Stephen Sondheim's score was to remain. The James Goldman book was to be adapted by off-Broadway playwright Jean Claude Van Itallie. The location was to be changed. Now a famous film studio was to be torn down and a lot of old Fox sets and film footage were to be used.

There were also conversations about the movie with Daniel Melnick at M-G-M. Hal Prince had the idea of gathering a group of bona fide old movie stars like Bette Davis and Joan Crawford who both agreed to do it. A real party would be created in an old soundstage and filmed in a cinema-verite style. But this version was not made. In January 2015, there was renewed interest in the property. It was reported that Rob Marshall had signed on to direct, with Meryl Streep rumored to star. John Logan expressed interest in writing the adaptation. In November 2019, it was announced that Dominic Cooke would adapt the screenplay as well as direct, following the successful 2017 National Theatre revival in London. But to date the film has not been made.

The actress appeared in the television crime drama pilot *Nightside* aka a Very Special Place which was broadcast on April 15 on ABC. Shot in New York, it had a teleplay by Pete Hamill and the director was Richard Donner. The story centred on three people whose careers required them to spend most of the night awake and on the prowl. They were press agent Carmine Kelly (John Cassavetes), private detective Aram Bessoyggian (Mike Kellen), and nightclub owner Smitty (Smith). The pilot was unsold.

The Women had a tryout in Philadelphia at the Shubert Theatre. It then opened on Broadway on April 25 after 7 previews from April 19 and ran till June 17. The actress played the role of Sylvia (Mrs. Howard Fowler). The show received a mixed reaction from Clive Barnes in *The New York Times* who wrote that she was adorable.

Smith ran the film version before she decided to do the play. The actress had seen it before but had forgotten it. She believed herself to be a feminist by degree, just by virtue of her independence. But Smith wasn't awfully interested in women en masse. Sometimes she wished the author had called her play "Mary's Trip to Reno". Then people wouldn't try to read so many profundities about women into it. Some people would be comfortable with the play as nostalgia, but you could go to 21 and see the same women there today. The actress reported the company followed the original play very closely. Claire Boothe Luce came to the first performance in Philadelphia, and she was a very formidable lady. If someone said an "if" instead of a "but" the author came backstage to correct it.

Business for the show was disappointing. The entire company was called in together and asked if they would take minimum wage to keep it going. Hopefully the show would then pick up momentum so that it became successful. According to Actors Equity everyone had to agree to do that which they did. But one day when Smith came to work, she realized everyone was making more money than her.

The actress was back on *The Tonight Show Starring Johnny Carson* for the episode broadcast on May 21. That night she had attended the International Diamond Jubilee, including a tribute to Sol Hurok, at the Metropolitan Opera in New York City.

On June 4 Smith appeared in "Golden Olden Days of Burlesque" directed by Michel Stuart for Phoenix House at Roseland Dance City. This was a benefit for Phoenix House.

For the week of August 14 she performed the part of Margo Channing in the stage musical *Applause* for John Kenley in Dayton, Ohio. The show was directed by Leslie B. Cutler.

On September 5 the actress appeared in the fall fashion show season presentation by Jacques Bellini held at the Plaza Hotel in New York. She wore men's clothes as part of the men's showing and Smith said she preferred them. They fitted her better, especially the pants. The actress modeled a navy satin pants suit with a ruffled shirt, and a shawl-collared sweater with a mink coat. She practiced the slouchy walk of model Elsa Peretti but was said to not manage to carry it off. Smith said the Russian wolfhound she had to lead inhibited her. The actress was told to keep saying 'Good Dog' and 'Heel' but forgot to walk like Elsa. She heard about Bellini's clothes from her hairdresser Joe Tubens.

On September 25 Smith attended the Hooray For Hollywood Benefit Gala at the Pub Theatrical in New York City. On October 23 she attended a Harvard Alumni Fundraising Dinner at the Beverly Hilton Hotel in Beverly Hills, California. On December 12 the actress attended a party at the Beverly Hills Hotel celebrating Ross Hunter's appointment as president of Brut Films.

The fiction novel *Rubyfruit Jungle* by Rita Mae Brown was published in 1973 and had a dedication to her. Brown described Smith as Actress, Wit, Beauty, Cook, Kindheart, and Irreverent Observer of Political Phenomena. Brown said the woman had taken the time to give her a playful push in the direction of her typewriter. The writer was reported to have seen *Follies* in 1971 and fell in love with Smith and wrote her a fan letter. She replied to the letter, and they met. Brown said the actress was warm, wise, and direct. Brown had never felt such lust in her life for that gorgeous creature and Smith bore it with good humor. Brown admitted that the crush must have been wearisome for the actress and her husband, but Smith nudged her along. She never loved Brown but saw a flash of talent and that was better than carnal love.

The actress was mentioned in an article about theatre dressers by Angela Taylor in *The New York Times* of January 2, 1974. This was entitled "In the Theater, The Best Dressers Don't Always Wear the Clothes". Fran Frank reported that she had dressed Smith who had a terrific sense of humor.

On January 3 she attended the opening of Habitation Leciere, a new retreat for the rich in Port-Au-Prince, Haiti. The actress was photographed with the retreat's president Olivier Coquelin by Henry Grossman for an article in *The New York Times*. It was written by Judy Klemesrud entitled "A New Retreat for the Rich – Surrounded by Tumbledown Shacks" and published January 6. It was reported that her airfare from her Californian home and as well as the hotel bill was paid for by the resort's management. Smith said she would go anywhere and if there was an arrow pointing in some direction the actress would always follow it.

She was a presenter at *The Annual National Sports Awards* which was held in Los Angeles and broadcast as a television special on February 4, 1974, on NBC.

Portrait of Smith for *"Jacqueline Susann's Once is Not Enough"* (1975)

Smith returned to films in the Paramount color romance *"Jacqueline Susann's Once is Not Enough"* (1975) which was shot from March 15 to June 24 on locations in Spain, Switzerland, New York and at the Paramount studios in Hollywood. The screenplay was by Julius J. Epstein based on the novel by Susann and the director was Guy Green. The story centred on January (Deborah Raffin) the teenage daughter of movie producer Mike Wayne (Kirk Douglas) who has a near fatal motorcycle accident in Europe.

Smith is billed second after the title and plays the supporting role of the wealthy Deidre 'Dee' Milford Granger who marries Mike. She also has a secret lesbian relationship with Karla (Melina Mercouri). Hair is by Vivienne Walker and costumes are by Moss Mabry that include a bathing suit and a towel worn in bed.

The role sees Dee handle a dog, laugh, be kissed by and kiss Karla, paint a landscape, and have an off-screen death in a plane crash. She gets a funny line. When Tom Colt (David Janssen) berates Mike for "fucking up" his best book as a movie, Dee comments, "I never saw the movie. Of course, I never read the book either."

The actress is to be congratulated for playing what is a bisexual character, since Dee says she also has sex with Mike. Director Green introduces her with a camera-tilt up Dee's whole body as she stands on a boat. He handles the lesbian love scene with restraint, with Karla's ethnicity and the food the pair eat post-coital adding more exoticism to the situation. Green has Dee turned away from Mike when he tells her he knows about the relationship. Dee pauses, and when Mike says there is no shock or reproach, she thanks him.

The film's release was delayed until June 20, 1975. It was released with the tagline "Jacqueline Susann's bold best seller that explored the avenues and darkest alleys of love among the international set". Another was "The Husband for sale - bought for $3 million. The Daughter - a virgin eager to make up for lost time. The Novelist who couldn't live the fantasies he wrote about." It won an Academy Award nomination for Best Actress in a Supporting Role for Brenda Vaccaro who plays Linda. The film was lambasted by Vincent Canby in *The New York Times* but received a mixed reaction from *Variety*, Pauline Kael in "5001 Nights At The Movies" and John Douglas Eames in "The Paramount Story".

The relationship of Dee and Karla was allegedly based on the heiress Barbara Hutton and film star Greta Garbo. Lana Turner was offered the part of Dee but balked at the scene where she kisses her female lover on the lips.

An article in *The Los Angeles Times* of July 8 reported that the love scene shot between Smith and Mercouri was deemed unusable and producer Howard K. Koch requested it be reshot. The new scene was rewritten by Jacqueline Susann but when it was shot, Guy Green decided he preferred Julius J. Epstein's version. The producer preferred Susann's version and directed it himself. The actress was said to have taken the part solely because of the opportunity to work with Mercouri. She was photographed at the Paramount studios gate on May 23 during production. Smith commented on her absence from the screen. She had not retired and wanted to act but nobody asked her to do a film.

Next the actress was back on *The Merv Griffin Show* for the episode broadcast on April 1. On the same date an article by Angela Taylor in *The New York Times* entitled "Color Your Hair Simply, or Turn It Blue – Salons Can Do It All" mentioned her. Leslie Blanchard of Clairol had Smith as a regular client.

On April 14 she attended the annual party of the American Theater Wing to inaugurate Tony Week at Sardi's Restaurant in New York. The party was to specifically honor the American musical and former Tony winners in the musical category.

Smith was mentioned in an article by Bernadine Morris in *The New York Times* of May 2 in the Fashion Talk column entitled "A Few Unexpected Moments at Fall Shows." She commented on Bill Blass' long skirts in his sportswear group. The actress loved them because she was tall, and they were good for tall girls.

Next Smith appeared in the episode of the television series *ABC Late Night* entitled "That's Entertainment: 50 Years of MGM" broadcast on May 29. The sixty-minute show captured the premiere of the documentary *That's Entertainment!* (1974). After the film was screened, the stars appeared in the Grand Ballroom of the Beverly Wilshire Hotel in a lineup in alphabetical order to have their photo taken. She was part of the lineup though, never having been an M-G-M contractee, only appearing in one film for the studio, and is not seen in the documentary.

On June 19 the actress attended a preview screening of the film *Chinatown* at the headquarters of the Directors Guild of America in Los Angeles, California. On June 24 she attended the Los Angeles opening of *A Little Night Music* at the Shubert Theater. On September 4 Smith attended the Los Angeles opening of *Seesaw* at the

Ahmanson Theatre. On November 15 she was a model for the Legends Fashion Show at the Waldorf Hotel in New York City.

The actress next appeared in the episode of the television biographical miniseries *The Lives of Benjamin Franklin* entitled "The Ambassador" broadcast on November 21 on CBS. The mini-series was made up of four plays, each showing Benjamin Franklin at a different stage in his life played by a different actor. The teleplay was by Howard Fast and was directed by Glenn Jordan. Smith played the role of Madame Helvetius, a female companion of the seventy-one-year-old Franklin (Eddie Albert) living in Paris in 1778.

The show won Emmy Awards for Outstanding Limited Series and Outstanding Writing for a Drama Series for "The Ambassador". It was nominated for Outstanding Directing for a Drama Series for The Ambassador" by Glenn Jordan and Outstanding Writing for a Drama Series for "The Whirlwind". The show was praised by John J. O'Connor in *The New York Times*.

On December 31 she attended a party in Malibu, California thrown by Polly Bergen. That year the actress reportedly appeared in the documentary *Busby Berkeley* (1974) directed by Russ Jones. The film paid tribute to Berkeley and featured candid interviews with his friends and associates. One source also has her reportedly in the Argentine film *Intriga de otros mundos* aka Intrigue from Other Worlds (1974).

On January 26, 1975 she attended a party celebrating the stage musical *In Gay Company* at the Hippodrome Theater in New York City. On February 3 Smith attended the St. Regis Roof to celebrate the seventy-fifth birthday of singer Mabel Mercer. The actress reported she was preparing for her first nightclub act by listening to Mercer's records.

On February 11 she attended a screening of the film *Shampoo* in New York City. On March 9 it was reported that Smith was the honorary chairman of Calvin Klein's boutique of his spring summer collection at Bloomingdale's on March 18. The event would benefit The Lighthouse, the New York Association for the Blind.

On April 11 it was said she was being considered for the role of publisher Katharine Graham in the historical thriller *All The President's Men* (1976). One source claims Geraldine Page was cast but a second says she declined the role. It was then decided to cut the one scene Graham had in the script at the request of Graham herself.

On April 18 the actress attended the National Academy of Television Arts and Sciences New York Chapter Presents - A Salute to Sir Lew Grade held at the New York Hilton Hotel. The event was televised as the British television special *Salute to Sir Lew - The Master Showman* broadcast on June 13 on ITV. The show was directed by Dwight Hemion. In the special she can be seen in the audience.

Smith was a performer at *The 29th Annual Tony Awards* aka The 1975 Tony Awards held at the Winter Garden Theatre and broadcast on April 20. The show was directed by Clark Jones. The theme was the Winter Garden Theatre and its history of shows and legendary stars. She was included in a tribute to *Follies* doing "The Story of Lucy and Jessie" with a chorus. After the number the actress introduced Clifton Davis to present the award for Best Play to *Equus*. She returned for the show's end to sing "Everything's Coming up Roses" with the cast.

The actress was back on *The Mike Douglas Show* for the episode broadcast on April 21.

She returned to the stage in the William Inge play *Summer Brave* which opened at the Eisenhower Theatre in Washington on September 8. The show was directed by Michael Montel. The play was a revised version of Inge's play *Picnic*. Smith played the part of Rosemary Sydney, the spinster schoolteacher played in the original show by Eileen Heckart. The new production received a mixed reaction from Mel Gussow in *The New York Times* who wrote that she gave the evening's strongest performance.

The show opened on Broadway at the ANTA Theatre on October 26 after 3 previews from October 24 and would only run till November 9. It received a mixed reaction from Clive Barnes in *The New York Times* who wrote that the actress was remarkably touching.

On November 7 she was crowned Miss Ziegfeld at the Ziegfeld Clan's 39th anniversary dinner dance held at the Waldorf-Astoria's Starlight Roof in New York. The event was held to benefit women entertainers in need.

Chapter 11. *The Little Girl Who Lives Down The Lane*

Smith appeared in the mystery film *The Little Girl Who Lives Down The Lane* (1976) shot from November 17 to December 30 in Canada. The screenplay was by Laird Koenig based on his novel and the director was Nicholas Gessner. The story centred on thirteen-year old Rynn (Jodie Foster) who lives with her absentee father but struggles against a predatory local neighbor.

The actress is billed third after the title and plays the supporting role of Mrs. Hallet, the village's realtor and Rynn's neighbor and landlady. Joe Tubens gets a credit for her hair and wardrobe by Valentino include reading glasses. The role sees Mrs. Hallett drive a car, slap Rynn, scream, and get knocked on the head dead by a cellar trapdoor.

Mrs. Hallet is a despicable character in the way she takes apples from the property Rynn is leasing, comes into the house uninvited, and moves the furniture around. The latter has an additional reason for Rynn to be defensive. The girl has her dead mother hidden there and Hallet wants to retrieve jelly glasses from storage. Hallet also makes racist remarks, threatens to report Rynn to the school board for not going to school and criticizes her supposed mocking tone. Hallet's threat to evict Rynn for no good reason prefigures her accidental death and director Gessner provides two shots of the bloodied corpse. Smith's natural likeability makes Hallet someone you love to hate. Gessner also gives her two close ups.

7622-27-6A `NOSY NEIGHBOR--Alexis Smith as Mrs. Hallet, emerges from the cellar of her 13-year-old neighbor, a young girl she suspects of inhabiting the house alone. In constantly trying to prove her theory, she runs into heavy problems in American International Pictures suspense-drama release, "The Little Girl Who Lives Down The Lane."

Smith in still for *The Little Girl Who Lives Down The Lane* (1976)

The film premiered at the Cannes Film Festival in May, 1976, but was not released in the United States until August 10, 1977. The taglines included "Ask Her No Questions And Nobody Dies" and "Thank heaven for little girls. Thank HELL for the little girl who lives down the lane!" It was lambasted by *Variety* and received a mixed reaction from Janet Maslin in *The New York Times*.

The actress bemoaned the fact that she had such a small role but was impressed with Jodie Foster's professionalism. For the face slap scene Foster told Smith it was okay to slap her hard. Nicholas Gessner said the casting of the actress helped secure Canadian tax incentives because she was Canadian. He reported Smith was nervous about the death scene, fearful of the trapdoor device, but she was not injured.

On October 28 the actress attended a charity party at the Carlyle Restaurant in New York City which was to benefit Leake Watts Children's Services. On December 11 she was at a party for the crime comedy film *Lucky Lady* (1975) held at 21 in New York City.

On January 22, 1976 Smith attended a party thrown by Ross Hunter celebrating Kaye Ballard's opening night at the Back Lot cabaret in West Hollywood, California.

She was mentioned in the article by Bernadine Morris in *The New York Times* of February 6 entitled "7th Ave: 3 Hits Bring Joy." The actress commented on the Halston collection in the week of summer fashion showings, as someone who was interested in clothes. She said the combination of crepe de chine and Ultrasuede was fantastic. Smith also stopped in at the showings of Geoffrey Beene and John Anthoy to gauge what was coming up in fashion.

The actress was the co-host for the episode of the sixty-minute television talk-show *Your Choice for the Film Awards* shot in Hollywood and broadcast on March 27. The show forecast winners of the Academy Awards to be held on March 28.

It was reported in an article by Bernadine Morris in *The New York Times* of April 27 entitled "Fashion – It's Just One Big Family" that she had recently attended the aerie of Calvin Klein. This was to celebrate Carrie Donovan's new job at Bloomingdale's as vice president. Smith wore a Cathy Hardwick knee-length dress over pants.

On June 4 it was reported that she had visited Divine backstage in his show *Women Behind Bars* at the Truck and Warehouse Theater in New York.

The actress was the narrator for the episode of television historical short series *Bicentennial Minutes* broadcast on June 23 on CBS. The series was a collection of one-minute-long on this day in history shorts, used as a countdown to America's bicentennial.

On July 9 she attended a party at Studio One in Los Angeles, California, celebrating the local opening of the *A Chorus Line* touring production.

On August 4 Smith and a dozen chorus boys presented a brief off-Broadway revue at the rotunda at 79th Street and the Hudson

River. The event was also described as a splashy party and token fashion show. It was sponsored by the men's clothing division of Yves Saint Laurent and the boys wore some of his clothes as they gyrated and did Rockette kicks. It was said she seemed to be vying for the crown of the darling of the camp followers. The actress sang, threw silver balls at the chorus, and tapped them with a riding crop. At one point the number became a striptease, as the boys took off their tops and threatened to remove the pants.

On August 12 it was announced that she was to appear in the film comedy "Casey's Shadow" playing a horse owner. It was written by Carol Sobieski and to be directed by Martin Ritt. Playing opposite her was Walter Matthau who said he always thought Smith was a very sexy looking woman. When Matthau recently met her, he thought she looked even sexier than before. The actress was sexy because she had no pomposity.

The Columbia family sports drama *Casey's Shadow* (1978) was produced by Ray Stark and shot from August 28 to October with reshoots @ late-April, 1977 on locations in Louisiana and New Mexico. The film had the working titles of A Horse of a Different Color, Cajun Colt, and Coon-Ass Colt. The screenplay was based upon the short story "Ruidoso" by John McPhee. Set in Louisiana the story centred on horse trainer Lloyd Bourdelle (Matthau) who purchases a mare that gives birth to the horse they call Casey's Shadow.

Smith is billed second after the title and plays the part of Sarah Blue, a horse breeder who wants to buy Casey. We wait 35 out of the 116 minutes running time to see her. She speaks with a Southern accent, with her hair by John Burt Reilly and costumes by Moss Mabry which include some large belt buckles and jeans. The role sees Sarah ride a horse and dress one for a race. However, the actress doesn't have any real acting challenge.

The film's released was delayed. It was screened at the USA Film Festival on March 13, 1978, then given a wide release on March 17. The taglines included "Thrill as they chase a dream . . . " and

"This crazy mixed-up family doesn't stand a chance of winning a million bucks. Wanna bet?" It was praised by Clive Hirschhorn in "The Columbia Story" but received a mixed reaction from Vincent Canby in *The New York Times*.

Smith was said to have been in the television documentary *The Making of 'Casey's Shadow"* which was broadcast on January 1, 1978. However, she is not in the viewed copy. It was directed by William Riead. Interestingly this shows one shot done with a slate dated July 4.

The actress admitted to feeling a bit uneasy getting back on a horse for the film, after her fall when making *The Young Philadelphians*. However, this time she would be using a Western saddle with the pommel. Smith liked what she did in the film and liked working with Walter Matthau and Martin Ritt. The actress was in love with Matthau, but the line was very long. He was such a delight, such a good actor and a joy to work with. Ritt was wonderful because he didn't have an ego that got in the way of the piece. The director was sensitive and, being an actor and a teacher, was aware of the actor's problem and was wonderfully supportive. She commented that the location had marvellous food. There were ten fine restaurants within an easy drive of the motel where the cast was housed. Specialities included catfish, hushpuppies, and jambalaya. Smith was grateful to not have a weight problem.

After making the film she returned to New York for a rest. One day shopping in the housewares department at Bloomingdale's the actress heard someone yelling her name. It was James Coco who said he had been looking for Smith everywhere. Coco was going to direct a new musical called *Sunset* that he thought was perfect for her. She would play a fading film star who tries to revamp her career by becoming a rock and roll singer. The show would have a variety of music from Big Band ballads to contemporary songs so the actress was interested. The book and lyrics were by Will Holt and the music by Gary William Friedman. The next day Holt and Friedman played her the songs. It was such an ego trip having a private hearing and was still fun even if the material was lousy. The score sounded good, and she started to think seriously about it.

On March 30, 1977, it was reported that a dinner party for her had been held at El Morocco in New York. Smith had flown in from California to escape the weather on the West Coast. The actress said she couldn't stand another morning of getting up to hear that it was another beautiful day. Smith denied that the evening was a celebration of her birthday since that was three months away. She was photographed at the event for an article by Enid Nemy in *The New York Times* entitled "Spring Buds: Wall-to-Wall People, and Tea with Grace."

On April 5 the actress attended the opening-night performance of Dolores Gray at Studio One's Backlot Room in Hollywood, California.

In June she was part of *The 24ᵗʰ Annual Milliken Breakfast Show* held in the Grand Ballroom of the Waldorf-Astoria Hotel in New York. It was sponsored by the textile manufacturer Milliken & Company. The show was written by Tom Eyen and directed by Frank Dunlop. It included a skit called "Who Dunnit". Smith played a store president who is one of the suspects for the murder of the designer Falston, killed at his own fashion show.

She commented that the Milliken show never failed to attract big name entertainers because of how well it paid. The two-week run was said to earn $25,000 for the big names. The actress doubted she would do any other industrial show but practically everyone in the theatre wanted to do this one. It had the best reputation, and the producers spoiled the talent. They stayed in suites at the Waldorf-Astoria, were provided with limousines and food, and got to keep all the clothes.

By the time rehearsals for *Sunset* were to begin James Coco had to withdraw because of a prior film commitment and Tommy Tune was the new director. The show premiered in Buffalo, New York at the Studio Arena Theater in September and ran for four weeks. It was thought that the musical had potential, but it needed a lot of work. On December 16 it was reported that it was now supposed to come to Broadway at the end of the season. The producers were currently negotiating with a new director since Tommy Tune had left the show.

On January 29, 1978, she attended a party for the 10th anniversary of the Ford Theatre in Washington, D.C.

On April 2 Smith was interviewed on the WMCA radio station. She was also interviewed by Tom Buckley in her pied-a-tierre in the Century on Central Park West for the April 13 "At the Movies" column in *The New York Times*.

On May 3 the actress attended a black tie gala benefit on the roof garden of the Lord & Taylor building in New York. The event was to honor Louis Auchincloss, the president of the Museum of the City of New York. She was offered a dare by Lee Guber to pinch an umbrella and put it down the back of her red dress. He said Smith carried herself so well that she could get away with it. But the actress refused. The event was reported in an article by Enid Nemy in *The New York Times* entitled "The Anatomy of Glitter, Bottom to Top."

On June 2 it was reported that the stage musical "Sunset" that had starred her as a 1940s musical comedy star rerecording her biggest hits with a disco beat had been retitled "Platinum". Sunset had referred to the Hollywood boulevard where the recording studio was as the centre of action. Platinum now referred to the platinum record that was awarded for sales of a million copies. The show had been revitalized by an input of funds by Paramount Pictures who were also providing a space for rehearsals to star on August 1.

The show was hoped to open in Philadelphia on September 11 for a two-week run. Then it would move to the Kennedy Center in Washington for five weeks from September 28 to October 28. The Broadway run would take place in November and there would eventually be a movie version. The show was being produced by Barry Brown and Fritz Holt in association with Gladys Rackmil.

The book was now by Will Holt and Bruce Vilanch. The new director was Joe Layton who would also stage the dance numbers.

Smith in portrait for *Platinum.*

On June 27 she attended the Party for New York Post Gossip Columnist Diane Judge held at the Il Cameretta Restaurant in New York City. This was to celebrate Mildred Newman's book *How To Take Charge Of Your Life.*

Between previews for *Platinum* Smith was interviewed by Robert Berkvist for The *New York Times* for an article that appeared on November 12 entitled "'Platinum' Is Everything I Never Did in Films." Accompanying the article was a Al Hirshfeld caricature of the cast. Berkvist noted that her name was above the title of the show in the marquee, evidence that she was regarded as a potent box office attraction. The actress was overjoyed at having a bunch of numbers in the show and she got to dance which was fun. Smith reported that the show had also done a run in Boston. Most of the music stayed the same but, apart from one or two scenes, everything else was changed. The title change had also been recommended as too many people were confusing *Sunset* with *Sunset Boulevard* and thought this was a musical version of the movie.

Doing a new show had its good and bad points. It was an original but untried and they could go in any direction they wanted to. But, given the multiplicity of choices, you had to be very sure to make the right one. It was an enormously delicate process and fascinating. She was a firm believer in involvement, not wanting anything to go by that the actress didn't know something about. She liked rock music, though said the music in the show was contemporary but not heavy rock, and disco dancing. Still Smith didn't want to do it nightly.

She preferred doing musicals to straight plays since musicals were her caviar. The actress danced all the time anyway, so she was usually in very good shape. Smith didn't consider acting the be-all and end-all of her life because there were so many other things in the world. She got into studying things – languages and seminars - and would have loved to go back to school. When the actress wanted to learn to do anything, like singing for example, she went and took lessons. Smith could have been a nuclear physicist if she wanted to because all the information was there for the taking. The actress would just start by going to the library and looking under N.

Whether it was in the theatre or in films Smith wanted everything she did to be really good or otherwise it was on to something else. People that complained that working in the theatre was boring because of the repetition irritated her. When you signed a contract, you knew you had to do your best eight times a week for the length of that agreement. That was part of the job and part of the challenge. To make the 400th performance as fresh as the first was fun.

The actress didn't want to try and think about the film version of the show just yet and whether she could beat out Barbra Streisand for the screen role. Smith would think about it if the time ever came but she may be busy. By then the actress may have been a nuclear physicist and couldn't have cared less about it.

After 12 previews from November 2 *Platinum* opened on Broadway at the Mark Hellinger Theatre on November 12 and ran till December 10. The show received a mixed reaction from Richard Eder in *The New York Times* who wrote that Smith brought a cheerful dignity to it. She was nominated for the Tony Award for Best Performance by a Leading Actress in a Musical. Richard Cox who played Dan Danger was nominated for Best Performance by a Featured Actor in a Musical. A cast recording was also made.

The actress described her character of Lila Halliday as a composite, part Rita Hayworth and Betty Grable. She had three solos: "Back with a Beat/Nothing But", "Destiny" and "Too Many Mirrors". The show's costumes were by Bob Mackie. They included leather pants and satin blouses, cashmere sweaters, and a silver curtain-call dress featuring bugle beads in a groove pattern reminiscent of a vinyl record. Mackie said he loved designing the latter and she looked stunning in it. However, the dress weighed a ton at about fifty pounds with the heavy beads. If Smith had ever fallen over on stage, she would never have been able to get up.

In his book *Not Since Carrie: Forty Years of Broadway Musical Flops* Ken Mandelbaum writes that the actress was not a big enough draw to carry the show. Its failure meant that producers stopped looking for musical vehicles for her.

Smith said that she did not expect such good reviews for herself and for the show and really couldn't deal with it. So, the actress just went on with her life. She liked to sing and dance. It beat playing Joan of Arc every night and it was more fun than making movies. Smith tried to treat opening night as just any other performance. But when she arrived at the theatre there were all these flowers and telegrams and people telling her not to be nervous. The actress reported doing the show was the best working experience she had ever had. Joe Layton loved actors which wasn't true of all directors. Smith had only had two days off since August and on the road they kept putting in new things in each performance. That was the creative part and she loved it.

The actress was back on *The Merv Griffin Show* for the episode shot on November 12 and broadcast on November 13. The show was directed by Dick Carson. She was there to promote *Platinum* though Smith did not perform any of her numbers. She wore an orange-colored bat-winged sweater with matching pants which was one of her Bob Mackie costumes for *Platinum*. Smith reported that the musical was marvellous, and she felt Griffin would love to perform "Too Many Mirrors".

On November 19 the actress attended the grand opening of Curtains Up Restaurant in Atlantic City, New Jersey.

She was a guest of the episode of the television news talk-show *Today* shot in New York and broadcast on November 21 on NBC.

Smith was interviewed about *Platinum* for John Corry's Broadway article for *The New York Times* of November 24. On November 29 she was honored with the good-luck gypsy robe by Gerriane Raphael for her work in the show. The robe had been passed from one musical dancer to another for more than a quarter-century. The actress was honored in recognition of the fact that she did almost all of the dancing in *Platinum*. Smith happily accepted the robe which was unwieldy and heavy. Each show cast traditionally attached to it a badge, bit of cloth, or ornament, autographed. Like its predecessors, the robe was soon to be retired to the Museum of the City of New York or the Library for the Performing Arts at Lincoln Center. Another would be put in circulation to carry on the tradition. The actress got to keep the robe until a new musical opened on Broadway.

On January 15, 1979, she attended Regine's in New York to celebrate both Imogene Coca's 50th anniversary in showbusiness and the 2nd year of New York State's "I Love New York" theatre promotion.

On April 13 it was reported that Smith would star in the national touring company of *The Best Little Whorehouse in Texas*. The musical with a book by Larry L. King and Peter Masterson and music and lyrics by Carol Hall had premiered off-Broadway at the Entermedia Theatre on April 17, 1978. It then re-opened on Broadway at the 46th Street Theatre on June 19 and would run till March 27, 1982.

One source claims that she appeared in a fashion layout for the April edition of *Harper's Bazaar* but this cannot be confirmed. The actress was reported to tell the magazine that she enjoyed her work so much more now than ten years ago. This was because it was in the proper perspective. Smith was not preoccupied with a burning desire for star billing, and now her energy was going in the right direction.

She attended *The 33rd Annual Tony Awards* aka 1979 Tony Awards that was held on June 3 at the Shubert Theatre in New York and broadcast as a television special on CBS. The actress lost Best Performance by a Leading Actress in a Musical to Angela Lansbury in *Sweeney Todd*. The show was directed by Clark Jones.

On August 28 she was photographed in New York rehearsing with Tommy Tune one of the dance numbers for *The Best Little Whorehouse in Texas*.

On September 12 it was reported that Smith had been in talks to star in Edward Albee's new play "The Lady From Dubuque" the previous season but the discussion failed to produce agreement on a contract.

On September 19 she attended the premiere of the war drama film *Yanks* (1979) in New York.

The national tour of *The Best Little Whorehouse in Texas* ran from September 29, 1979, to February 1, 1981. The actress played the role of Mona Stangley during the entire run. The tour travelled from Boston, Philadelphia, Miami, Atlanta, Washington, Detroit, Chicago, San Francisco, Los Angeles. San Diego and back to Los Angeles. The show was staged by Peter Masterson and Tommy Tune who had also done the Broadway show.

She said it was fun to do though it wasn't a particularly good show. The company was wonderful, and Smith enjoyed being with them. The dancing was marvellous due to Tommy Tune's great contribution. Audiences adored it though the critics were not too thrilled. She hadn't toured in a long time and found that very interesting, spending time in the major cities of the country and getting to know it again. The actress reported on being miked for the show, where her body pack was in the back of her form-fitting dress. Someone backstage asked if she had a pacemaker which Smith found very funny.

In *The Whorehouse Papers* Larry L. King writes that she proved to be a great lady. There was no haughty star quality about her, or phoniness or looking down the nose. The cast members loved the actress because she treated them as equals. Smith was not afraid to cut loose with a hearty, earthy laugh even if the joke was on her. King had dinner several times with she and Craig Stevens.

However, King made an awful comment that was published in *Women's Wear* Daily. This is something he later regretted and attributed to alcohol and the betrayal of confidence of someone thought to be a friend. Reporter Lois Romano asked him to compare the different leading ladies in the various companies and specifically asked if he was satisfied with the actress as a singer. King's answer was she was the best one who auditioned for the national company but he and Romano both knew Smith couldn't carry a tune in a goddamn sack. But she was a great draw on the road and made a lot of money for the show.

Immediately after King said it, he asked Romano to not quote him, but she quoted him exactly. King decided if the actress found out, and she was certain to, he would lie. King would say he was misquoted and had said that *he* was the one who couldn't carry a tune. King felt he would rather have Lois Romano mad at him that Smith. But the quote spread, and King rang his son who was playing in the show with her in Detroit. King didn't know if she had seen the article because everyone in the company was tearing up every copy they could find. He had also tipped off her dresser and driver to keep it away from the actress. But who knew how long these tactics could last?

Smith in portrait for *The Best Little Whorehouse in Texas*

She was a guest on the television talk-show *Over Easy* broadcast on January 14, 1980.

Smith was profiled by Anthony Cassa in the March edition of *Hollywood Studio* Magazine in an article entitled "Alexis Smith – A star who has it all together."

A new film part interested her. This was actress Sally Ross in the horror thriller *The Fan* (1981) but Lauren Bacall was cast instead.

On September 5 the actress attended the grand re-opening of Studios 54 on September 15, 1981, in New York City.

She was back on *The Merv Griffin Show* for the episode that was shot in Los Angeles and broadcast on November 20. The show had multiple writers and was again directed by Dick Carson. Smith wore a plum-colored sparkly dress by Luis Estevez with a magenta-colored jacket. She was there to promote *The Best Little Whorehouse in Texas* as well as host a fashion show of evening wear worn by some of the female cast. The actress had been on the road for a year. She joked that the wonderfully warm reception offered from the studio audience was from a number of the cast.

Smith said the *Whorehouse* company was exceptional and it was a lovely thing to be able to travel the country. She got to meet new people and visit museums and learn about those cities. The doctor the actress consulted in Boston envied her travel. It was true that most people spent their nine to five job in the same location. She had managed to cram in quite a lot of holidaying before the tour. Smith had gone to Monte Carlo, London, and Greece.

She commented about playing a madam in the show, saying when you had been a lady as long as the actress had, it was really nice to go slumming. The show received different reactions. In some cities they refused to say the title on the air or in television commercials and bleeped it out. Some newspapers also refused to print the word and changed the title to The Best Little Chicken Ranch in Texas. Smith didn't know before starting in the show that whorehouse was a dirty word. It was such a surprise to her considering the permissiveness that existed in the culture today. She acknowledged there was some dialogue in the show that made people react negatively. However, the actress considered it very innocent and a wholesome show. The language was an integral part of the piece. When you have a redneck Texan sheriff, he could not speak like a choir boy.

She was a guest on the television family talk-show *Hour Magazine* for the episode that was broadcast on November 25.

After the completion of the *Whorehouse* tour in February, 1981 Smith headed home to California.

On March 8 she attended the Turn to the Right Opening Night Party held at Chasen's Restaurant in Beverly Hills, California. On April 3 the actress was at A Tribute to L. Arnold Weissberger held at the Mark Taper Forum, Los Angeles Music Center. On April 26 she attended a cocktail and dinner party given for Elizabeth Taylor at the New York restaurant Jim McMullen. The event was given by Florence Klotz, the costume designer for *The Little Foxes* that starred Taylor and was to begin previews on April 29 at the Martin Beck Theater.

In the summer Smith played the role of Claire Zachanassian in the stage play *The Visit* by Friedrich Dürrenmatt which was done in Canada. The play had premiered in Zurich in 1956 and a touring production in Britain that ran from 1957 to 1958, was then transferred to Broadway. The show starred Lynn Fontanne as Claire and ran from May 5 to November 29, 1958.

After the death of William Holden on November 12 she was among those who came to the house of Stefanie Powers in Benedict Canyon the following Sunday to reminiscence.

Chapter 12. *La Truite*

Her next film was the French romance *La Truite* aka The Trout (1982) shot from January 26, 1982, on location in France and Japan. Craig Stevens is also in the film and plays Carter. Since he has some scenes in outdoor locations in Japan it is possible that the actress' scenes were also filmed in Japan at the Fuji View Hotel. The screenplay was by Monique Lange and Joseph Losey adapted from the novel by Roger Vailland. Losey was also the director. The story centred on Frédérique (Isabelle Huppert), who leaves her family's small-town trout farm to embark on a journey taking her to Japan and into the arms of a man.

She is billed twelfth in the end credits and plays the supporting role of Gloria, an American woman married to a Japanese man that Frederique meets at her Tokyo hotel. We wait 35 out of the 103 minutes running time to see her. Gloria is revealed with her back to the camera as she exits an elevator. Hair by Ludovic Paris and Max Guerin is a new look, worn short and off the forehead. Costumes are by Annalisa Nasalli Rocca. The role sees her laugh and speak in French. Smith is funny delivering Gloria's monologue about how she has made love 33,000 times, in thirteen world capitals, never in cities with populations under 100,000.

The film premiered at the Venice Film Festival on September 4 and was given a wide release in the United States on May 27, 1983. It received a mixed reaction from Janet Maslin in *The New York Times* and Roger Ebert in the *Chicago Sun-Times*.

In *Joseph Losey: A Revenge on Life*, David Caute describes the actress' French accent as thick as a tatami mattress.

She was in the *Night Of 100 Stars* shot at Radio City Music Hall on February 14 and broadcast as a television special on March 8 on ABC. The event celebrated the centennial of the Actors' Fund of

America. It was written by Hildy Parks and directed by Clark Jones. The show actually featured 200 stars and Smith was number 132. She is in the Broadway part of the show and in the medley sings a few lines from "Could I Leave You?" as the representative of *Follies*. The actress comes back for the cast curtain-call where they sing "The Lullaby of Broadway". She is also seen under the end credits when the entire cast gathers to be photographed. The show's hair was by Joe Tubens and the costumes by Alvin Colt.

It won the Emmy Awards for Outstanding Variety, Music or Comedy Program and Outstanding Achievement in Music Direction. The show was nominated for Outstanding Achievement in Music and Lyrics, Outstanding Directing in a Variety or Music Program and Outstanding Lighting Direction (Electronic).

Smith was in *Broadway Plays Washington on Kennedy Center Tonight* held at the John F. Kennedy Center for the Performing Arts in Washington on March 13 and broadcast as a television special. This was a musical celebration honoring the 10th Anniversary of the Center written by Stephen Dick and directed by Stan Lathan. She performed the song ""We Have Nothin' But Style".

On September 5 the actress appeared in the revue "Broadway Salutes Sage" at the Fire Island Pines Pavilion in New York.

On October 12 or 19 she attended The State Dinner for Indonesia's President and his wife Mrs. Suharto held by President Reagan and Mrs. Reagan at the White House.

Smith was a guest on the television romantic comedy series *The Love Boat* for the two-part episode entitled "The Spoonmaker Diamond/Papa Doc/The Role Model/Julie's Tycoon". This was shot on location in Greece, Turkey, and Egypt and at the 20th Century Fox Hollywood studios, and broadcast on November 13 on ABC. The show was directed by Robert Scheerer. As the guest stars are listed alphabetically, she is billed tenth and appears in the "Papa Doc" subplot which was written by Mike Marmer. The actress plays the part of wealthy Amanda Drake, whose daughter Sabrina (Jan Smithers) is secretly dating crusading reporter Joe Novak (Kiel Martin). Her hair is by Naoma Cavin and clothes by Nolan Miller. The role sees Amanda ride a camel and laugh.

She is meant to have an acerbic sense of humor but the closest thing to a funny line comes in an exchange with Joe as Amanda learns he has married Sabrina. Joe comments that perhaps in the scathing article he wrote about Amanda he went too far. She replies, "Well if you didn't then, you certainly have now." Smith isn't given any great acting challenges here. Her scenes include all the foreign locations and on board the ship the Stella Solaris that is not filmed at the Fox studio, as well as one interior obviously done at Fox.

On November 29 she attended a black-tie anniversary party at the Metropolitan Museum of Modern Art's Englehard Court thrown by Fifth Avenue jeweler Harry Winston. The biggest attention-getter was the deep blue oval shaped Hope Diamond located at the foot of Rodin's "Gates of Hell" which amused the actress. This was because some of the diamond's previous owners reportedly met their deaths by wild dogs, at the hands of a mob, by beheadings, in motor accidents, and from an overdose of drugs.

On December 6 she was at the opening of a costume exhibit "La Belle Epoque" at the Metropolitan Museum of Art in New York City.

In 1982 she appeared in the television special *Showstoppers: The Best of Broadway* broadcast on the pay cable Entertainment Channel. It was later broadcast as an episode of the television musical series *Great Performances* entitled "The Best of Broadway" on May 4 or 24 on PBS. The show had multiple writers and was directed by Rob Iscove. Smith performed "Could I Leave You? from *Follies*.

On April 27, 1983, she attended a dinner held in L'Orangerie of Le Cirque in New York. The occasion was to celebrate the new edition of the Italian publication *Capital Magazine* which featured America's most successful Italians. The hosts were Mario D'Urso of Lehman Brothers and the designers Lella and Massimo Vignelli. On April 29 the actress was at a party to celebrate the Broadway stage revival of *Private Lives* then in previews at the Lunt-Fontanne Theatre. The party was held at the Jockey Club inside the Ritz-Carlton Hotel in New York City.

On May 8 she attended the Cloud Nine Opening Night Performance held at the Los Angeles Stage Company West in Beverly Hills, California.

In the summer Smith appeared in a tour of *Pal Joey* produced by John Kenley and directed by Tom O'Horgan. The musical had a book by John O'Hara and songs by Richard Rodgers and Lorenz Hart. It had originally run on Broadway from December 25, 1940, to November 29, 1941 and had received subsequent Broadway revivals in 1952 -1953 and 1976. In the new tour she played the role of Vera Simpson which had been originated by Vivienne Segal. The tour ran from June 28 to July 3 and the show appeared in Dallas, Atlanta, St. Louis and Akron, Ohio.

The actress was a guest on the television show *Cinema Showcase* for the episode broadcast on July 14 on WETV. This was an Atlanta show, and the interview was shot when she was in the city doing *Pal Joey*. The director was Lance Lipman. Smith agreed to a degree that shows like *Pal Joey* were not written anymore though thought Stephen Sondheim compared very favourably to Rodgers and Hart. Sondheim embodied the two and was the genius of our time. His lyrics were superior to Hart's because he had such great wit and profundity.

She thought *Pal Joey* had staying power because it was ahead of its time because the hero was an anti-hero. Prior to that musicals were upbeat with a happy ending. In the new show they used some of the song lyrics that could not be used in the original because then they were considered too raunchy and shocking. The part of Vera was something that so many people had said over the years the actress should do. So, when the opportunity came up Smith felt she may as well do it and get it out of the way. Being cast as another sophisticated and wealthy lady amused her. This is how the actress seemed to be typecast though she didn't see herself like that. Smith especially denied having a bored sophistication which she thought was not an attractive quality. The actress didn't know how this type-casting got started though she assumed a great deal of it had to do with her height where Smith was often described as statuesque. She felt the phenomena was an example of how one's physical being often affected how you were cast and your career.

The actress recalled being told Broadway was dying when she did *Follies* and felt it was presently in a slump after a few healthy and productive seasons. People were always saying theatre was dying and it never did. While there seemed to be a dearth of new material the major problem was economical. Even *Follies* would not be economically feasible to be staged today. There were rising costs which meant leaner production values and less risk on productions that might close in one night. Smith blamed the unions and not the creatives who were willing to take salary cuts and do anything to get a show on. But as the unions would not make any concessions, companies were forced to only pay minimum wages which some performers resented.

It was shocking how theatres were being torn down and hotels, like the Helmsley Hotel, could not be built around theatres to save them. There was also the problem of the new large community complexes that were designed to accommodate a circus, an intimate play, and a motorcycle race. Theatres in London like the Haymarket were built for acting. But the new American buildings were unfortunate as they certainly hurt the artist who performed there.

Acting on the road was an entirely new ballgame. Before actors might object to doing shows in what they considered to be unsuitable venues. She believed one should be able to project and fill the house. That was part of your technique and equipment. But there were two factors that now came into it – big theatres and how the ear of the public had changed considerably. People were used to seeing television and film and going to concerts that were heavily miked. They wouldn't accept seeing theatre that wasn't miked or had artificial amplification although miking could distort the sound.

In *Pal Joey* the actress wore a chest microphone and a body pack, and the theatre was miked. Some of the other cast did not have microphones and sometimes her dialogue sound liked she was yelling. They were reliant upon a sound man to do a mix. There were other problems like when the microphone went off during the performance. Smith said it was a trap and dangerous to depend upon it because then your energy level dropped. She personally played the show at the same vocal level the actress would if she didn't have a microphone.

On August 16 Smith attended a party at the Park Avenue apartment of Jerry Silverman and Shannon Rodgers in New York to celebrate the birthday of theatrical agent Milton Goldman. On August 21 she was at the opening night of the new stage musical *La Cage aux Folles* at the Palace Theatre in New York. The actress also attended the after-show party held at the Pan Am Building.

On November 11 she was at an event benefitting the Damon Runyon-Walter Winchell Cancer Fund, held in Dallas, Texas. In December Smith attended the Costume Institute's Met Ball Benefit held at the Metropolitan Museum of Art in New York.

On January 31, 1984, she was at the opening of *Sugar Babies* at the Pantages Theater in Hollywood, California.

Smith in portrait for *Dallas*

The actress began a series of recurring successive guest appearances on the television series *Dallas* which was shot on locations in Texas, California and at the M-G-M Hollywood studios and broadcast on CBS. The series centred on J.R. Ewing (Larry Hagman), a Texas oil baron, who uses manipulation and blackmail to achieve his ambitions, both business and personal. Her first episode was entitled "The Unexpected" and broadcast on March 16. The teleplay was by Arthur Bernard Lewis and the director was Nick Havinga.

She isn't billed till the end credits of the show as the fifth of the guest stars. Smith plays the part of Jessica Montford, the sister of Clayton Farlow (Howard Keel). She comes to the Ewing home for her brother's wedding to J.R.'s mother Miss Ellie Ewing (Barbara Bel Geddes). Hair is by Greg Mitchell and Generio Gugliemotto though there is no credited costume designer.

We have to wait 41 out of the 49 minutes running time to see her. The actress uses a Southern accent since Jessica is originally from Texas though has been living in London. She gets a funny line to Miss Ellie, "Sometimes I come on a little strong. If I do, slap me down." The role sees her laugh and handle a sword. Smith is styled beautifully. In line with the drama of the show Jessica gets a camp transition from smiling at Miss Ellie to a grimace. Talking to herself, she says, "I wouldn't count on you marrying Clayton, Miss Ellie. I wouldn't count on it at all." However, the actress adds vulnerability to her expression which suggest Jessica is somehow unstable.

"Strange Alliance" was broadcast on March 23. Written by Leonard Katzman and directed by Larry Hagman it saw J.R. and Jessica allied in their objection to the wedding. Smith slips to the sixth billed in the end credits guest stars. We get to see Jessica in jeans in one scene. Her fiddling with a bracelet in another where Jessica talks with Miss Ellie perhaps suggests mental instability. Jessica is also slightly hysterical talking about her past. She scores a laugh with her fake smile about the wedding when saying "What a happy day that will be for everyone when it happens." Director Hagman gives Jessica a private moment in a dialogue scene with J.R. She has her back to him as Jessica talks about being estranged from Clayton with a sad look on her face.

On March 20 the actress attended a party at the Corcoran Gallery in Washington, D.C. This was a preview for the *George Washington* television miniseries which was to premiere on April 8.

Next on *Dallas* was "Blow Up" broadcast on April 6 written by David Paulsen and directed by Patrick Duffy. Now her credit slips to seventh of the guest stars in the end credits. Jessica tells J.R., when the time comes, she will know what to do to stop the wedding. When Clayton and Miss Ellie are being photographed director Duffy uses a slow zoom in on Jessica's unhappy reaction. She gets more camp moments in this episode. When asked to join the family for a toast, Jessica says, "How could I not toast such a lovin' couple." She picks up a large knife when asked by Miss Ellie to cut up vegetables in the kitchen, with Jessica's point of view shown as Miss Ellie's back. The photograph and the knife get a payoff when Jessica uses a nail file to tear Miss Ellie's face out of the photograph of Ellie and Clayton.

"Turning Point" was broadcast on April 13. It was written by Arthur Bernard Lewis and directed by Gwen Arner. Smith's billing is back to sixth in the end credits. In this episode Jessica has a denim jacket to go with her jeans. Clayton describes her as a little too outspoken, a little too wild, and unpredictable. This both explains the actress' performance and foreshadows Jessica's future actions. She is angry that he has sold their property The Southern Cross, and believes she was banished to England. Her anger leads Jessica to reveal a secret to J.R. that he thinks he can use to stop the wedding. The property had a mysterious fire and Jessica says that Clayton's former wife Amy died so they could keep the ranch. This suggests that Amy was murdered.

"Love Stories" was broadcast on May 4. It was written by Leonard Katsman and directed by Michael Preece. Smith is back to billed seventh of the guest stars at the end credits. Jessica explains to J.R. that Amy's trust fund allowed Clayton to save The Southern Cross, but she is still angry feeling Clayton has deprived his son Dusty of his birthright.

She was back *The Love Boat* for another two-part episode entitled "Dreamboat/Gopher, Isaac & the Starlet/The Parents/The Importance of Being Johnny/Julie and the Producer". It was shot at the Warner Hollywood studios and broadcast on May 5. The actress is billed sixth among the alphabetically listed guest stars. She plays faded movie star Angela Lovett, the mother of rock star Johnny Lovett (James A. Osmond), who is romanced by the Captain (Gavin MacLeod). The story centres on how a Hollywood movie "Dream Boat" is being shot onboard the Pacific Princess. Angela's subplot appears to have written by Ray Jessell and Cynthia Thompson and the episode was directed by Robert Scheerer. Her hair by Mary Hadley and Joan Phillips is worn mostly in a side part though also off the forehead in one scene, and costumes are by Nolan Miller.

Angela gets some funny lines. When Faye Marsh (Juliet Prowse) says "I do so admire a woman who doesn't try to hide her age", Angela replies, "How could I? You've taken all the hiding places." Faye comments on how she had replaced Angela in a movie with "Cream always rises to the top". Angela replies, "Yes dear. So does hot air." At dinner the Captain says "Angela, if you haven't decided yet may I suggest the Captain's Special" to which she replies, "He certainly is." When Johnny and Vicki (Jill Whelan) walk by hand-in-hand after having been previously antagonists, Angela says a shocked and deadpan "Hi" in response to theirs.

The role sees her throw streamers as the ship leaves port, be kissed by the Captain and Bennett Barton (Ben Vereen), laugh, and sing and dance. Angela duets with the Captain on "I'm Old Fashioned" by Johnny Mercer, has the solo "I'm Still in This Race" by Ray Jessel, and duets with Faye on "Dear Friends" by Jessel.

"I'm Old Fashioned" has Angela fiddling with her costumes beads in one shot which is distracting. Angela performing "I'm Still in this Race" is done as a good-natured ploy to get Faye to come back to the film after she has quit, since the song had been written for her. This gives context to the cutaways director Scheerer uses as reactions of Faye and Bennett. Angela performs the song with a dancing chorus which Scheerer sometimes has in the foreground. There is also the camera in the foreground that is supposed to be recording the number for the film. The ploy to get Faye to come back does not work but it is Angela telling her that she is costing jobs for the crew that changes Faye's mind. Faye also demands that Angela be given a part in the film, so that both Faye and Angela are presented as being ultimately generous and not cliched Hollywood divas.

"Dear Friends" is shot at Imperial Studios after the film crew has left the ship. It is part of the "Dreamboat" medley by Ray Jessel and has Angela and Faye dressed in male drag tuxedos. They sing and dance the number though Scheerer uses one medium shot that cuts off their legs as they move. Angela, now wearing a dress, joins the cast to sing and dance "Dreamboat" for the end of the finale. Again, Scheerer uses cutaways of the observing crew, a tilted camera angle, and medium shots of the movement. The show's choreography is by Walter Painter.

Smith was back on *Dallas* for the next episode "Hush, Hush, Sweet Jessie" broadcast on May 11. It was written by David Paulsen and directed by Gwen Arner. Jessica's actions of hitting Donna Culver Crebbs (Susan Howard) with a telephone, and then kidnapping Miss Ellie at gunpoint are described by Donna but not shown. Clayton reveals that Jessica is not Dusty's aunt but his mother, which explains why she is more excited about him coming to the wedding. Clayton is Dusty's uncle, and his true father is unknown. Amy and Clayton took the child in as Jessica had an emotional depression and needed to be cared for in a rest home. Then Jessica came back to Texas when Amy fell ill. J.R. reads Jessica's diary where she admits to setting fire to The Southern Cross.

"End Game" was broadcast on May 18. It was written by Arthur Bernard Lewis and directed by Leonard Katzman. Now the actress slips to the ninth place for the guest stars in the end credits. Jessica is seen driving a car. Her talking to herself is evidence of emotional instability as is her fantastical assessment of the situation. We later see that she has Miss Ellie bound and gagged in the car's boot so we could have been shown how Jessica accomplished that. Smith handles a gun when Jessica is found by the Ewing's at a motel where her hair is dishevelled to add to her perceived instability. The actress gets a monologue of Jessica's desire to have a picnic with Clayton and Dusty. We are told that she is taken to a sanatorium and has been declared not competent to stand trial.

Smith said that since the show was number one in the ratings it was not bad to go into it. She described her character as bad and that was the best kind of role to play. The writers hadn't said what happened to Lord Montford, Jessica's husband, so perhaps he would turn up in the future. Everyone on the set would sit around and guess what might happen to the characters because very little information was given out in advance.

On November 9 it was reported that the actress was being considered for the role of the wife in the new Garson Kanin play "Peccadillo" to be premiered February 26 at the Royal Poinciana Theater in Palm Beach. The play told the story of a great maestro in his late sixties who, though married, falls in love with a younger woman. Kanin was also directing, and production was planned to move to Broadway in the fall.

On November 27 she attended a gala for James Watter's book *Return Engagement: Faces To Remember - Then And Now* held at the Century Plaza Hotel in Century City, California. On November 28 Smith was at a party for the book held at 385 North Restaurant in West Hollywood, California.

On December 3 she attended The Metropolitan Museum's Costume Institute Gala Exhibition of Man and the Horse held at The Metropolitan Museum of Art in New York City.

On February 14, 1985, the actress was at the Time Covers Hollywood 1923-1985 Exhibition at the Academy Theater in Beverly Hills, California.

She appeared in the television special *The Hollywood Reporter Salutes Radie Harris* held at the Beverly Hills Hotel and broadcast on March 21 on NBC. Harris was an American journalist and newspaper columnist.

On May 1 Smith attended Luis Esteves Fashion Party at the Visage in New York City.

She was next in the television miniseries *A Death In California* shot on locations in California and broadcast on May 12. This had a teleplay by E. Jack Neuman based on the book by Joan Barthel and was directed by Delbert Mann. The story was set in Chicago in 1973 and centred on Hope Masters (Cheryl Ladd), a Beverly Hills socialite. She embarks on a love/hate relationship with the psychotic D. Jordan Williams (Sam Elliott). Smith is top-billed among the special guest stars and plays the supporting role of Honey Niven, Hope's mother. Hair is by Rita Bellissimo but there is no credited costume designer.

Honey is prepared to believe the paranoid delusions of Jordan, as opposed to her husband Van (Fritz Weaver) who has doubts. She gets some funny lines. To Hope, "Stop that damn pacing up and down. It's hard on my rug and my nerves". "You keep saying Mother, Mother, Mother. My God Hope, you haven't called me mother in twenty years and now you've called me Mother a dozen times in the last twenty-four hours." And "Is there some kind of impediment in your thought process that won't let you free of him?" The role sees her interact with children and cry, though Honey has minor impact on the plot. The actress makes Honey funny and supplies emotion when appropriate.

The show was nominated for Emmy Awards for Outstanding Cinematography and Outstanding Art Direction for a Limited Series or a Special. It received a mixed reaction from Lawrence Van Gelder in *The New York Times*.

Smith was back on television's *The Love Boat* for the two-part episode "The German Cruise: The Villa/The Racer's Edge/Love or Money/The Accident" broadcast on November 2, 1985. The show was shot on locations in West Germany, Italy, and France, on the Vistafjord ship, and interiors at the Warner Hollywood studios. It had multiple writers and was directed by Richard Kinon. She is billed eighth among the alphabetically listed guest stars. Smith plays Justina Downey whose family estate was taken by Viktor Lucas (Craig Stevens) but reunites with an old flame Jack Powers (Mel Ferrer). This subplot is "The Villa" which was written by Michael L. Grace. A June 10 auction sign at the villa suggests this was when some of the show's shooting was done.

Hair is now by Mary Hadley and Lola 'Skip' McNalley with Nolan Miller as the wardrobe consultant. The role sees her kissed by Anton (Ulrich Matschoss) and Jack. The only notable plot point is that Justina steals one auction item before the sale. Smith has nothing challenging to do here in terms of acting.

She appeared in the television special *The 2th Annual American Cinema Awards* broadcast on November 22.

In 1985 the actress and Dorothy Collins were invited to Houston where a producer mounted a production of *Follies* to open a new theatre. During a break in the show Smith reportedly grabbed Collins by the arm and pulled her out of the seat. She took Collins into the ladies room because actress said she had to apologize. Seeing the show now, Smith said she had no idea how good Collins was in the original.

Chapter 13. *Tough Guys*

The actress returned to films for the crime comedy *Tough Guys* (1986) shot from February 10 to April 27, 1986, on locations in California. The screenplay was by James Orr and Jim Cruickshank and the director was Jeff Kanew. The tough guys are Harry Doyle (Burt Lancaster) and Archie Long (Kirk Douglas), two elderly gangsters released from prison who have trouble fitting into modern society.

She is billed fourth after the title and plays the supporting part of sixty-year-old Belle who lives at the Golden Sunset home where Harry is placed. Belle is a former showgirl who now teaches aerobics and tap dance. Hair is by Yolanda Toussieng. Clothes by Erica Phillips include a backless evening gown which is quite shocking for a sixty-three-year-old actress to be so exposed.

Leon B. Little (Eli Wallach) scores a laugh at her expense when he calls Belle "Jane Fonda" when she is doing aerobics in her room. Belle gets a funny line. Leon says if he lived in the home he calls a rat hole, he would kill himself in an hour. She replies, "You've been here forty-five minutes." Belle gets involved in the exploits of Harry and Archie when she is nearly kidnapped by Leon.

The role also sees her handle a bicycle, dance with Harry, karate-chop the arm of Deke Yablonski (Charles Durning) when he appears in the home with a gun and handle the gun. Smith gets to play slapstick in the karate chop scene. Director Kanew has the camera behind her as she bends over doing aerobics.

Joining Burt Lancaster and Kirk Douglas in the action-comedy "Tough Guys" are: Darlanne Fluegel (left), as the shapely aerobics instructor who gives Douglas a few lessons in the sport of love; and Alexis Smith, as Lancaster's former girlfriend with whom he rekindles a romance. The movie was directed by Jeff Kanew and produced by Joe Wizan from an original screenplay written by James Orr and Jim Cruickshank. "Tough Guys" is a Touchstone Pictures presentation in association with Silver Screen Partners II and will be distributed by Buena Vista. (TG86)
PHOTO CREDITS: (left) STEVE SCHAPIRO; (right) CHRISTINE LOSS

Permission is hereby granted to magazines and newspapers to reproduce this picture on condition that it is accompanied by: ©MCMLXXXVI Touchstone Pictures. All rights reserved.

Smith on right in portrait for *Tough Guys* (1986)

The film was premiered at ShowEast on September 9, 1986, and received a wide release on October 3. The taglines included "After 30 years in jail, breaking the law is more fun than ever!" and "Friends for years. Legends for life. Tough guys forever." It was a box office success. The film was lambasted by *Variety* but received a mixed reaction from Walter Goodman in *The New York Times* who wrote that Smith looked mighty good, and Roger Ebert in the *Chicago Sun-Times*. In his book, *Against Type: The Biography Of Burt Lancaster*, Gary Fishgall said there was rumors of a sequel but it was not made.

Debbie Reynolds and Ruth Roman were considered to play Belle.

In his autobiography *A Ragman's Son*, Kirk Douglas wrote that the actress looked stunning, and it was good to work with her.

In her book, *Burt Lancaster: An American Life*, Kate Buford wrote that Smith was a welcome companion and seemed to calm the actor with her graceful manner. She had to endure take-after-take of the scene where the couple danced due to Lancaster's physical limitations.

The actress was back on television in the crime mystery miniseries *Dress Gray* shot on location in New Mexico and at the Warner Bros Hollywood studios and broadcast on March 9 and 10 on NBC. The teleplay was by Gore Vidal based on the novel by Lucian Truscott IV. The director was Glenn Jordan. The story centred on the murder of David Hand (Patrick Cassidy), a cadet at the U.S. Grant Military Academy. Smith is billed seventh among the alphabetically listed stars. She plays the role of Mrs. Iris Rylander, the wife of the Academy's Superintendent General Axel Rylander (Lloyd Bridges). Hair is by Jan Brandow and costumes by Shari Feldman and Lucille Cusolito. The actress only has two audible lines, otherwise she speaks in the background, and the part is negligible.

The show was nominated for Emmy Awards for Outstanding Miniseries, Outstanding Writing in a Miniseries or a Special and Outstanding Achievement in Costuming for a Miniseries or a Special. It received a mixed reaction from John J. O'Connor in *The New York Times* who wrote that Smith was wasted.

On April 26 she attended A Birthday Bash for Carol Burnett's 53rd Birthday held at UCLA's Pauley Pavilion in Westwood, California.

On October 10 it was reported that the actress had recently gone to a party at the Wyndham Hotel apartment of Suzanne and John Mados in New York to honor Robert Lindsay. He was the acclaimed star of the stage musical *For Me and My Girl* which had opened on Broadway on August 10.

On January 2, 1987, it was reported that she and Ann Miller were the front-runners to replace Carol Channing and Mary Martin in "Legends". The current stars were to leave the show after their final performance in Palm Beach on January 18. The new duo would begin rehearsals in mid-February for an opening somewhere in the following month. A Broadway run was hoped for afterward. The James Kirkwood comedy about two aging and battling film stars had toured the country from January, 1986. However, it was reported on January 1, 1988, that the plan for "Legends" to star Miller and Smith was abandoned apparently permanently.

She appeared in the television special *The 5th Annual American Cinema Awards* held at the Beverly Hilton Hotel and broadcast on January 30 on NBC.

On April 30 the actress attended the Hollywood Salutes The Kennedy Center Honorees Gala to Benefit The John F. Kennedy Center for the Performing Arts held at the Beverly Hilton Hotel.

On May 21 she appeared in a concert at the Theater Royal in London of "Nymph Errant". The Cole Porter musical with book by Romney Brent, based on the novel by James Laver, was first staged in England in 1933. The show told of the romantic adventures of Evangaline Edwards, a properly reared young woman who is lured by a French revue producer to the resort of Neauville. It was directed by Christopher Renshaw. Smith played the part of Clarissa and got the solo song "The Cocotte".

On June 20 it was reported that she would appear in a new dramatic television series to debut on June 30. "Hothouse" centred on a small family-owned psychiatric hospital. The show's creator was Jay Presson Allen with the actress playing the ex-wife of the doctor in charge, Sam Garrison (Josef Sommer). The premiere episode would be a two-hour opener and the following episodes would run for one hour for six weeks.

The first episode of *Hothouse* was entitled "The Good Family" and was written by Nina Shengold and directed by Stephen Gyllenhaal. It was broadcast on ABC. The story centred on Sheriff Joe Gates (Franklin Cover), an old friend of Sam whose wife Ida (Augusta Dabney) suffers from depression and kleptomania. In addition, the social worker Ginny Loudon (Madi Weland) feels that a patient is after her.

Smith is billed thirteen in the opening credits as part of the Family, after the Doctors and The Staff. She plays the part of Lily Garrison Shannon. The locale was New England. Lily is described as a fancy woman who left Sam to run off with a wealthy businessman after thirty-seven years of marriage. The show was lambasted by John J. O'Connor in *The New York Times*.

"The Subject of Sex" was broadcast on July 7. It was written by Donald Margulies and directed by Gyllenhaal, but Smith does not appear in this episode.

"The Actress" was broadcast on July 14. It was written by Jay Presson Allen and directed by Jeff Bleckner. An actress has a breakdown on the set of a movie. This episode originally served as the pilot for the show with the shooting title of "The Clinic."

"Nancy: Part 1" was broadcast on July 28. It was written by Jay Presson Allen and directed by Bill Hays. Nancy (Amy Locane), a sixteen--year-old patient of Dr. Art Makter (Michael Jeter) reminds him of a girl he had a crush on, and the friendship between Claudia Garrison (Susan Diol) and Lily's blossoms.

"Nancy: Part 2" was broadcast on August 4, written by Presson Allen, and directed by Bill Hays. Dr. Ved Lahari (Art Malik) talks to Art about his intense feelings for a patient, and Dr. Marie Teller (Michael Learned) doesn't know how to get through to Jakie Guyer (Nicholas Strouse).

"His Mother" was broadcast on August 11, and written by Presson Allen. It was directed by Jonathan Sanger. Marie wants Jakie's mother to come to the center, and Claudia complains about having no privacy.

"Love and Taxes" was broadcast on August 25, written by Presson Allen, and directed by Sanger. Sam wants his son to move back home from London.

HOTHOUSE

Alexis Smith portrays Sam's
ex-wife Lily.

Smith in still for *Hothouse*

On September 16 she attended a party at Halston's New York City residence celebrating the collaboration of Martha Graham with Mikhail Baryshnikov and Rudolf Nureyev.

On December 3 the actress was at the History of Hollywood Costume Exhibition held at the Natural History Museum of Los Angeles County in Los Angeles, California.

She appeared in the television movie *Marcus Welby, M.D.: A Holiday Affair* which was shot in October and broadcast on December 19 on NBC. This followed the television series *Marcus Welby, M.D.* that ran from 1969 to 1976. The new teleplay was by Steven Gethers who was also the director. The story had Welby (Robert Young) take a holiday to Europe where he finds romance with fifty-nine-year-old Tessa Menard (Smith), a wealthy American divorcée in Switzerland who runs a perfumery boutique in Paris.

She is billed second after the title and plays a supporting part. Hair is by Thomas Nellen and Diane Rietsch and costumes by Tin

Anderson. The actress looks thinner here, perhaps because Tessa is a former dancer and is health conscious about her diet.

She gets some funny lines. When Marcus comments he spent a short period of time in Paris, Tessa comments "No one should spend a short period of time in Paris." About the blind Anna Depuy (Delphine Forest), "She wants to dance. But she can't. What's she supposed to do – weave baskets?" Tessa tells Marcus her ex-husband was great in bed, "Not only with me I discovered". When Marcus tells her she is a very erotic woman, Tessa replies, "You are a very neurotic man."

However, she also gets some howlers. When Marcus asks for a last dinner before he goes home, Tessa tells him, "Last dinners are like What should we order before the execution? I don't believe in capital punishment." When a customer says she wants a perfume that is lively, Tessa tells her, "Maybe I can deliver Michael Jackson to your doorstep." She tells Anna to "Become an architect" and "Construct a mental floor plan of the world". And Tessa has an unfortunate line to her when she catches the girl dancing, "Well look at you."

The role sees her be a guide to the blind Anna, brush Anna's hair, laugh, run, speak French, hold hands with and kiss and be kissed by Marcus, and be kissed by Frank Poston (Craig Stevens). A ride in a hot air balloon has the possible use of a stunt double. This is the most sizeable part Smith has had in a long time. She makes Tessa funny. Tessa has some nice reflective moments as when she looks at herself in the mirror. The character also has dimension as demonstrated when Tessa is irritated at Anna's need for attention.

The actress commented that the movie was very much like a 1940s film. It was a mature love story, and it was high time it happened in the nation that venerated youth. It was lovely that some attention was being put upon older people as there were a lot of them around.

She made a guest appearance in the television comedy *Cheers* for the episode entitled "Sammy and the Professor" broadcast on

January 4, 1990, on NBC. It was shot at the Paramount Hollywood studios. The series centred on the regulars of the Boston bar Cheers where everybody knows your name. The episode was written by Brian Pollack and Mert Rich and was directed by James Burrows. It saw Alice Anne Volkman (Smith), the old college professor and mentor of Rebecca Howe (Kirstie Alley) come by the bar to meet up with her. She gets a Special Guest Star billing in the show's end credits. Hair is by Marilyn Patricia Phillips but there is no credited costume designer. The role sees her sleep with Sam Malone (Ted Danson) though it occurs off-screen.

Alice has some funny lines. She tells Rebecca, "You don't have to impress. You never have." Rebecca calls her a slut for sleeping with Sam, and Alice says, "That's the first time I've heard you make a stand without worrying about offending someone." Rebecca continues that Alice is a "soulless pig of a rotten slut", and Alice says, "Now I'm offended." The actress makes Alice funny though she is alarmingly thin. Smith was nominated for an Emmy Award for Outstanding Guest Actress In A Comedy Series.

On January 27 she attended the Seventh Annual American Cinema Awards held at the Beverly Hilton Hotel in Beverly Hills, California.

The actress returned to the television series *Dallas* for another recurring guest spot for the episode "Jessica Redux" broadcast on April 6. The teleplay was by Leonard Katzman and the director was Irving J. Moore. This time she is billed thirteen in the opening credits after the main cast. Clayton (Howard Keel) is told that Jessica has been released from the SunnyVale Sanitarium. She is heard on the telephone with him. Jessica is seen from the back, dressed as a maid who gives coffee to the policeman guard (Michael Francis Clark) of the hotel room where Clayton and Miss Ellie (Barbara Bel Geddes) are hiding. Then we see Jessica in the room holding a hypodermic needle.

"Family Plot" was broadcast on April 13. The teleplay is by Lisa Seldman and the director is Patrick Duffy. Jessica is trying to murder Clayton and she reveals that Dusty's father is Atticus Ward (John Larch). Jessica's gleeful admission to Clayton and the police of her murders demonstrates her emotional instability. She gets the crazy attitude of wanting to kill Clayton but telling him the poison would have been painless as Jessica wouldn't do anything to hurt him. The role sees her handling poison, and costumes include widow's black. Director Duffy gives us an extreme close-up of Smith's eyes and white-frosted camera for Jessica's memory.

Next was the two-part "Three, Three, Three". Part 1 was broadcast on May 4. The teleplay was by Leonard Katzman who was also the director. J.R. (Larry Hagman) has himself committed to an insane asylum to coerce Jessica into signing over to him her shares of WestStar stock. Part 2 was broadcast on May 11 and was also written and directed by Katzman. J.R. is successful in his plan. The episode sees her handled by guards and the actress is funny as Jessica primps her hair when awoken by J.J. at night. She asks, "Why couldn't you have picked a more respectable hour?" though still wears full make up and lipstick in bed.

Smith in still for *Dallas*

She appeared in the television documentary *Warner Bros. Celebration of Tradition* shot at the Warners Hollywood studios and broadcast on June 2. It was written by Diana Lowenstein and Stanley Ralph Ross and directed by Terry Donohue and Gary Halvorson.

On June 23 Smith attended the American Cinema Awards Foundation Hosts Senator George Murphy's 88th Birthday Party/65th Anniversary in Show Business held at the Regent Beverly Wilshire Hotel in Beverly Hills.

She was in the episode of the biographical documentary television series *American Masters* entitled "You're the Top: The Cole Porter Story" broadcast on July 23 on PBS. The show was written and directed by Allan Albert and was a portrait of one of Broadway's most brilliant songwriters. The actress talked about *Night And Day* and the day Porter visited the set. The show received a mixed reaction from Walter Goodman in *The New York Times*.

Smith was next in the made for TV movie comedy *Lola* aka *Escape from 212* broadcast on August 1 on CBS. It had a teleplay by Chris Thompson and was directed by Ellen Gittelsohn. Lola Baltic (Lesley Ann Warren) was a New York businesswoman who trades Wall Street for suburban Connecticut but finds country life has its own absurdities. The actress played the part of Phoebe.

On September 16 she attended the 42nd Annual Primetime Emmy Awards held at the Pasadena Civic Auditorium in Pasadena, California. This was presumably because of her Emmy Award nomination for the guest appearance on *Cheers*.

On April 18, 1991, Smith was at the opening night of *A Little Night Music* held at the James A. Doolittle Theatre in Hollywood, California. On May 1 she attended the opening night of *The Will Rogers Follies* at the Palace Theatre in New York City.

On June 9 the actress appeared in a musical revue at Carnegie Hall to celebrate the 100th anniversary of Cole Porter's birth. This was part of the 1991 New York Festival of the Arts.

On December 10 she attended the Glitter and Be Giving Fine Jewelry Auction to Benefit AmfAR held at the Regent Beverly Wilshire Hotel in Beverly Hills.

Her next and what would be last appearance in film was the romance *The Age Of Innocence* (1993). It was shot on locations in New York and Paris and Philadelphia and at the Kaufman Astoria studios in New York from March 24 to June 26, 1992. The Edith Wharton novel had been previously filmed as a Warner Bros. 1924 silent and an RKO 1934 talkie. The new screenplay was by Jay Cocks and Martin Scorsese with Scorsese also the director. The story was set in 1870s New York. It told how lawyer Newland Archer (Daniel-Day Lewis) falls in love with Ellen Olenska (Michelle Pfeiffer) while he is engaged to her cousin May Welland (Winona Ryder).

Smith is billed fourteenth after the title since the supporting players are billed alphabetically. She plays Louisa van der Luyden, the wife of Henry (Michael Gough), the most powerful figures in New York society. The character apparently does not appear in either earlier film. The actress presumably wore a wig by Peter Owen and costumes were by Gabriella Pescucci. The part is negligible, but she looks pale, and her teeth are period yellow like the other characters.

The film premiered at the Venice Film Festival on August 31, 1993, and then given a wide release on October 1. The tagline was "In a world of tradition. In an age of innocence. They dared to break the rules." It was a box office success. The film won the Academy Award for Best Costume Design. It was nominated for Best Supporting Actress for Ryder, Best Writing, Screenplay Based on Material Previously Produced or Published, Best Art Direction-Set Decoration, and Best Music, Original Score. The film received a mixed reaction from Todd McCarthy in *Variety* but was praised by Vincent Canby in *The New York Times* and Roger Ebert in the *Chicago Sun-Times*.

Smith commented that her billing was bigger than the role.

In 1992 she and Craig Stevens did a reading of the A.R. Gurney play *Love Letters* as a benefit.

The actress was admitted to a hospital near her home in California for minor female surgery that was meant to be just an overnight stay. But it was discovered she had double vision after the operation. Test results showed that Smith had a brain tumor which was successfully removed. Frances Rafferty reported that she visited her friend after the tumor operation. Smith wanted Rafferty to see all the well-wishing cards she had received. Doctors said the prognosis was healthy and the actress was released from hospital.

Craig Stevens said his wife was doing great – eating and looking fine. She underwent radiation treatment, and it was thought the condition was under control. Smith was said to be cheery and very positive.

On February 17, 1993 she was photographed arriving at the Los Angeles International Airport.

On April 10 it was reported the actress had recently attended a party held by Rosemary Clooney in Beverly Hills to honor the release of Dolores Reade Hope's first album.

A friend gave Smith and Craig Stevens about twenty-six of their films on videocassette to watch. However, they didn't look at any of them. He specifically wanted her to watch *The Constant Nymph*, but she refused. Stevens said this was because his wife didn't care about the past. What she was interested in was the future and what new things could be learned.

Then on Sunday of the Memorial Day weekend of May the actress fell apart. She couldn't handle herself and neither could her husband. He had a hard time getting the doctor, but they got Smith to a hospital. The doctors discovered that cancer had spread throughout her entire body. She took it well. The actress lasted another week, on oxygen. It was said she didn't suffer and that was the one thing Stevens was grateful for.

They celebrated Smith's seventy-second birthday on June 8 with her husband saying she looked fifty-two. The actress died at the Cedars-Sinai Hospital in Los Angeles on June 9, one day after her birthday. By Smith's side was her husband of nearly forty-nine years, Frances Rafferty, and Rafferty's daughter. Stevens was the sole survivor.

There was an obituary by Ronald Sullivan in June 10 of *The New York Times*. He defined her as a Hollywood actress of the 1940's and 50's who later won a Tony Award as a star of the Broadway musical *Follies*. She had an image as a strong-willed actress who often played tempestuous romantic leads opposite many of Hollywood's most glamourous male stars. Smith was known for her beauty, with penetrating blue-green eyes and a low, throaty voice. But she managed to submerge it when asked to play a vengeful woman or a cold, calculating seductress. On stage and film sets, the actress was widely known as an easygoing professional who loved her craft. She was a favorite among crews and stagehands.

Smith was cremated and her ashes scattered over the Pacific Ocean, 3 miles off San Pedro, California.

In his 1994 *Films in Review* two-part profile of the actress Jerry Vermilye reported that a local New York television station ignorantly accompanied her obituary with photographs of Jane Wyman. They later apologized for the error.

In September Craig Stevens was interviewed by Skip E. Lowe for cable television. Stevens reported how losing his wife was just impossible and the worse experience he had ever gone through. It was harder than losing his parents because Stevens and Smith were so close. It was now so lonesome. All he could do was put one foot in front of the other every day and just do the best possible. Stevens was sure he would never get over the loss but had to learn how to live with it. Life had to go on.

She had no star on the Hollywood Walk of Fame. This was particularly galling because of how long the actress had been in the industry and how he considered her a major star in film and theatre. She had not been recognised yet there were people he had never heard of, like rock stars, who had been given stars. Smith didn't care about not being offered one as she was never really pushy about publicity. Previously Stevens had disinclined to ask for one for her but now he would do everything possible to make it happen. The actor quipped he would go there and dig the hole himself. Stevens refused to pay since he said that was not what it was about. However, to date there is no star for her.

As a couple they hadn't socialised a lot though they had a lot of friends in the business. They also had friends in all works of life. The couple had no children but had six godchildren Stevens felt they had practically raised. This is because the children would go to the couple for help before their own parents. His happiest memories with his wife came from the fact that they had grown up together. This was very rare, and they had shared so much.

The actress was included in the In Memoriam part of *The 66th Academy Awards* held on March 21 at the Dorothy Chandler Pavilion in Hollywood.

Appendix

Shorts

Alice in Movieland (1946). Part: Herself.
So You Want to Be in Pictures (1947). Part: Herself.
Camera Angles (1948). Part: Herself.

Films

"She Couldn't Say No" (1940)
"Flight From Destiny" (1941)
The Great Mr. Nobody (1941)
Here Comes Happiness (1941)
"Affectionately Yours" (1941)
"Singapore Woman" (1941). Part: Uncredited Miss Oswald.
Three Sons o' Guns (1941). Part: Actress
"Dive Bomber" (1941). Part: Linda Fisher.
"The Smiling Ghost" (1941). Elinor Bentley Fairchild.
Passage from Hong Kong (1941). Part: Uncredited Nightclub Dancer.
"Steel Against The Sky" (1941). Part: Helen Powers.
"Gentleman Jim" (1942). Part: Victoria Ware.
"The Constant Nymph" (1943). Part: Florence Creighton.
"Thank Your Lucky Stars" (1943). Part: Herself.
"The Adventures of Mark Twain" (1944). Part: Olivia Langdon
    Clemens.
The Doughgirls (1944). Part: Nan Curtis Dillon.
hollywood canteen (1944). Part: Herself.
"The Horn Blow At Midnight" (1945). Part: Elizabeth.
"Conflict" (1945). Part: Evelyn Turner.

"Rhapsody In Blue" (The Story of George Gershwin) (1945). Part: Christine Gilbert.

"San Antonio" (1945). Part: Jeanne Starr.

"One More Tomorrow" (1946). Part: Cecelie Henry.

Night And Day (1946). Part: Linda Lee Porter.

W. Somerset Maugham's Of Human Bondage (1946). Part: Nora Nesbit.

"The Two Mrs. Carrolls" (1947). Part: Cecily Latham.

Stallion Road (1947). Part: Rory Teller.

"Always Together" (1947). Part: Uncredited The Bride.

"The Woman In White" (1948). Part: Marian Halcombe.

"The Decision of Christopher Blake" (1948). Part: Evelyn Blake.

"Whiplash" (1948). Part: Laurie Durant.

"South Of St. Louis" (1949). Part: Rouge de Lisle.

"One Last Fling" (1949). Part: Olivia Pearce.

Any Number Can Play (1949). Part: Lon Kyng.

"Montana" (1950). Part: Maria Singleton.

Wyoming Mail (1950). Part: Mary Williams.

Undercover Girl (1950). Part: Christine Miller.

Frank Capra's Here Comes The Groom (1951). Part: Winifred Stanley.

Cave Of Outlaws (1951). Part: Elizabeth Trent.

The Turning Point (1952). Part: Amanda Waycross.

Split Second (1953). Part: Kay Garven.

The Sleeping Tiger (1954). Part: Glenda Esmond.

The Eternal Sea (1955). Part: Sue Hoskins.

Beau James: The Life and Times of Jimmy Walker (1957). Part: Allie Walker.

This Happy Feeling (1958). Part: Nita Hollaway.

The Young Philadelphians (1959). Part: Carol Wharton.

"Jacqueline Susann's Once is Not Enough" (1975). Part: Deidre Milford Granger.

Busby Berkeley (1974). Part: Herself.

Intriga de otros mundos (1974). Part: Unknown.

The Little Girl Who Lives Down The Lane (1976). Part: Mrs. Hallet.

Casey's Shadow (1978). Part: Sarah Blue.

La Truite (1982). Part: Gloria.

Tough Guys (1986). Part: Bella.

The Age Of Innocence (1993). Part: Louisa van der Luyden.

Radio

Lux Radio Theatre: "The Constant Nymph" (January 10, 1944). Part: Florence Creighton.

The Jack Benny Program For Grape-Nuts and Grape-Nuts Flakes (January 16, 1944). Part: Herself.

The Screen Guild Theater: "Gentleman Jim" (February 14, 1944). Part: Victoria Ware.

The Screen Guild Theater: "The Constant Nymph" (March 10, 1944). Part: Florence Creighton.

Lux Radio Theater: "Old Acquaintance" (May 29, 1944). Part: Kit.

Command Performance (March 1, 1945). Part: Herself.

The Screen Guild Theater: "My Reputation" (July 7, 1947). Part: Jessica.

Lux Radio Theater: "One More Tomorrow" (June 9, 1947). Part: Cecelia Henry.

Lux Radio Theater: "Stallion Road" (October 4, 1948). Part: Rory Teller.

Command Performance (October 18, 1949). Part: Herself.

The Screen Guild Theater: "Any Number Can Play" (October 12, 1950). Part: Lon Kyng.

Twenty Questions (September 22, 1951). Part: Herself.

Bing Crosby Chesterfield Show (November 21, 1951). Part: Herself.

Family Theater: "Grandpa's Marvelous X-Ray" (November 28, 1951). Part: Hostess.

Bing Crosby Chesterfield Show (December 12, 1951). Part: Herself.

The Dean Martin And Jerry Lewis Show (January 25, 1952). Part: Herself.

Stars Over Hollywood: "It's a Man's Game" (November 1, 1952). Part: Susan Douglas.

Lux Radio Theater: "Submarine Command" (November 17, 1952). Part: Carol.

WMCA (April 2, 1978). Part: Herself.

Theatre

Private Lives (dates unknown, 1952). York and Lakewood Park Theatre in Barnesville, Pennsylvania. Part: Unknown.

Bell, Book and Candle (dates unknown, 1953). Lakewood Park Theatre in Barnesville, Pennsylvania; Ogunquit Playhouse in Ogunquit, Maine. Part: Unknown.

Plain and Fancy (August 29, 1955 – February 11, 1956). Los Angeles Philharmonic Auditorium, Chicago. Part: Ruth Winters.

Wonderful Town (July, 1957). Paul Winston's Music Theatre Memorial Hall, Dayton, Ohio. Part: Ruth.

Critic's Choice (September, 1961 - date unknown, 1962). Tour. Part: Unknown.

Mary, Mary (Summer, 1965). Veterans Memorial Theatre, Columbus and Packard Music Hall Theatre, Warren, Ohio.

The Coffee Lover (August 8 to September 3, 1966). Westport Country Playhouse, Connecticut; Falmouth Playhouse, Massachusetts; Ogunquit Playhouse, Maine.

Cactus Flower (August, 1968 to March 1, 1969). Ogunquit Playhouse, Maine; National Tour. Part: Stephanie.

Follies (April 4, 1971 to July 1, 1972). Wintergarden Theatre, New York. (July 2 to 9). St. Louis Municipal Opera House, Missouri. (July 22 to October 1). Shubert Theatre, Los Angeles. Part: Phyllis Rogers Stone.

Party Musical (March 10, 1973). Shubert Theatre, New York. Part: Herself.

The Women (April 25 to June 17, 1973). 46th Street Theatre, New York. Part: Sylvia.

Golden Olden Days of Burlesque (June 4, 1973). Roseland Dance City. Part: Herself.

Applause (August 14 to unknown). Dayton, Ohio. Part: Margo Channing.

Summer Brave (September 18, 1975 to Unknown). Eisenhower Theatre, Washington. (October 26 to November 9, 1975). ANTA Theatre, New York. Part: Rosemary Sydney.

The 24th Annual Milliken Breakfast Show: "Who Dunnit" (June, 1977). Waldorf-Astroria Hotel Grand Ballroom, New York. Part: Store President.

Sunset (September, 1977). Studio Arena Theater, Buffalo, New York. Part: Lila Halliday.

Platinum (September 11, 1978 to unknown). Philadelphia. (September 28 to October 28, 1978). Kennedy Center, Washington. (November 12 to December 10, 1978). Mark Hellinger Theatre, New York. Part: Lila Halliday.

The Best Little Whorehouse in Texas. National Tour. (September 29, 1979 to November 04, 1979). Shubert Theatre at the Boch Center, Boston, Massachusetts. (November 06, 1979 to December 16, 1979). Forrest Theatre, Philadelphia, Pennsylvania. (December 18, 1979 to January 06, 1980). Jackie Gleason Theater Of Performing Arts, Miami, Florida. (January 08, 1980 to January 20, 1980). Fox Theatre, Atlanta, Georgia. (January 22, 1980 to March 02, 1980). Warner Theatre, Washington, DC. (March 04, 1980 to May 18, 1980). Fisher Theatre, Detroit, Michigan. (May 20, 1980 to August 03, 1980). CIBC Theatre, Chicago, Illinois. (August 05, 1980 to August 16, 1980). Ellie Caulkins Opera House, Denver, Colorado. (August 19, 1980 to September 28, 1980). Golden Gate Theatre, San Francisco, California. (September 30, 1980 to November 22, 1980). Pantages Theatre - Los Angeles, California. (November 25, 1980 to December 14, 1980) Copley, San Diego,

California. (December 30, 1980 to February 01, 1981). Wilshire Theatre, Los Angeles, California. Part: Mona Stangley.

The Visit (Dates unknown, Summer, 1981). Unknown theatre, Canada. Part: Claire Zachanassian.

Broadway Salutes Sage (September 5, 1982). Fire Island Pines Pavilion, New York. Part: Herself.

Pal Joey (June 28 to July 10, 1983). Music Hall at Fair Park, Dallas, Texas. (July 12 to July 17, 1983). Atlanta Civic Center, Atlanta, Georgia. (July 18 to July 24, 1983). St. Louis Municipal Opera House, St. Louis, Missouri. (July 26 to July 31, 1983). E. J. Thomas Hall, Akron, Ohio. Part: Vera Simpson.

Nymph Errant (May 21, 1989). Theater Royal, London. Part: Unknown.

Cole Porter's 100th Birthday Celebration (June 9, 1991). Carnegie Hall, New York. Part: Herself.

Television

The Star and The Story: "W. Somerset Maugham's The Back of Beyond" (March 5, 1955). Part: Violet Saffrey.

Stage 7: "To Kill a Man" (March 6, 1955). Part: Caroline Taylor.

The 20th Century-Fox Hour: "The Hefferan Family" (June 13, 1956). Part: Emily Hefferan.

Robert Montgomery Presents: "September Affair" (October 8, 1956). Part: Unknown.

Lux Video Theatre: "The Gay Sisters" (November 22, 1956). Part: Fiona.

Lux Video Theatre: "To Have and Have Not" (January 17, 1957). Part: Herself.

Lux Video Theatre: "Death Do Us Part" (May 16, 1957). Part: Lilly.

The Steve Allen Plymouth Show (June 30, 1957). Part: Herself.

Schlitz Playhouse: "I Shot A Prowler" (March 28, 1958). Part: Vivian Braxton.

The United States Steel Hour: "The Last Autumn" (November 18, 1959). Part: Barbara Welch.

James A. Michener's Adventures in Paradise: "Somewhere South of Suva" (December 28, 1959). Part: Loraine Lucas.

Person to Person (May 20, 1960). Part: Herself.

To Tell the Truth (September 21 – 25, 1964). Part: Herself.

Michael Shayne: "A Night with Nora" (October 7, 1960). Part: Nora Carroll.

The Defenders: "Impeachment" (March 18, 1965). Part: Carol Defoe.

To Tell the Truth (March 29 – April 2, 1965). Part: Herself.

Gypsy (July 2, 1965). Part: Herself.

The Mike Douglas Show (February 26, 1969). Part: Herself.

The Governor & J.J.: "State of Reunion" (December 9, 1969). Part: Leslie Carroll.

The Governor & J.J.: "Once Upon a War" (January 6, 1970). Part: Leslie Carroll.

The Tonight Show Starring Johnny Carson (June 11, 1971). Part: Herself.

The David Frost Show (June 23, 1971). Part: Herself.

The Dick Cavett Show (August 5, 1971). Part: Herself.

The Dick Cavett Show (January 6, 1972). Part: Herself.

The Tonight Show Starring Johnny Carson (April 4, 1972). Part: Herself.

The Dick Cavett Show (April 17, 1972). Part: Herself.

The 26th Annual Tony Awards (April 23, 1972). Part: Herself.

The Dick Cavett Show (June 22, 1972). Part: Herself.

The Tonight Show Starring Johnny Carson (July 28, 1972). Part: Herself.

The Merv Griffin Show (July 31, 1972). Part: Herself.

This Is Your Life (September 24, 1972). Part: Herself.

Rowan & Martin's Laugh-In (September 25, 1972). Part: Herself.

The Bob Hope Special (October 5, 1972). Part: Herself.

The Tonight Show Starring Johnny Carson (November 30, 1972). Part: Herself.

The 27th Annual Tony Awards (March 25, 1973). Part: Herself.

Nightside (April 15, 1973). Part: Smitty.

The Tonight Show Starring Johnny Carson (May 21, 1973). Part Herself.

The Annual National Sports Awards (February 4, 1974). Part: Herself.

The Merv Griffin Show (April 1, 1974). Part: Herself.

ABC Late Night: "That's Entertainment: 50 Years of MGM" (May 29, 1974). Part: Herself.

The Lives of Benjamin Franklin: "The Ambassador" (November 21, 1974). Part: Madame Helvetius.

The 29th Annual Tony Awards (April 20, 1975). Part: Herself.

The Mike Douglas Show (April 21, 1975). Part: Herself.

Salute to Sir Lew - The Master Showman (June 13, 1975). Part: Herself.

Your Choice for the Film Awards (March 27, 1976). Part: Herself.

Bicentennial Minutes (June 23, 1976). Part: Herself.

The Merv Griffin Show (November 13, 1978). Part: Herself.

Today (November 21, 1978). Part: Herself.

The 33rd Annual Tony Awards (June 3, 1979). Part: Herself.

Over Easy (January 14, 1980). Part: Herself.

The Merv Griffin Show (November 20, 1980). Part: Herself.

Hour Magazine (November 25, 1980). Part: Herself.

Night Of 100 Stars (March 8, 1982). Part: Herself.

Broadway Plays Washington on Kennedy Center Tonight (March 13, 1982). Part: Herself.

The Love Boat: "The Spoonmaker Diamond/Papa Doc/The Role Model/Julie's Tycoon" Part 1 and 2. (November 13, 1982. Part: Amanda Blake.

Showstoppers: The Best of Broadway (date unknown, 1982). Part: Herself.

Cinema Showcase (July 14, 1983). Part: Herself.

Dallas: "The Unexpected" (March 16, 1984). "Strange Alliance" (March 23, 1984). "Blow Up" (April 5, 1984). "Turning Point"

(April 13, 1984). "Love Stories" (May 4, 1984). Part: Jessica Montford.

The Love Boat: "Dreamboat/Gopher, Isaac & the Starlet/The Parents/ The Importance of Being Johnny/Julie and the Producer" (May 5, 1984). Part: Angela Lovett.

Dallas: "Hush, Hush, Sweet Jessie" (May 11, 1984). "End Game" (May 18, 1984). Part: Jessica Montford.

The Hollywood Reporter Salutes Radie Harris (March 21, 1985). Part: Herself.

A Death In California (May 12, 1985). Part: Honey Niven.

The Love Boat: "The German Cruise: The Villa/The Racer's Edge/ Love or Money/The Accident" (November 2, 1985). Part: Justina Downey.

The 2th Annual American Cinema Awards (November 22, 1985). Part: Herself.

Dress Gray (March 9 and 10, 1986). Part: Mrs. Iris Rylander.

The 5th Annual American Cinema Awards (January 30, 1987). Part: Herself.

Hothouse: "The Good Family" (June 30, 1988). "The Actress" (July 14, 1988). "Nancy: Part 1" (July 28, 1988). "Nancy: Part 2" (August 4, 1988). "His Mother" (August 11, 1988). "Love and Taxes" (August 25, 1988). Part: Lily Garrison Shannon.

Marcus Welby, M.D.: A Holiday Affair (December 19, 1988). Part: Tessa Menard.

Cheers: "Sammy and the Professor" (January 4, 1990). Part: Alice Anne Volkman.

Dallas: "Jessica Redux" (April 6, 1990). "Family Plot" (April 13,1990). "Three, Three, Three: Part 1" (May 4, 1990). "Three, Three, Three: Part 2" (May 11, 1990). Part: Jessica Montfort.

Warner Bros. Celebration of Tradition (June 2, 1990). Part: Herself.

American Masters: "You're the Top: The Cole Porter Story" (July 23, 1990). Part: Herself.

Lola (August 1, 1990). Part: Phoebe.

Recordings

Follies Original Broadway Cast (1971).
Sondheim: A Musical Tribute (1973).
Platinum (1978).
Nymph Errant (1989).

Bibliography

Abel. "Night and Day". *Variety*. July 10, 1946. Retrieved June 25, 2023 from http://www.variety.com.

Adams, Val. "Pat Hingle Is Cast". *The New York Times*. September 29, 1959. Retrieved July 31, 2023 from http://www.nytimes.com.

Alexander, Ron. "The Honored Guests Were Jewels." *The New York Times*. December 1, 1982. Retrieved August 27, 2023 from http://www.nytimes.com.

__________. "Opulent Opening Party for 'La Cage'". *The New York Times.* August 23, 1983. Retrieved August 28, 2023 from http://www.nytimes.com.

Archerd, Army. "Showbiz family will miss Alexis Smith." *Variety*. June 10, 1993. Retrieved September 9, 2023 from http://www.variety.com.

Arden, Eve. *Three Phases Of Eve: An Autobiography*. New York: St. Martin's Press, 1985.

Arnold, Jeremy. "Article: The Constant Nymph." *Turner Classic Movies*. June 3, 2011. Retrieved June 5, 2023 from http://www.tcm.com.

__________. "Article: The Two Mrs. Carrolls." *Turner Classic Movies*. July 27, 2005. Retrieved June 24, 2023 from http://www.tcm.com.

__________. "Article: Montana." *Turner Classic Movies*. June 17, 2014. Retrieved July 4, 2023 from http://www.tcm.com.

__________. "Article: Any Number Can Play." *Turner Classic Movies*. October 27, 2004. Retrieved July 5, 2023 from http://www.tcm.com.

Astor, Mary. *A Life on Film*. Delacorte Press, 1971.

A.W. "At the Capitol." *The New York Times*. July 1, 1949. Retrieved July 5, 2023 from http://www.nytimes.com.

___. "The Screen In Review." *The New York Times*. October 23, 1950. Retrieved July 8, 2023 from http://www.nytimes.com.

Barbour, Alan G. *Humphrey Bogart. Illustrated History Of The Movies*. London: W. H. Allen, 1974.

Barnes, Clive. "Stage: 'Follies' Couples. Years Later." *The New York Times*. April 5, 1971. Retrieved August 5, 2023 from http://www.nytimes.com.

__________. "Stage: A Not So Naughty 'Women'". *The New York Times*. April 26, 1973. Retrieved August 13, 2023 from http://www.nytimes.com.

Bawden, James and Miller, Ron. *Conversations with Classic Movie Stars. Interviews From Hollywood's Golden Era.* Lexington, KY: University Press of Kentucky, 2016.

Berkvist, Robert. "'Platinum'". *The New York Times*. November 12, 1978. Retrieved August 22, 2023 from http://www.nytimes.com.

Blau, Eleanor. "TV Notes: 'Hothouse' Drama." *The New York Times*. June 20, 1988. Retrieved September 3, 2023 from http://www.nytimes.com.

Bogarde, Dirk. *Snakes And Ladders*. London: Chatto and Windus, 1978.

Bookbinder. Robert. *The Films of Bing Crosby*. Secaucus, N.J.: Citadel Press, 1977.

Brady, Thomas F. "3 Author's Work…". *The New York Times*. August 1, 1947. Retrieved June 29, 2023 from http://www.nytimes.com.

__________. "WARNERS REPLACE DIRECTOR." *The New York Times*. August 18, 1947. Retrieved June 29, 2023 from http://www.nytimes.com.

__________. "U-I WILL PRODUCE WESTERN." *The New York Times*. January 8, 1948. Retrieved June 30, 2023 from http://www.nytimes.com.

__________. "-- Elkins to Do 'Sunburst'". *The New York Times*. February 27, 1948. Retrieved July 1, 2023 from http://www.nytimes.com.

__________. "SANTANA TO FILM STORY OF CONVICT." *The New York Times*. May 26, 1948. Retrieved July 1, 2023 from http://www.nytimes.com.

__________. "ALEXIS SMITH GETS LEAD IN METRO." *The New York Times*. December 24, 1948. Retrieved July 4, 2023 from http://www.nytimes.com.

__________. "LEAD IN RKO FILM." *The New York Times*. March 29, 1949. Retrieved July 6, 2023 from http://www.nytimes.com.

__________. "FOX BUYS RIGHTS." *The New York Times*. April 11, 1949. Retrieved July 6, 2023 from http://www.nytimes.com.

__________. "MYRNA LOY MAY DO LEAD." *The New York Times*. September 21, 1949. Retrieved July 6, 2023 from http://www.nytimes.com.

__________. "LEE J. COBB TO BOW." *The New York Times*. April 16, 1950. Retrieved July 6, 2023 from http://www.nytimes.com.

__________. "PREMINGER SIGNS NEW FOX CONTRACT." *The New York Times*. June 28, 1950. Retrieved June 27, 2023 from http://www.nytimes.com.

__________. "METRO WILL FILM OLD CAPRA STORY." *The New York Times*. November 20, 1950. Retrieved July 9, 2023 from http://www.nytimes.com.

__________. "METRO IS LIMITING 'RED BADGE'". *The New York Times*. March 7, 1951. Retrieved July 12, 2023 from http://www.nytimes.com.

__________. "MAYER IS REPORTED LEAVING FILM POST." *The New York Times*. April 6, 1951. Retrieved July 12, 2023 from http://www.nytimes.com.

__________. "LADD, PARAMOUNT DISCUSS CONTRACT." *The New York Times*. September 13, 1951. Retrieved July 12, 2023 from http://www.nytimes.com.

Brog. "Film Reviews." *Variety*. June 13, 1945. Retrieved June 13, 2023 from http://www.variety.com.

___. "Film Reviews." *Variety.* January 4, 1950. Retrieved July 4, 2023 from http://www.variety.com.

Brozan, Nadine. "The Evening Hours." *The New York Times.* October 10, 1986. Retrieved September 3, 2023 from http://www.nytimes.com.

___________. "Chronicle." *The New York Times.* April 10, 1993. Retrieved September 9, 2023 from http://www.nytimes.com.

Bubbeo, Daniel. *The Women of Warner Brothers. The Lives And Careers Of 15 Leading Ladies.* Jefferson, NC: McFarland, 2002.

Buckley. Tom. "At The Movies…She felt just a bit uneasy.. " *The New York Times.* April 14, 1978. Retrieved August 21, 2023 from http://www.nytimes.com.

_______________________________. *The New York Times.* June 3, 1978. Retrieved August 21, 2023 from http://www.nytimes.com.

Buford, Kate. *Burt Lancaster: An American Life.* Cambridge, MA : Da Capo Press, 2001.

Calta, Louis. "…Considerable progress…. *The New York Times.* June 18, 1955. Retrieved July 20, 2023 from http://www.nytimes.com.

___________. "… "Follies". *The New York Times.* May 29, 1972. Retrieved August 11, 2023 from http://www.nytimes.com.

Canby, Vincent. "Film:If Once Is Not Enough,Then . . . " *The New York Times.* June 19, 1975. Retrieved August 14, 2023 from http://www.nytimes.com.

___________. "Film: Matthau in 'Casey's Shadow'". *The New York Times.* March 17, 1978. Retrieved August 20, 2023 from http://www.nytimes.com.

___________. "Review/Film." *The New York Times.* September 17, 1993. Retrieved September 8, 2023 from http://www.nytimes.com.

Cannon, Lou. *Governor Reagan: His Rise To Power.* New York : Public Affairs, 2003.

Capra, Frank. *The Name Above The Title*. New York, Macmillan, 1971.

Capua, Michelangelo. *Jean Negulesco: The Life and Films*. Jefferson, NC: McFarland, 2017.

Cars. "San Antonio". *Variety*. November 21, 1945. Retrieved June 21, 2023 from http://www.variety.com.

Casper, Drew Dr. and Sherman, Vincent. The Young Philadelphians DVD Audio Commentary. Warner Bros, 2014.

Cassa, Anthony. "Alexis Smith – A star who has it all together." *Hollywood Studio Magazine*. March, 1981: 13 – 15.

Caute, David. *Joseph Losey: A Revenge on Life*. London: Faber, 1994.

Chapin, Ted. *Everything Was Possible: The Birth of the Musical Follies*. New York : Applause Theatre & Cinema Books, 2005.

Ciment, Michael. *Conversations With Losey*. London; New York: Methuen, 1985.

Coldstream, John. *Dirk Bogarde: The Authorised Biography*. London: Weidenfeld & Nicolson, 2004.

Collins, Glenn. "Festival Of Arts." *The New York Times*. February 27, 1991. Retrieved September 7, 2023 from http://www.nytimes.com.

Corry, John. "Broadway." *The New York Times*. June 4, 1976. Retrieved August 19, 2023 from http://www.nytimes.com.

__________. ________________________. December 16, 1977. Retrieved August 20, 2023 from http://www.nytimes.com.

________________________. November 24, 1978. Retrieved August 22, 2023 from http://www.nytimes.com.

________________________. April 13, 1979. Retrieved August 22, 2023 from http://www.nytimes.com.

__________. "Feistiness of Lauren Bacall Is Still Film and Stage." *The New York Times*. July 10, 1980. Retrieved August 23, 2023 from http://www.nytimes.com.

__________. "TV Weekend: In 'Best of Broadway'" *The New York Times*. May 3, 1985. Retrieved August 30, 2023 from http://www.nytimes.com.

Cox, Amy. "Article: "The Doughgirls." *Turner Classic Movies*. July 27, 2005. Retrieved June 17, 2023 from http://www.tcm.com.

Crowther, Bosley. "…'Lady With Red Hair,' at the Palace." *2. New York Times*. December 6, 1940. Retrieved September 13, 2022 from http3://www.nytimes.com.

__________. "" Dive Bomber"". *The New York Times*. August 30, 1941. Retrieved May 31, 2023 from http://www.nytimes.com.

__________. "Poor Ghost." *The New York Times*. September 26, 1941. Retrieved June 2, 2023 from http://www.nytimes.com.

__________. "" Thank Your Lucky Stars"". *The New York Times*. October 2, 1943. Retrieved June 8, 2023 from http://www.nytimes.com.

__________. "The Screen." *The New York Times*. May 4, 1944. Retrieved June 10, 2023 from http://www.nytimes.com.

__________. "THE SCREEN; 'Horn Blows at Midnight'". *The New York Times*. April 21, 1945. Retrieved June 15, 2023 from http://www.nytimes.com.

__________. "THE SCREEN; 'Conflict'". *The New York Times*. June 16, 1945. Retrieved June 13, 2023 from http://www.nytimes.com.

__________. "THE SCREEN; 'Rhapsody in Blue'". *The New York Times*. June 28, 1945. Retrieved June 15, 2023 from http://www.nytimes.com.

__________. "" Hollywood Canteen"". *The New York Times*. December 16, 1944. Retrieved June 17, 2023 from http://www.nytimes.com.

__________. "THE SCREEN." *The New York Times*. December 29, 1945. Retrieved June 21, 2023 from http://www.nytimes.com.

__________. "THE SCREEN; 'Of Human Bondage'". *The New York Times*. July 6, 1946. Retrieved June 18, 2023 from http://www.nytimes.com.

__________. "' The Two Mrs. Carrolls'". *The New York Times.* April 7, 1947. Retrieved June 24, 2023 from http://www.nytimes.com.

__________. "' Stallion Road'". *The New York Times.* April 5, 1947. Retrieved June 27, 2023 from http://www.nytimes.com.

__________. "The Screen." *The New York Times.* December 11, 1947. Retrieved June 29, 2023 from http://www.nytimes.com.

__________. "' The Woman in White'". *The New York Times.* May 8, 1948. Retrieved June 28, 2023 from http://www.nytimes.com.

__________. "THE SCREEN IN REVIEW." *The New York Times.* December 11, 1948. Retrieved June 30, 2023 from http://www.nytimes.com.

__________. "'South of St. Louis'". *The New York Times.* March 7, 1949. Retrieved July 3, 2023 from http://www.nytimes.com.

__________. "THE SCREEN." *The New York Times.* February 4, 1950. Retrieved July 4, 2023 from http://www.nytimes.com.

__________. "THE SCREEN IN REVIEW." *The New York Times.* September 21, 1951. Retrieved July 11, 2023 from http://www.nytimes.com.

__________. "Screen: 'Happy Feeling'". *The New York Times.* June 19, 1958. Retrieved July 28, 2023 from http://www.nytimes.com.

Curtis, Charlotte. "Dinner at the White House." *The New York Times.* October 19, 1982. Retrieved August 26, 2023 from http://www.nytimes.com.

Davis, Ronald L. *Zachary Scott: Hollywood's Sophisticated Cad (Hollywood Legends Series).* University Press of Mississippi, 2013.

Deschner, Donald. *The Films of Cary Grant.* Secaucus, N. J.: Citadel, 1975.

De Vries, Peter. "Show Business: The Once and Future Follies." *Time.* May 3, 1971. Retrieved August 10, 2023 from http://www.content.time.com.

Dietz, Dan. *The Complete Book Of 1970s Broadway Musicals*. New York: Rowman & Littlefield, 2015.

Dixon, Wheeler Winston. *The Films of Reginald LeBorg: Interviews, Essays, and Filmography*. Metuchen, N.J.: Scarecrow Press, 1992.

D'Onofrio, Joseph. "Article: Night And Day." *Turner Classic Movies*. December 22, 2003. Retrieved June 25, 2023 from http://www.tcm.com.

Douglas, Kirk. *The Ragman's Son: An Autobiography*. New York: Pocket Books, 1989.

Duka, John. "Elizabeth Taylor Previews at a Party." *The New York Times*. April 27, 1981. Retrieved August 24, 2023 from http://www.nytimes.com.

Eames, John Douglas. *The MGM Story: The Complete History Of Over Fifty Roaring Years*. New York : Crown Publishers, 1975.

__________________. *The Paramount Story. The Complete History Of The Studio And Its 2,805 Films*. London: Octopus Books, 1985.

Ebert, Roger. "Reviews: The Trout." June 8, 1983. Retrieved August 25, 2023 from http://www.rogerebert.com.

__________. "Reviews: Tough Guys". October 3, 1986. Retrieved September 2, 2023 from http://www.rogerebert.com.

__________. "Reviews: The Age of Innocence." September 17, 1993. Retrieved September 8, 2023 from http://www.rogerebert.com.

Eder, Richard. "Stage: Alexis Smith Stars in 'Platinum'. *The New York Times*. November 13, 1978. Retrieved August 22, 2023 from http://www.nytimes.com.

Edwards, Russell. "Future Social Events." *The New York Times*. March 4, 1973. Retrieved August 13, 2023 from http://www.nytimes.com.

______________________________. May 26, 1973. Retrieved August 13, 2023 from http://www.nytimes.com.

______________________________. March 9, 1975. Retrieved August 15, 2023 from http://www.nytimes.com.

__________________________. November 2, 1975. Retrieved August 17, 2023 from http://www.nytimes.

Eliot, Marc. *Cary Grant: A Biography.* New York: Random House Large Print, 2004.

Eells, George. *Final Gig: The Man Behind The Murder.* San Diego : Harcourt Brace Jovanovich, 1991.

Essoe, Gabe. *The Films of Clark Gable.* New York, Citadel Press, 1970.

Eyman, Scott. *Cary Grant: A Brilliant Disguise.* New York: Simon & Schuster, 2020.

Fagen, Herb. *The Encyclopedia Of Westerns.* New York: Facts on File, 2003.

Faith, William Robert. *Bob Hope: A Life in Comedy.* London: Grandad Publishing, 1983.

Feaster, Felicia. "Article: The Little Girl Who Lives Down The Lane." *Turner Classic Movies.* November 10, 2006. Retrieved August 18, 2023 from http://www.tcm.com.

__________________. "Article: The Age Of Innocence (1993)." *Turner Classic Movies.* January 21, 2003. Retrieved September 8, 2023 from http://www.tcm.com.

Ferrara, Greg. "Article: The Age Of Innocence." *Turner Classic Movies.* February 8, 2016. Retrieved September 8, 2023 from http://www.tcm.com.

Fishgall, Gary. *Against Type: The Biography Of Burt Lancaster.* New York : Scribner, 1995.

Flatley. Guy. "Three Show-Biz Girls and How They Grew." *The New York Times.* April 4, 1971. Retrieved August 5, 2023 from http://www.nytimes.com.

__________________. "At The Movies." *The New York Times.* August 13, 1976. Retrieved August 19, 2023 from http://www.nytimes.com.

Flynn, Errol. *My Wicked, Wicked Ways.* New York: G.P. Putnam's Sons, 1959.

Fontaine, Joan. *No Bed of Roses.* New York: Morrow, 1978.

Freedland, Michael. *The Two Lives Of Errol Flynn. The Legends and the Truth about a Loveable Outrageous Rogue.* New York: W. Morrow, 1979.

Funke, Lewis. "…Separate Paths." *The New York Times.* June 26, 1966. Retrieved August 2, 2023 from http://www.nytimes.com.

__________. "News of the Rialto." *The New York Times.* December 6, 1970. Retrieved August 4, 2023 from http://www.nytimes.com.

__________. __________. __________. October 7, 1972. Retrieved August 12, 2023 from http://www.nytimes.com.

__________. "…Round-Up." *The New York Times.* March 11, 1973. Retrieved August 13, 2023 from http://www.nytimes.com.

Gardner, Paul "Curtain Rises on Shubert Alley West." *The New York Times.* July 23, 1972. Retrieved August 12, 2023 from http://www.nytimes.com.

Goldberg, Lee. *Unsold Television Pilots Vol.1: 1955 - 1976.* Lincoln, NE: iUniverse, 2001.

Goodman, Walter. "SCREEN: 'TOUGH GUYS'". *The New York Times.* October 3, 1986. Retrieved September 2, 2023 from http://www.nytimes.com.

__________. "Cole Porter: Still De-Lovely." *The New York Times.* July 23, 1990. Retrieved September 6, 2023 from http://www.nytimes.com.

Grater, Tom. "'Follies': …Getting Film Treatment." *Deadline.* November 14, 2019. Retrieved August 9, 2023 from http://www.deadline.com.

Gussow, Mel. "Prince Recalls the Evolution of 'Follies'". *The New York Times.* April 9, 1971. Retrieved August 5, 2023 from http://www.nytimes.com.

__________. "'Summer Brave', Revised 'Picnic' Is Staged." *The New York Times.* September 8, 1975. Retrieved August 16, 2023 from http://www.nytimes.com.

Haberman, Clyde and Krebs, Albin. "Notes on People." *The New York Times*. November 30, 1978. Retrieved August 22, 2023 from http://www.nytimes.com.

Hagen, Ray and Wagner, Laura. *Killer Tomatoes: Fifteen Tough Film Dames*. Jefferson, N.C.: McFarland, 2004.

Harris, Warren G. *Cary Grant: A Touch Of Elegance*. New York: Doubleday, 1987.

Henreid, Paul. *Ladies Man: An Autobiography*. New York: St. Martin's Press, 1984.

Hetrick, Adam. "Is a Follies Film With Meryl Streep in the Works?" *Playbill*. January 16, 2015. Retrieved August 9, 2023 from http://www.playbill.com.

H.H.T. "At the Palace." *The New York Times*. July 1, 1949. Retrieved July 1, 2023 from http://www.nytimes.com.

______. "'The Sleeping Tiger'". *The New York Times*. October 9, 1954. Retrieved July 17, 2023 from http://www.nytimes.com.

______. "'Beau James'". *The New York Times*. June 27, 1957. Retrieved July 21, 2023 from http://www.nytimes.com.

Higham, Charles. *Errol Flynn: The Untold Story*. New York: Dell, 1981.

______________. *Sisters: The Story Of Olivia De Havilland & Joan Fontaine*. New York: Coward-McCann, 1984.

______________, and Greenberg, Joel. *Hollywood in The Forties*. London, A. Zwemmer; New York, A.S. Barnes, 1968.

______________ Moseley, Roy. *Cary Grant: The Lonely Heart*. San Diego : Harcourt Brace Jovanovich, 1989.

Hirschhorn, Clive. *The Columbia Story*. London: Pyramid Books, 1989.

______________. *The Universal Story*. New York: Crown, 1983.

______________. *The Warner Bros. Story*. London: Octopus, 1986.

Holden, Stephen. "The Pop Life." *The New York Times*. November 21, 1990. Retrieved September 6, 2023 from http://www.nytimes.com.

__________. "Recordings View." *The New York Times.* December 9, 1990. Retrieved September 6, 2023 from http://www.nytimes.com.

Ilson, Carol. *Harold Prince: A Director's Journey.* Limelight Editions, 2000.

Jewell, Richard B. with Harbin, Vernon. *The RKO Story.* London: Octopus Books, 1982.

Johnston, Laurie. "Original Cast Looks Back at 'Women'". *The New York Times.* April 25, 1973. Retrieved August 13, 2023 from http://www.nytimes.com.

Jordan, Rene. *Clark Gable. Pyramid Illustrated History Of The Movies.* New York: Pyramid Publications, 1973.

Josefsberg, Milt. *The Jack Benny Show. The Life and Times of America's Best-Loved Entertainer.* New Rochelle, N.Y.: Arlington House, 1977.

Kael, Pauline. *5001 Nights At The Movies. A Guide from A to Z.* New York: Holt, Rinehart and Winston, 1984.

Kalat, David. "Article: Split Second." *Turner Classic Movies.* April 9, 2011. Retrieved July 16, 2023 from http://www.tcm.com.

Kanfer, Stefan. *Tough Without a Gun: The Life and Extraordinary Afterlife of Humphrey Bogart.* New York: Alfred A. Knopf, 2011

Kennedy, Matthew. *Edmund Goulding's Dark Victory: Hollywood's Genius Bad Boy.* Madison, WI: University of Wisconsin Press, 2004.

King, Larry L. *The Whorehouse Papers.* New York: Viking Press, 1982.

Kjolseth, Pablo. "Article: The Trout on DVD." *Turner Classic Movies.* April 26, 2004. Retrieved August 25, 2023 from http://www.tcm.com.

Klemesrud, Judy. "The Happy Marriage." *The New York Times.* June 1, 1971. Retrieved August 5, 2023 from http://www.nytimes.com.

______________.”Even Before Her Movie, Face Was . . .” *The New York Times.* January 11, 1971. Retrieved August 10, 2023 from http://www.nytimes.com.

______________. "A New Retreat for the Rich". *The New York Times.* January 6, 1974. Retrieved August 14, 2023 from http://www.nytimes.com.

______________. "Weaving Stars And Stripes Together." *The New York Times.* June 8, 1977. Retrieved August 20, 2023 from http://www.nytimes.com.

Land. "Film Reviews: Beau James". *Variety.* June 12, 1957. Retrieved July 21, 2023 from http://www.variety.com.

L.B.F. "THE SCREEN; ' The Constant Nymph'". *The New York Times.* July 24, 1943. Retrieved June 5, 2023 from http://www.nytimes.com.

Landazuri, Margarita. "Article: "Thank Your Lucky Stars." *Turner Classic Movies.* March 24, 2005. Retrieved June 8, 2023 from http://www.tcm.com.

______________. "Article: "The Horn Blows At Midnight." *Turner Classic Movies.* October 28, 2003. Retrieved June 15, 2023 from http://www.tcm.com.

______________. "Article: Whiplash." *Turner Classic Movies.* October 22, 2013. Retrieved June 29, 2023 from http://www.tcm.com.

______________. "Article: Here Comes The Groom." *Turner Classic Movies.* November 23, 2005. Retrieved July 11, 2023 from http://www.tcm.com.

Lawson, Carol. "News of the Theater." *The New York Times.* September 12, 1979. Retrieved August 23, 2023 from http://www.nytimes.com.

Littauer, Joelyn. "Three Of A Kind". *The New York Times.* February 17, 1946. Retrieved June 26, 2023 from http://www.nytimes.com.

LoBianco, Lorraine. "Article: One Last Fling." *Turner Classic Movies.* June 17, 2014. Retrieved July 1, 2023 from http://www.tcm.com.

McBride, Joseph. *Frank Capra: The Catastrophe Of Success*. New York : Simon & Schuster, 1992.

McCarthy, Todd. "Film: Reviews: The Age of Innocence." *Variety*. August 31, 1993. Retrieved September 8, 2023 from http://www.variety.com.

McClelland, Doug. *Eleanor Parker: Woman of a Thousand Faces*. Lanham, MD: Scarecrow Press, 1989.

McKittrick, Christopher. Interviews. *creative screenwriting*. May 19, 2017. Retrieved August 9, 2023 from http://www.creativescreenwriting.com.

McNulty, Thomas. *Erroll Flynn: The Life and Career*. Jefferson, NC: McFarland, 2004.

Mandelbaum, Ken. *A Chorus Line And The Musicals Of Michael Bennett*. St. Martin's Press, 1989.

_____________. *Not Since Carrie: Forty Years of Broadway Musical Flops*. St. Martin's Press, 1992.

Maslin, Janet. "Screen: But When She Was Bad . . . " *The New York Times*. August 11, 1977. Retrieved August 18, 2023 from http://www.nytimes.com.

_________. "ISABELLE HUPPERT IN LOSEY'S 'TROUT'". *The New York Times*. October 1, 1982. Retrieved August 25, 2023 from http://www.nytimes.com.

Miller, Frank. "Article: "The Great Mr. Nobody." *Turner Classic Movies*. January 5, 2017. Retrieved September 19, 2022 from http://www.tcm.com.

_________. "Article: "Affectionately Yours". *Turner Classic Movies*. July 26, 2012. Retrieved September 21, 2022 from http://www.tcm.com.

_________. "Article: "The Adventures of Mark Twain." *Turner Classic Movies*. October 27, 2003. Retrieved June 10, 2023 from http://www.tcm.com.

_________. "Article: "Rhapsody In Blue." *Turner Classic Movies*. March 26, 2003. Retrieved June 15, 2023 from http://www.tcm.com.

__________. "Article: "Hollywood Canteen." *Turner Classic Movies.* December 17, 2004. Retrieved June 17, 2023 from http://www.tcm.com.

__________. "Article: "Of Human Bondage (1946)." *Turner Classic Movies.* September 24, 2008. Retrieved June 18, 2023 from http://www.tcm.com.

__________. "Article: The Young Philadelphians." *Turner Classic Movies.* September 6, 2011. Retrieved July 30, 2023 from http://www.tcm.com.

Mordden, Ethan. *One More Kiss: The Broadway Musicals In The 1970s.* St. Martin's Publishing Group, 2015

Morella, Joe and Epstein, Edward Z. *Jane Wyman: A Biography.* New York: Delacorte Press, 1985.

Morley, Sheridan. *Dirk Bogarde: Rank Outsider.* London: Bloomsbury, 1999.

Morris, Bernadine. "Fashion Talk." *The New York Times.* September 8, 1973. Retrieved August 13, 2023 from http://www.nytimes.com.

__________. __________. __________. May 2, 1974. Retrieved August 15, 2023 from http://www.nytimes.com.

__________. "7th Ave: 3 Hits Bring Joy." *The New York Times.* February 6, 1976. Retrieved August 18, 2023 from http://www.nytimes.com.

__________. "Fashion – It's Just One Big Family." *The New York Times.* April 27, 1976. Retrieved August 18, 2023 from http://www.nytimes.com.

Morris, Edmund. *Dutch: A Memoir of Ronald Reagan.* New York: Random House, 1998.

Morris, George. *Errol Flynn. Pyramid Illustrated History Of The Movies.* New York: Pyramid Publications, 1975.

Neibaur, James. *The Bob Hope Films.* Jefferson, NC: McFarland & Company, 2004.

Nelson, Nancy. *Evenings With Cary Grant: Recollections In His Own Words And By Those Who Knew Him Best.* New York, N.Y.: Warner Books, 1993.

Nemy, Enid. "Spring Buds . . . Once upon a time . . ." *The New York Times.* March 30, 1977. Retrieved August 20, 2023 from http://www.nytimes.com.

__________. "The Anatomy of Glitter, Bottom to Top." *The New York Times.* May 5, 1978. Retrieved August 21, 2023 from http://www.nytimes.com.

__________. "The Evening Hours." *The New York Times.* April 29, 1983. Retrieved August 28, 2023 from http://www.nytimes.com.

__________. "Broadway." *The New York Times.* November 9, 1984. Retrieved August 30, 2023 from http://www.nytimes.com.

____. January 2, 1987. Retrieved September 3, 2023 from http://www.nytimes.com.

__________. "On Stage". *The New York Times.* January 1, 1988. Retrieved September 3, 2023 from http://www.nytimes.com.

Nixon, Rob. "Article: Conflict." *Turner Classic Movies.* September 25, 2003. Retrieved June 13, 2023 from http://www.tcm.com.

__________. "Article: "San Antonio." *Turner Classic Movies.* January 26, 2005. Retrieved June 21, 2023 from http://www.tcm.com.

Norden, Martin F. *Cinema of Isolation: A History Of Physical Disabilities In The Movies.* Rutgers University Press, 1994.

O'Connor, John J. "TV: Beyond the Reruns." *The New York Times.* June 23, 1971. Retrieved August 5, 2023 from http://www.nytimes.com.

__________. "TV: Sly, Amusing Benjamin Franklin." *The New York Times.* November 21, 1974. Retrieved August 15, 2023 from http://www.nytimes.com.

__________. "TV WEEKEND; 'DRESS GRAY'". *The New York Times.* March 7, 1986. Retrieved September 3, 2023 from http://www.nytimes.com.

__________________. "Review/Television: Mental Institution." *The New York Times*. June 30, 1988. Retrieved September 3, 2023 from http://www.nytimes.com.

Orriss, Bruce W. *When Hollywood Ruled The Skies. The Aviation Classics Of World War II*. Hawthorne, CA: Aero Associates, 1985.

Passafiume, Andrea. "Articles: Lady with Red Hair (1940)." *Turner Classic Movies*. October 28, 2003. Retrieved September 13, 2022 from http://www.tcm.com.

__________________. "Article: One More Tomorrow." *Turner Classic Movies*. June 8, 2010. Retrieved June 12, 2023 from http://www.tcm.com.

__________________. "Article: Always Together." *Turner Classic Movies*. June 29, 2009. Retrieved June 29, 2023 from http://www.tcm.com.

Patillo, Dawn. Skip E. Lowe interviews Craig Stevens. Continental Cablevision. 1993.

Perry, Hart. *Sondheim: A Musical Tribute*. 1973.

Peterson, Deborah C. *Fredric March: Craftsman First, Star Second*. Westport, CT: Greenwood Press, 1996.

Porter, Darwin. *Paul Newman, The Man Behind the Baby Blues: His Secret Life Exposed*. Blood Moon Productions, 2009.

Powe. "Film Reviews: This Happy Feeling." *Variety*. March 19, 1958. Retrieved July 28, 2023 from http://www.variety.com.

P.P.K. "'The Doughgirls'". *The New York Times*. August 31, 1944. Retrieved June 17, 2023 from http://www.nytimes.com.

Prince, Harold. *Contradictions: Notes on Twenty-six Years in the Theatre*. New York : Dodd, Mead, 1974.

Pryor, Thomas M. "…Victor Jory." *The New York Times*. August 19, 1952. Retrieved July 18, 2023 from http://www.nytimes.com.

__________________. "…R.K.O." *The New York Times*. October 23, 1952. Retrieved July 18, 2023 from http://www.nytimes.com.

________________. "Court Opens Way…". *The New York Times.* October 13, 1958. Retrieved July 31, 2023 from http://www.nytimes.com.

Raymond, Maria. "American Original". *Photoplay.* October, 1943: 58, 110 – 112.

Quirk, Lawrence J. *Paul Newman: A Life.* Dallas, TX: Taylor Publishing Company, 1996.

________________. *The Films of Fredric March.* New York: Citadel Press, 1971.

________________. *The Films Of Paul Newman.* Secaucus, N.J. : Citadel Press, 1973.

________________. *The Films of William Holden.* Secaucus, N.J.: Citadel Press, 1973.

Robertson, James C. *The Casablanca Man: the cinema of Michael Curtiz.* London ; New York : Routledge, 1993.

Rode, Alan K. *Michael Curtiz: A Life in Film.* University Press of Kentucky, 2017.

Sayre, Norma. "Kirk Douglas and Crew Roam Town." *The New York Times.* April 15, 1974. Retrieved August 15, 2023 from http://www.nytimes.com.

Scherle, Victor and Turner Levy, William. *The Complete Films of Frank Capra.* New York, N.Y.: Carol Publishing Group, 1992.

Schickel, Richard. *Cary Grant: A Celebration.* Thorndike, Me.: Thorndike Press, 1984.

Schiro, Anne-Marie. "The Evening Hours". *The New York Times.* August 19, 1983. Retrieved August 28, 2023 from http://www.nytimes.com.

Schwartzman, Arnold. Interview with Guy Green. *History Project.* November 19, 1991. Retrieved August 14, 2023 from http://www.historyproject.org.uk.

Secrest, Merlye. *Stephen Sondheim: a life.* New York : Alfred A. Knopf, 1998.

Shanley. J.P. "Choate, Ross Plan To Stage Thriller." *The New York Times.* February 7, 1953. Retrieved July 18, 2023 from http://www.nytimes.com.

__________. "On Summer Stages." *The New York Times.* June 20, 1953. Retrieved July 18, 2023 from http://www.nytimes.com.

__________. "TV Review". *The New York Times.* November 19, 1959. Retrieved July 31, 2023 from http://www.nytimes.com.

Shavelson, Mel and Rose, Jack. "On Hailing His Honor." *The New York Times.* June 15, 1957. Retrieved July 22, 2023 from http://www.nytimes.com.

Shepard, Richard F. "Imogene Coca's Golden Jubilee." *The New York Times.* January 16, 1979. Retrieved August 22, 2023 from http://www.nytimes.com.

Sherman, Vincent. *Studio Affairs: My Life as a Film Director.* University Press of Kentucky, Lexington, ©1996.

Silver, Alain et al. *Film Noir: The Encyclopedia.* New York, London: Overlook Duckworth, 2010.

Slate, Libby. "Take 2: Warner Bros. Reclaims Its Studio." *Los Angeles Times.* June 1, 1990. Retrieved September 5, 2023 from http://www.latimes.com.

Smith, Richard Harland. "Articles: Flight from Destiny." *Turner Classic Movies.* June 2, 2015. Retrieved September 18, 2022 from http://www.tcm.com.

__________. "Articles: The Smiling Ghost." *Turner Classic Movies.* June 18, 2014. Retrieved June 2, 2023 from http://www.tcm.com.

__________. "Article: Stallion Road." *Turner Classic Movies.* March 21, 2008. Retrieved June 27, 2023 from http://www.tcm.com.

Stafford, Jeff. "Article: The Woman in White (1948)." *Turner Classic Movies.* September 27, 2002. Retrieved June 28, 2023 from http://www.tcm.com.

Stanley, Fred. "JESSE L. LASKY AGAIN ON BIOGRAPHICAL TRAIL." *The New York Times*. August 8, 1943. Retrieved June 14, 2023 from http://www.nytimes.com.

Steinberg, Jay. "Article: Dive Bomber." *Turner Classic Movies*. May 20, 2003. Retrieved June 1, 2023 from http://www.tcm.com.

__________. "Article: Gentleman Jim." *Turner Classic Movies*. March 29, 2005. Retrieved June 4, 2023 from http://www.tcm.com.

Sterritt, David. "Article: Steel Against The Sky (1941)." *Turner Classic Movies*. October 31, 2012. Retrieved June 3, 2023 from http://www.tcm.com.

Swindell, Larry. *Charles Boyer: The Reluctant Lover*. Garden City, N.Y.: Doubleday, 1983.

Tanitch, Robert. *Dirk Bogarde: The Complete Career Illustrated*. London: Ebury Press, 1988.

Taravella, Steve. *Mary Wickes: I Know I've Seen That Face Before*. Jackson : University Press of Mississippi, 2013.

Tatara, Paul. "Article: Casey's Shadow." *Turner Classic Movies*. June 8, 2010. Retrieved August 20, 2023 from http://www.tcm.com.

Taylor, Angela. "Stars Turn Out for 'Fabulous 40's' Party". *The New York Times*. June 6, 1972. Retrieved August 11, 2023 from http://www.nytimes.com.

__________. "In the Theater, The Best Dressers Don't…". *The New York Times*. January 2, 1974. Retrieved August 14, 2023 from http://www.nytimes.com.

__________. "As a Fashion Show, It Was a Good Party." *The New York Times*. August 6, 1976. Retrieved August 19, 2023 from http://www.nytimes.com.

Thomas, Bob. *Golden Boy: The Untold Story Of William Holden*. New York, N.Y.: Berkley Pub. Group, 1984.

Thomas, Tony. *The Dick Powell Story*. Burbank, California : Riverwood Press, 1993.

__________. *Errol Flynn: The Spy Who Never Was*. New York, NY: Carol Pub. Group, 1990.

__________, et al. *The Films of Errol Flynn*. New York: Citadel Press, 1969.

Thompson, Howard H. "Anti-Crime Film at Globe." *The New York Times*. November 1952. Retrieved July 14, 2023 from http://www.nytimes.com.

__________. "Screen: 'Eternal Sea'". *The New York Times*. June 10, 1955. Retrieved July 19, 2023 from http://www.nytimes.com.

T.M.P. "At The Strand." *The New York Times*. November 26, 1942. Retrieved June 4, 2023 from http://www.nytimes.com.

__________. "THE SCREEN IN REVIEW." *The New York Times*. May 25, 1946. Retrieved June 11, 2023 from http://www.nytimes.com.

__________. "The Screen: 'Night and Day'". *The New York Times*. July 26, 1946, Retrieved June 25, 2023 from http://www.nytimes.com.

__________. "At the Globe." *The New York Times*. December 27, 1948. Retrieved June 29, 2023 from http://www.nytimes.com.

__________. "Alexis Smith Starred in Film at Rivoli." *The New York Times*. November 8, 1950. Retrieved July 9, 2023 from http://www.nytimes.com.

Tornabene, Lyn. *Long Live The King: A Biography Of Clark Gable*. New York : Putnam, 1976.

Torregrossa, Richard. *Cary Grant: A Celebration Of Style*. New York : Bulfinch Press, 2006.

Van Gelder, Lawrence. "Death in California." *The New York Times*. May 10, 1985. Retrieved August 31, 2023 from http://www.nytimes.com.

Vermilye, Jerry. *Barbara Stanwyck. Pyramid Illustrated History Of The Movies*. New York: Pyramid, 1975.

__________ "Alexis Smith." *Films In Review*. March - April, 1994: 2 -13.

______________. "Alexis Smith Part 2." *Films In Review*. May-June 1994: 22 - 34.

Vlastnik, Frank and Ross, Laura. *The Art Of Bob Mackie*. New York: Simon & Schuster, 2021.

Weiler. A.H. "…Versatile." *The New York Times*. March 30, 1947. Retrieved June 28, 2023 from http://www.nytimes.com.

______________. "THE SCREEN IN REVIEW." *The New York Times*. May 13, 1953. Retrieved July 16, 2023 from http://www.nytimes.com.

______________. "Young Philadelphians'". *The New York Times*. May 22, 1959. Retrieved July 30, 2023 from http://www.nytimes.com.

______________. "Hal's 'Follies'". *The New York Times*. April 14, 1973. Retrieved August 13, 2023 from http://www.nytimes.com.

Weinman Lear, Martha. "Clare Boothe Luce." *The New York Times*. April 21, 1973. Retrieved August 13, 2023 from http://www.nytimes.com.

Willis, Donald C. *The Films of Frank Capra*. Scarecrow Press, 1974.

Wilson, John S. "The Score of 'Follies'". *The New York Times*. April 16, 1971. Retrieved August 5, 2023 from http://www.nytimes.com.

______________. "Mabel Mercer, Storyteller in Song." *The New York Times*. February 3, 1975. Retrieved August 15, 2023 from http://www.nytimes.com.

Wise Jr., James E. and Wilderson III, Paul W. *Stars In Khaki : Movie Actors in the Army and the Air Services*. Annapolis, Md.: Naval Institute Press, 2000.

Wolfe, Charles. *Frank Capra: A Guide to References and Resources*. G.K. Hall, 1987.

Zadan, Craig. *Sondheim & Co*. New York: Harper & Row, 1986.

Zolotow, Sam. "…Pretty Packages." *The New York Times*. May 29, 1968. Retrieved August 2, 2023 from http://www.nytimes.com.

Index

Italic titles are shorts, films, television, theatre, radio shows, and magazines. **Bold** numbers are images.

About the author

Peter Shelley is a playwright, screenwriter, and author of several film books. He lives in Gosford, Australia.